A Memoir of the
Paris Peace Conference
1919

Sir James Headlam-Morley,
about the time of the Peace Conference

Sir James Headlam-Morley

A MEMOIR
OF THE PARIS
PEACE CONFERENCE
1919

Edited by
Agnes Headlam-Morley
Russell Bryant, Anna Cienciala

METHUEN & CO LTD
11 New Fetter Lane, London EC4

First published 1972
by Methuen & Co Ltd
11 New Fetter Lane London EC4
© *1972 by Agnes Headlam-Morley*
Printed in Great Britain by
Butler & Tanner Ltd
Frome & London

SBN 416 75470 8

Distributed in the USA by
HARPER & ROW PUBLISHERS, INC.
BARNES & NOBLE IMPORT DIVISION

CONTENTS

ACKNOWLEDGEMENTS
AND SOURCES

Our thanks are due above all to the Hon. Margaret Lambert for her constant encouragement and for her help in making possible the publication of this Memoir and of Sir James Headlam-Morley's History of the Peace Conference. We are grateful also to Miss Campbell and her staff at Chatham House, to the librarians of the Polish library, St Hugh's College and St Antony's College, Oxford,[1] and to those who have given information about the people mentioned, especially the late Dr Norman Bentwich (who gave generous help and advice until his last illness), Lady Namier, Miss Sybil Crowe, Miss Carolyn Morrison, the Rt. Hon. Philip Noel-Baker, Professor Hugh Seton-Watson and Mr Hugh Cecil.

We have given references to contemporary sources covering the same events. The most important of these sources are Sir Maurice Hankey's Minutes published by the State Department: *Papers relating to the Foreign Relations of the United States: Paris Peace Conference 1919*, 13 vols. (Washington, D.C.: United States Printing Office, 1942–7). These are referred to as P.P.C. Monsieur Paul Mantoux, the official interpreter, subsequently published the notes he had taken at meetings of the Council of Four. These include a number of early meetings at which no secretary was present and of which there is no other record. Our reference is to the French edition: Paul Mantoux, *Les Délibérations du Conseil des Quatre*, 2 vols. (Paris: Éditions du Centre de la Recherche Scientifique, 1955). There is also an English translation of the first volume: *Paris Peace Conference 1919: Proceedings of the Council of Four* (March–April 1919). Sir James Headlam-Morley's Memoranda on the History of the Peace Conference will, we hope, soon be published as a further volume. They are here cited as P.C.M. with the official number. We have given references also to some collections of unpublished documents. The most important are the Lloyd

---

[1] Since this was written some papers of my father have been made available by the New University of Ulster, Coleraine. For this we are most grateful.

George Papers in the Beaverbrook Library and the Marquess of Lothian Papers (Scottish Record Office, Edinburgh, G.D. 40/17/72). These are referred to as the Lothian Papers. There are occasional references also to *Recueil des actes de la Conférence de la Paix 1919–1920*, 36 vols. (Paris, 1924–1934), cited as *Recueil*.

INTRODUCTION
by Agnes Headlam-Morley

The editors of this Memoir are, or have been, active teachers in the field of international relations and recent history. We have found, especially among young graduates, an increasing interest in the causes and consequences of the First World War. This is particularly true of American research students at their own universities and at Oxford. They are eager to investigate the causes of their involvement in the tangled history of Europe. We have found also a very wholesome interest in original sources. The evidence now available for the Peace Conference of Paris is very large. We venture to add to it this Memoir which recounts the experiences and reflections of a Civil Servant who was also a historian and who, as a member of the British Delegation, came to play an active part in some of the most important and most controversial aspects of the territorial settlement. We hope that it may prove of interest also to a wider public.

The work of a higher Civil Servant was strenuous and the remuneration far from bountiful. But my father had one inestimable advantage – the full-time service of a highly skilled secretary, Miss Mary Hughes. Miss Hughes was not only a first-rate stenographer and typist. She could read my father's handwriting, an almost unique accomplishment, and guide him in the use of the telephone, an instrument with which he never really came to terms. She was also a lady of intellectual accomplishment who in our parlance would have been called a research assistant. Miss Hughes, after my father's death, put together the Memoir which we have now had permission to publish. We have altered nothing except to make a few minor corrections. We have given references to sources covering the same events and have added occasional footnotes[1] and an appendix giving some biographical information about the people mentioned. We thought this might be useful to a younger generation to whom these are not necessarily household names and that it might be interesting to call to mind the kind

[1] Miss Hughes's footnotes in the original manuscript are initialled M.H.

of people who took part in the making of the Peace. I am solely responsible for the essay on my father, but have relied heavily on information
supplied by my co-editors.

James Wycliffe Headlam was the younger son of the Rev. Arthur William
Headlam of Whorlton Hall near Barnard Castle. He was born there on
24 December 1863. His elder brother Arthur Cayley became a distinguished theologian – for twenty-three years he was Bishop of Gloucester.[1]
Headlam's second name was taken from the old family home at Wycliffe,[2]
a small hamlet in the meadows a mile or so downstream on the Yorkshire
side of the Tees. There Wycliffe worshipped in the flat-roofed Gothic
church, there the grey wagtails feed in the stony shallows and the dipper
flies low over the fast-running, clear, brown water.

In 1918 Headlam took by royal licence the additional name and arms
of Morley. This was in accordance with the will of his cousin and god-
father, George Morley. A gentle unassuming clergyman, he came of an old
West-Riding family. The last of his line, he set great store by its survival.
In due course Headlam inherited some small sheep-raising farms near
Settle – the farmers' wives insisted on a few cows for dairy produce.

When Headlam was a boy at Whorlton a family of cousins came to live
at the Grange, a rambling, unpretentious sort of house on the other side of
the village green. His closest companion was the eldest son John. (Afterwards Major-General Sir John Headlam. He commanded the guns at the
retreat from Mons and was a member of the last military mission to
Russia at the outbreak of the revolution.) As boys they explored the source
of the Whorlton Beck (it has never been discovered) or scrambled about
the rocky banks on the steep Durham side of the Tees – now and then an
oxlip can be found among the primroses and forget-me-nots. Sometimes
they would follow the great river upstream past falls and pools to the
junction with the Greta at Rokeby – there Brignall Banks are fresh and
fair and Greta Woods are gay.

In due course Headlam was sent to a preparatory school at Reading.
Although not given to reminiscence about his own early life he did some-
times refer to the unhappiness of those childhood days in an alien place.
He always, I think, retained some prejudice against that kind of establish-
ment. (When the time came he sent his own son to a day school at
Wimbledon and then as an oppidan to Eton. It paid out all right as he won

1 See Appendix, p. 161.
2 Pronounced with a long first syllable as in 'wine'.

an open scholarship to New College.) However, the Reading school did its job efficiently and he went as a colleger to Eton.

At Eton he was happy. There, as afterwards at Cambridge, he responded to the delicate beauty of the place. The physical hardships did him no harm – breaking the ice to pump water for his fag master on cold winter mornings. In 1877 he wrote home a spirited account of the visit of the Queen for the marriage at Windsor of the Princess Louise. The boys had a whole holiday on the understanding that they would turn out and cheer. As a wet bob without athletic ambitions he was left in peace to wander, read and row casually along the river banks. He worked well, was well taught and won a scholarship to the sister house, King's College, Cambridge.

At King's he took part in the lively intellectual and artistic interests of his contemporaries, Lowes Dickinson,[1] C. R. Ashbee, Roger Fry. His closest friends were his cousin Walter Headlam, the classical scholar,[2] and J. K. Stephen, who had been his fag master at school. People's ages even out a bit as they grow up. Headlam took a first class in both parts of the classical tripos and then started to investigate a hitherto neglected aspect of Athenian democracy. In 1887 he went for the first time to Germany and continued work first at Göttingen, then at Berlin.

As a result of this research he was able to show that in post-Periclean Athens the lot was not, as most scholars had assumed, an archaic survival. According to the older religious conception, acceptance of 'chance' implied submission to the will of the gods. This had given way to a secular view of democracy: all citizens were members of the assembly, they all had the right – and the duty – to serve on the Council and to share the responsibility of office. All appointments, except in the army, were made by the drawing of lots, every citizen was expected to take his turn in the exercise of authority. To the Greeks our modern system of representation with party alignment would be a corrupt kind of oligarchy. Headlam pointed out that their own ideal of direct democracy was essentially aristocratic. It assumed that every citizen was capable of acting in the public interest and taking part in administration. The hard manual labour was done by slaves. In the modern world some approach to it would be possible only 'if the use of machinery were so far developed that the greater part of society had leisure to devote themselves not only to the discussion but to the management of public business'.[3]

1 See E. M. Forster, *Goldsworthy Lowes Dickinson* (London: Arnold, 1934), p. 63.
2 He edited the *Plays of Aeschylus* (London: John Bell, 1909).
3 *Election by Lot at Athens*, 1st ed. (Cambridge University Press, 1891); 2nd ed., ed. D. C. Macgregor (1933); a third edition is about to appear.

During these years of study in Berlin Headlam became engaged to Else Sonntag who, with her eldest sister Hedwig, lived in a rather shabby flat in the Potsdammer Strasse. Else, young, graceful, a little shy, had been a pupil of Liszt. Now, since Liszt was dead, she had joined the school of Zawa Schavenka in Berlin. Schavenka, when he heard of the engagement was far from pleased ... 'Ist ein langer Engländer gekommen will Elsbetchen[1] heiraten – heisst Scharfskopf.' But the 'langer Engländer' had his way. They were engaged for four years and married in 1892.

Hedwig – Heide, as she was always called – was fifteen years older than Else. Their father August Sonntag had been a successful doctor in Lüneburg. He attended *das gute Bürgertum* but preferred to ride about the heath visiting his patients in the scattered farms. Dr Sonntag was a National Liberal who looked forward to the unification of Germany. None the less he was loyal to the king of Hanover and it annoyed him to see the Prussian eagles carried through the streets of Lüneburg. Thinking to give his children greater artistic opportunities he moved to Dresden. He lost his money in the *Wiener Krach*. Heide studied with Marie Wieg, the sister of Clara Schumann. She was the first to recognize that Else's talent was of an entirely different order. When she was eleven Else was taken to see Liszt. She played to him the *Wanderer Fantasie* of Schubert-Liszt and was accepted as a pupil. So the sisters moved to Weimar. Their parents died soon afterwards. *Der liebe Meister* – as his pupils called him, always addressing him in the third person – gave no formal instruction. Two or three times a week they assembled in the music room with the great hanging curtains. Those who were asked to play and allowed to finish thought themselves lucky. They were expected to practise at least eight hours a day. Else gained much from the help of older pupils, Alexandre Silotte, Friedheim and Richard Burmeister, who were already established artists. As she grew up she was recognized as one of the favoured group who were invited to travel with Liszt and to perform in public. She played for him in Budapest and put in some time with Eppstein in Vienna. She could not afford to go to Rome. *Der liebe Meister* never knew of the piano pieces she had composed as a child.

Now in Berlin Heide kept house and earned the money by giving German lessons to foreign visitors. Later she made quite a bit out of her novels; they show no great imaginative power but give a sympathetic picture of life as she knew it in Lüneburg and in Weimar. She was a brilliant conversationalist, sophisticated, witty – with deeper tones of understanding. My father had moved almost entirely in academic circles;

[1] She had been christened Elisabeth.

Heide introduced him to a different kind of society. Many of the friends who met in her modest sitting-room were Englishmen. An odd assortment: Harry Cust – the most faithful and affectionate of her admirers – Cecil Spring-Rice, Leo Strachey, Graham Wallas, Sydney Webb, Walter Freer. Bernard Shaw, then quite unknown, carried on a spasmodic flirtation. Later in London he used to take the sisters to the Opera on his free tickets as a critic. Finally he sent to Heide a post card: 'Es ist eine Frau gekommen. Will mich heiraten.' So that was the end of that.

In the meantime my father had completed his dissertation. It was awarded the Prince Consort Prize in 1890 and led to a fellowship at King's. In his preface to the second edition (1933) Mr Macgregor wrote that *Election by Lot at Athens*, which quickly won an international reputation, had enabled Headlam 'to take his place in the small but good company of notable Hellenists . . . but he did not keep it long'. He adds with a note of reproach that 'this no doubt was partly due to his defection to other fields of study'.

So indeed it was. He worked with Hans Delbrück and attended Treitschke's lectures. In Treitschke he was astonished – and repelled – by the dichotomy between the wealth of his knowledge and the narrow, distorted interpretation. Headlam turned with relief to the philosophers and poets. Kant and Goethe, the greatest of all, had the humility to accept the limitations of the human mind. Hegel in attempting to build a universal system had overloaded a sound foundation. Nietzsche came to grief because, determined to pursue the source of evil, he forsook the firm path of reason. In this world we must leave the ultimate problem unresolved.

At this time and during later visits he became interested also in the social legislation of the Bismarkian era and especially in the general provision of secondary education – so different from our own haphazard arrangements depending on the financial resources of the parents or the accidental proximity of a grammar school.

Headlam's family suffered from the strange illusion that he was inclined to be lazy and would do better if left to his own resources. The reverse in fact was true. He was sometimes careless, even indifferent, about private business affairs. But in his work he was always fortunate and he showed great powers of concentration. Else, as it turned out, was not very practical in domestic matters. All he needed was peace of mind and relief from financial anxiety. At last the fellowship at King's made marriage possible. Their love survived all the stress and strains, the joys and griefs of the years to come.

After his marriage Headlam was for a short time Professor of Greek at Queen's College, London. But his classical studies were gradually pushed aside by increasing interest in modern Europe. He contributed articles on German history to the *Encyclopaedia Britannica* and gave extension lectures on Goethe and the later Romantics. His life of Bismarck[1] appeared in 1899. Headlam never got round to doing a second edition but in spite of all that has been published since, the book is still worth reading for the account it gives of Bismarck's character and personality. Headlam came to think that succeeding generations of German writers and politicians had betrayed the Bismarckian tradition of moderation and limited aims. For this Bismarck himself was much to blame. After the unification of Germany he preserved the peace of Europe by skilful diplomatic manipulation – in secrecy and isolation. He left a legacy of distrust. He gave no impulse to inspire the quest for a new European order.[2]

Once more at Cambridge, Headlam took an active part in the life of his college. Else too had made friends with Jim Stephen. When she first left Germany she had been taken to visit his father, Sir James Fitzjames Stephen, in Ireland. She never forgot the drive from the station sitting sideways in a jaunting-car. J. K. S. had already shown signs of mental disturbance. Headlam helped to nurse him through his last tragic illness. The children were born at Cambridge. As soon as we were old enough Walter Headlam, who enjoyed my mother's company, used to help her out by romping with us in the little dining-room at Benet Place. He too died young.

Headlam presented a report on secondary education in Germany to the Bryce Commission, of which he was an honorary assistant member.[3] He began work for the newly constituted Board of Education in 1902 and two years later was appointed a Permanent Staff Inspector. The Inspectors were centred in Whitehall but travelled all over the country, examining and comparing small grammar schools in country towns, the newly established secondary schools, ancient foundations at Manchester and Birmingham, and, by invitation, many public schools. They were concerned not with administration but with teaching methods and curriculum. It was an original and daring venture in government activity, due chiefly to the enterprise and inspiration of Robert Morant. Headlam as always was interested in the connection between history and literature. He advised the

[1] J. W. Headlam, *Bismarck*, Heroes of the Nations Series (London: Putnam, 1899).
[2] See review of *Die grosse Politik der europäischen Kabinette*, in *The Times Literary Supplement*, August 1922.
[3] The Royal Commission on Secondary Education sat from 1894 to 1895 under the chairmanship of Mr (afterwards Viscount) Bryce.

Board to encourage sixth-form work in selected periods which would make possible the correlation of history, literature and modern languages.[1] Naturally patient and good-tempered, Headlam proved himself a popular Inspector. Sometimes he would take over a class; his own interest in the subject, the vigour and clarity of his presentation seldom failed to stimulate the interest of even the dullest pupils and the most exhausted teacher.[2]

It was a happy time. Since he had to be within reach of the office in Whitehall he bought a house at Wimbledon with a large untidy garden. He made a rock garden, a pond and for reasons best known to himself a large, grass-covered hill. Togo, an old wire-haired terrier, came with us from Cambridge. Tusnelda and her daughter Jemmima produced a succession of kittens. When good and reliable homes could not be found the population increased. We children rode our bicycles recklessly over the hill and round about the elm trees. In our more rational moments, my father encouraged us, with the help of an older friend, Hubert Laughton,[3] to build up a natural history museum and a chemical laboratory – highly scientific. We all three spoke German to my mother but not amongst ourselves. By the time I knew him my father – Cliffchen as she called him – was as fluent in German as in English. He was away a good deal inspecting schools, but whenever he could he would read to us in the evenings: Walter Scott from *Quentin Durward* to the *Heart of Midlothian*, *Barnaby Rudge*, *Oliver Twist*, *The Newcomes* (this was a great favourite) and the whole of Carlyle's *French Revolution*. Children will take in much more when read aloud to than they can on their own. We always clamoured for more and had to be driven to bed.

After her marriage, when she gave up concert-playing, Else developed her powers as a composer. She had the gift of melody. As all artists must she spent long hours in concentrated work. Headlam, like most of his family, was quite unmusical. This was a purely physical defect in hearing. He had a true understanding of poetry and as a young man wrote quite a lot of verse. It was he who suggested to his wife most of the English and German words which she set to music. In Heine's hymn to the angels, the greatest lyric of a great poet, she found a perfect partnership:

Bei allen Tränen die ihr jeh
Geweint um unser Menschen Weh,
Beim Wort das nur der Priester kennt,

---

[1] In 1917 after he had left the Board he was asked to submit a report on the topic.
[2] *The Times*, 9 September 1929.
[3] The youngest son of the naval historian, Sir John Laughton. He fought right through the war and having been slightly wounded died of influenza in hospital just after the armistice.

Und niemals ohne Schauder nennt,
Bei eurer eichnen Schönheit Huld und Milden
Beschwör ich euch ihr Engel schützt Mathilden.[1]

On the outbreak of war Headlam was transferred from the Board of Education to the newly constituted Propaganda Department at Wellington House. He served there with G. M. Masterman and afterwards as assistant director of the Intelligence Bureau under Count Gleichen.[2] In addition to his official duties he set to work at once on an investigation into the causes of war. *The History of Twelve Days* was completed and published in 1915.[3]

The book begins with a brief account of the historical background. In August 1913 the long-drawn crisis in the Balkans seemed at last over. Sir Edward Grey could tell the House of Commons that the concert of Europe was firmly established; that the great powers in spite of their differences could live at peace without apprehension. Within a year they were at war. The murder of the Archduke Franz Ferdinand and his consort on 28 June 1914 was a crime as purposeless as it was wicked. He had been looked upon as an enemy of the Magyars, as a friend of the Slavonic peoples. All Europe responded in horror at the deed and in sympathy for the aged emperor. Why then did the restraining influence of Germany on Austria, of Russia on the Balkan Slavs fail to preserve peace as it had done in the past? Headlam argued that the Austrian Chancellor Count Berchtold had come to believe that war against Serbia, the forcible repression of the pan-Serb movement, was essential for the survival of the monarchy as a great power. In this he was probably influenced by Count Forgach, a relentless enemy of the Slavs who had played a leading part in the Friedjung and Agram trials. The Austrian ultimatum of 25 July was intended not to secure reparation but as a pretext for the military occupation of Serbia. Such a policy would involve the immediate danger of war with Russia. It could be pursued only with German support. For Germany the military situation was at least for the time being favourable. To the Government, and above all to the military party, it might well seem the given opportunity to establish a German domination from Vienna to Constantinople. The people, stirred by an exultant patriotism, subject at the same time to a vague fear of Russian power, would follow without

[1] 'By all the tears that you have shed for all the sorrows of mankind; by the word that no one but the priest can know and never utters without dread; by your own beauty, grace and kindness, you angels, I beseech you guard Mathilde.'
[2] Afterwards Lord Edward Gleichen.
[3] *The History of Twelve Days* (T. Fisher Unwin, 1915).

question. Russia at this time had no desire for war. To Zazanov it was evident from the first that Germany in seeking to isolate the Serbian issue was determined on the humiliation of Russia, the defeat of her vital interests. The only hope of preventing war between the Franco-Russian and German-Austrian alliances was a firm warning in which Great Britain should take part. The French, though consistently conciliatory in method, took the same view. Sir Edward Grey from the first maintained that we were not concerned in the merits of the dispute between Austria–Hungary and Serbia. The strong line urged by Russia and by France might involve Great Britain in a major war on an issue rejected by the majority in Parliament and in the country. But if – as all the contestants asserted – there was a genuine desire for peace then Great Britain and Germany, acting together, might mediate between Austria and Russia. Alternatively they could encourage the direct negotiations proposed first by Russia then by Austria. The surmounting of an unparalleled danger might establish the peace of Europe on a firmer foundation.

Headlam sought to elucidate the problem, to test these general conclusions, by a detailed examination of the official documents issued by the belligerent Governments. It may well happen that the immediate occasion for war is of comparatively small importance. This was not the case in 1914. The diplomatic correspondence of the last crucial days would reveal the purposes of the contestants both before and during the conflict. (In this if in nothing else he agreed with G. Lowes Dickinson in *The European Anarchy*.)[1] The British White Paper published on 6 August[2] gives the texts, in some cases a full summary, of the relevant dispatches. It is possible to follow consistently the development of the crisis as seen in the actions taken, the advice given by the British Government. The French Yellow Book corroborates the British account; there are differences of outlook, sometimes a fuller, more dramatic version, no indication of concealment. Both the Russian and the Austrian documents contain some useful information but there are considerable omissions. The German Government did not publish the evidence. On 4 August the Chancellor, Herr von Bethmann-Hollweg, presented to the Reichstag a statement explaining the course of events; a selection of documents was appended, some undated and in a truncated form. The correspondence between the German Emperor and the Tsar is given in full. There is a complete absence of information about the relations between Germany and Austria. On this the Austrians also were silent. But oddly enough there was printed

1 First published by Macmillan in New York in 1916.
2 Cmd. 7467, Misc. No. 6, 1914.

B

in the *Westminster Gazette* on 1 August a single telegram dated 30 July in which Bethmann-Hollweg urged the Austrians to exchange views with St Petersburg and warned that Germany could not be drawn into a world conflict because Austria–Hungary would not follow her advice.

The publication of *The History of Twelve Days* led to a controversy at long distance with Professor Delbrück and other writers in the *Preussische Jahrbücher*.[1] Eventually Bethmann-Hollweg produced further spasmodic items of information. This confirmed Headlam's view that the real turning point had come on 29 July. The Serbian reply, in spite of its moderation, had been rejected, Belgrade had been bombarded, Serbian territory invaded. After the crown council on that day there were signs of hesitation in Berlin. Sir Edward Grey was approached. In the strongest terms he refused to commit Great Britain to neutrality. He drew attention to the fact that the fleet had not been demobilized after the recent manœuvres. It is possible that Bethmann-Hollweg now backed away from what would be a world war. The military party and, Headlam assumed, the Emperor pressed forward. The Russian Government had decided on 25 July that an attack on Serbia would mean mobilization. In this they were fully justified. The German Government, Headlam supposed, were intent to prove, at least to their own people, that the mobilization, which they knew to be inevitable, was the cause of war. He was confirmed in this by further evidence that both Austria and Russia had been prepared to negotiate after mobilization. The war was deliberately precipitated by the German attack in the west. England declared war on 4 August; Grey did not threaten to do so until the invasion of Belgium had actually taken place. He was of course influenced by the need to preserve national unity. Headlam did not think that the cautious policy he followed ran counter to Grey's own judgement. Later Headlam wrote critically of Mr Gladstone because in 1870 and again in 1872 he wrongly asserted that the guarantee of Belgian neutrality gave us the right to intervene but did not impose an obligation.[2] At this time he did not reproach Sir Edward Grey for his unwillingness to use this obligation as a means of deterrence. The German Chancellor afterwards asserted that Britain, while posing as the pacifier, had secretly encouraged Russian mobilization. This was the source of violent anti-British propaganda. It is a sheer fabrication for which there is not a shred of evidence.

[1] J, W, Headlam-Morley, *The German Chancellor and the Outbreak of War* (T. Fisher Unwin, 1917).
[2] 'Treaties of Guarantee 1926', in J. W. Headlam-Morley, *Studies in Diplomatic History* (London: Methuen, 1930), p. 120.

Writing, as he said, in the middle of a great war, faced by an enemy more powerful and more implacable than any the country had met in the past, it would be foolish to claim the merit of impartiality. But he had written no word that he did not believe to be true. (He proved himself always ready to amend his views as new evidence appeared.) Had he in the course of his work discovered that the result would be unfavourable to the British cause, he would have remained silent till the war was over. The German Government had deliberately rejected the established means of conciliation, a continental conflict became a world war because they failed to recognize that the independence of the Low Countries, the security of the opposite shores of the Channel against the domination of a single great power was then, as in the past, a vital British interest.

In his work Headlam was successful. But the distress of war brought to him also much hardship and private sorrow. His wife had already got into trouble with his family for supporting unpopular causes. Now in all seriousness she turned in love and loyalty to her own country.[1] She made no secret of it. She spent the war years in almost complete isolation and paid no attention to the background rumble of 'Hun' and 'bloody German'. We children did not take it too tragically. My mother assumed that we would wish Britain to win the war, but we were brought up not to deny our German ancestry. It was an open battle. Unlike so many children of mixed marriages we had no secret sense of shame in being half-German.

After the first year when her son was gravely ill Else turned once more to composition. For her songs she had always written a strong accompaniment; next to Beethoven, Schubert was her favourite composer. She now developed an increasing interest in a daring counterpoint.[2] In the concerto, *Deutschland*, the outpouring of a stricken heart, she once more found inspiration in the words of Heine. 'Ich bin das Schwert, ich bin die Flamme. Ich hab euch erleuchtet in der Dunkelheit.'[3]

Headlam was from the first convinced that an agreed peace would be tantamount to defeat. In *The Issue* – a collection of articles published in 1917 – he argued that an undefeated Germany would attain her immediate purpose, the establishment of an irresistible power in central Europe. The other objectives would follow after: the overthrow of British sea power, which had captured the imagination of the German people; the destruction of the British Empire; the satisfaction of extra-European ambitions

[1] She was from the first totally opposed to Hitler. During the Second World War she hoped for a British victory.
[2] The conductor, Ernst Kunwald, so described it.
[3] 'I am the sword, I am the flame. In the darkness I gave you light.'

to be achieved by the unholy alliance between the German and Turkish military. Bethmann-Hollweg and the former Chancellor Count Bülow might disguise their aims in superficially moderate language. Essentially they were the same as those of the Pan-Germans, the Conservative and Liberal parties, the leaders of professional and academic associations who demanded annexations in the west and in the east, the appropriation of the sources of production, the planting of German colonists in the conquered Polish territories. Most dangerous to the liberties of Europe were the seemingly constructive proposals of Friedrich Naumann, an intellectual of the Catholic Centre Party.[1] The new continental union of *Mitteleuropa*, though nominally free, would in fact be dominated by a German army, a German administration, a German agricultural and industrial organization.

The purpose of the allies was to establish in the concert of Europe the free and friendly competition of independent states, great and small. There would be no annexation of territories that were purely German, frontiers would be altered only in accordance with the wishes of the inhabitants. But more important than the terms of peace was the outcome of the conflict. If the German army remained undefeated, the German people could claim that they had defied Europe with impunity. Their ambitions unsatisfied, they would prepare for the next war. It would be war between Germany and Britain, a Britain which would not be able to depend upon the help of her present allies. Our object therefore must be the destruction of militarism; 'the spirit of militarism can be eradicated from the heart of the German people only by the defeat of the German army'. A compromise peace would mean only a renewal of the struggle and the suffering.

In 1917 Lord Beaverbrook was appointed Minister of Information, which was really a pseudonym for propaganda. He took over the direction of Wellington House. At the same time it was determined to start an intelligence department at the Foreign Office. The members of the Intelligence Bureau, who had in fact been working closely with the Foreign Office, were asked to join. The Minister of Information objected on the grounds that no government office could invite the transfer of officials from another department. When they heard of it the staff of the Intelligence Bureau resigned.[2] They were then reappointed to the F.O.[3] There was one exception. R. W. Seton-Watson, in accordance with his

[1] See Appendix, p. 202.
[2] *The Issue* (London: Constable, 1917), p. 23.
[3] The P.I.D. was finally constituted in April 1918. Confidential 4428, Record Office 371/4382.

own choice, was transferred to the Enemy Propaganda Department. My father much regretted the loss of his expert advice on central and south-eastern Europe.

The Political Intelligence Department of the Foreign Office was nicknamed the 'Ministry of all the Talents'. They were indeed a gifted crew. My father was assistant director under Sir William Tyrrell. The members included Arnold Toynbee, Lewis Namier, Alfred Zimmern, Rex and Allen Leeper, Edwyn Bevan, George Saunders. The number of inquiries and the output of memoranda constantly increased. They were frequently shown papers and invited to comment before action was taken.

On 3 October 1918 Prince Max Von Baden, the newly appointed German Chancellor, addressed to President Wilson the request for an immediate armistice and for peace negotiations on the basis of the President's announcements to Congress[1] (the 'Fourteen Points' of 8 January, and 'Subsequent Addresses'). These pronouncements had been carefully examined in the P.I.D. My father presented a series of memoranda in which he pointed out that many of the proposals were outdated, that in some cases the general statements were mutually incompatible and that on certain points – the freedom of the seas and indemnities – they were contrary to British interests. It would be possible to substitute a few clear, general principles which would strengthen rather than weaken the President's underlying intention.[2] On 11 November the Germans accepted unconditionally the imposition of the armistice terms on the understanding that the subsequent peace would be in accordance with the President's principles as defined in the pre-armistice note of 5 November. Neither Headlam nor any of his colleagues doubted that apart from the specified exceptions we were legally and morally bound by the President's statements. They had been voluntarily accepted by the Allies and must be given a just and impartial interpretation. The obligation was all the stronger since, as a result of the change in circumstances, including the disorganization in Germany, a breach of the agreement on our part could not be resisted by force. It might well have been to our interest to impose unconditional surrender. This had not been done. 'The whole honour and reputation of the allies and of this country in particular is involved in our carrying out in the strictest manner the undertakings which we have made.'[3]

It was presumed that a short, preliminary treaty would be imposed on

[1] *The Memoirs of Prince Max von Baden*, 11 vols. (London: Constable, 1928), p. 23.
[2] 'Memorandum on President Wilson's Speeches as a Basis of Negotiations', 12 October 1918, 4400, FO 371/4368.
[3] 'Memorandum on Settlement with Germany' (26 November, revised 23 December), Confidential 4523, FO 371/4354. Headlam wrote the chapter on 'The Political Aspects of

the defeated enemy in a matter of weeks rather than months. This was on the analogy of the Treaty of Paris after the Napoleonic Wars. (Headlam drew attention to Professor Webster's essay on Castlereagh's policy.)[1] The state of war would end, the blockade would be lifted, normal trade would be resumed. In doubtful cases – including the German colonies – territories would be held in trust by the Allied and Associated Powers. This would make careful investigation possible before final decisions were reached. Germany would take part in the subsequent Peace Conference. Austria–Hungary, which had ceased to exist as a sovereign state, would not be represented.

The experts in the P.I.D. prepared detailed statements on all the possible issues that might arise. They also correlated the work done in other Government departments and examined the proposals made by the French Ministers at the beginning of December. Headlam summarized the conclusions reached in a 'Memorandum on the Settlement with Germany'.[2] Alsace-Lorraine would be ceded to France with the frontier of 1871. It would be a service to peace and reconciliation if the French allowed their right to be confirmed by a vote of the inhabitants. But it was unlikely that they would agree to this. Further French claims to annexation or control of territory on the left bank of the Rhine should be rejected as contrary to the principle of self-determination and detrimental to the long-term interests of France. Germany must accept that the populations concerned be consulted in regard to rectification of the frontiers with Belgium and Denmark. Areas with a predominantly Polish population in Posnania and Silesia would be ceded to the Allies. Germany would take part in the final drawing of the frontiers at the Peace Conference. Danzig would remain in Germany.

In regard to reparations the French demand for the total cost of the war must be rejected since it ran counter to the accepted terms of the pre-armistice agreement. Germany could be charged for restoring the occupied territories and for damage done to civilians. Since Germany's capacity to pay might not cover the whole amount it was in the interests of this country to state her claims clearly and precisely. They would be limited to loss of merchant shipping and damage by air raids. The Dominions would get nothing. The largest share would go to France and Belgium, and rightly

---

the Armistice Negotiations' in Sir H. V. Temperley's *History of the Peace Conference*, 4 vols. (London: Institute of International Affairs, 1920-4), Vol. I. See also P.C.M., 'The End of the War', Confidential 13680.

[1] *The Congress of Vienna*, Foreign Office Handbooks, nos. 165/165a, Vol. XXIV.

[2] Confidential 4523, FO 371/4354.

so, for they had suffered most. Headlam had arranged that the Treasury memorandum[1] should be circulated in the Foreign Office – it was not at that time attributed to Keynes. Headlam commented: 'This is an admirable memorandum'; he gave some elucidation of the indemnity paid by France in 1871 and pointed out that Germany could not claim as part payment the value of natural resources in the ceded territories. He urged acceptance of the Treasury view that allied claims should be limited to civilian damage and suggested that a capital payment over a few years would be to the general advantage rather than a long-drawn-out tribute. This was minuted 'I agree' by Eyre Crowe and initialled by Robert Cecil. In his own Memorandum Headlam suggested that the coalfields in the Saar Valley might be transferred to France to meet the shortage caused by the destruction of the mines in the Pas de Calais. He appears to have thought that the Germans might consent to this as a major act of reparation.

Valuable work was done in the Foreign Office on the League of Nations by Alfred Zimmern, Noel-Baker and Eustace Percy. This was afterwards put to good use by Lord Robert Cecil. In commenting on proposals put forward by the War Office Headlam argued that the League of Nations if firmly established would provide effective security and bring to an end the pre-war system of conflicting armed alliances.[2] He did not think it wise to impose on its members – and among these he included Germany – any particular system of defence. In a 'Memorandum on Conscription and Militarism'[3] he pointed out that compulsory service was not the source of militarism. A short-service militia might be the ideal system but the League of Nations could scarcely interfere in the details of domestic legislation. Militarism in Prussia and in Germany had resulted from the privileged position of the Officers' Corps. It might well be fostered in a long-service professional army. Lord Robert Cecil commented on this that although he did not desire to identify himself altogether with the conclusions, they seemed to him to justify great caution in dealing with the disarmament question. The paper should be circulated to the Cabinet.

For reasons best known to himself Lloyd George decided that General Smuts, not the Foreign Office, should prepare the British proposals for the Peace Conference. Smuts had no adequate staff and so far as Europe was concerned little knowledge. He worked himself nearly to death, but

[1] Confidential 4386, FO 371/4369.
[2] Minute on 'Memorandum on the Future Franco-German Frontier', communication by the General Staff, 15 January 1917, 4409, FO 371/4377.
[3] Confidential 4699, 6 January 1919, PC/020, FO 371/4356.

did not even read most of the papers submitted to him. He produced a League of Nations scheme and a plan for establishing mandated territories in the former Habsburg and Turkish lands – not in Africa. In regard to Europe the Government did not, before the meeting of the Conference, produce any agreed policy or plan of action. That some of the expert advice did reach the heads of delegation was due to the unremitting labours of Lloyd George's private secretary, Philip Kerr.

The Memoir describes Headlam's interests and activities as a member of the British Delegation at Paris. He became involved in most of the territorial problems of the settlement with Germany in both the west and in the east – Belgium, Slesvig, the Saar Valley, Alsace-Lorraine, Danzig and the Polish Corridor. He was the British representative on the *ad hoc* committee which after the presentation of the Treaty to Germany revised the terms in regard to Upper Silesia. As early as February he expressed interest in the position of minorities. It was largely due to his efforts that the Polish Treaty for the Protection of Minorities was ready for signature on the same day as the Treaty of Versailles. Towards the end he was principally concerned in the work of the New States Committee.

In the United States work on a programme for peace had begun as early as April 1917. The members of the 'Inquiry'[1] were for the most part academic figures. They had no experience of politics and were isolated from the State Department. Their researches were finalized in two reports which were submitted to the President. Headlam took part in the first exchange of views with the American experts. This did not take place till February. He and his colleagues were then given copies of the American 'case' in exchange for some P.I.D. reports.

Several members of the Inquiry played an important part at Paris. My father found their interpretation of the President's principles oddly inconsistent. None the less he was firmly convinced that the peace of the world would depend on the united efforts of Great Britain and America. In this he found a sympathetic partner in Professor Shotwell. They did all they could to promote intellectual as well as political understanding.

When the conference met it was still assumed that this was a preliminary meeting to prepare a preliminary treaty. But for weeks on end nothing was done to achieve this purpose. The leaders of the major powers were burdened with the immediate problems arising from the war. Wilson insisted that the League of Nations must come first, the new states were encouraged to state their claims, committees got to work on the details

[1] L. E. Gelfand, *The Inquiry* (New Haven, Conn.: Yale University Press, 1963).

of the final settlement. In the Memoir there is no mention of the Fontaine-bleau Memorandum of 25 March in which Lloyd George defined the British policy for peace with Germany. But in answer to criticism from his colleagues in the P.I.D. Headlam was able to tell them at the beginning of April that at last things had begun to move and that important decisions had been taken.[1] The almost haphazard changes in organization, the establishment of the Council of Four which gave direct instructions to a small number of experts did in fact lead to greater speed and efficiency.[2] Towards the end the work was done under enormous pressure: there was little possibility of correlation. Wilson seems at last to have realized that he was not prepared – never had been prepared – to get two treaties through the Senate. The idea of a preliminary treaty went by the board. When the Germans finally arrived they were faced with a single comprehensive settlement to be imposed, not negotiated.

My father had a great personal regard for Mr Balfour and gave him full credit for speeding up the conference whilst Lloyd George was away in February. None the less he held him chiefly to blame for the earlier delays and confusions. When the Prime Minister was otherwise occupied it was for him to propose that the Foreign Ministers should meet and pre-pare the preliminary treaty.[3] At Paris he should have insisted that the organization, so far as the British delegation was concerned, should be entrusted to the official head of the Foreign Office who had diplomatic experience and knowledge of the matters in hand.

In spite of the unnecessary difficulties caused by faulty organization – delay at the beginning, haste at the end – Headlam enjoyed the work at Paris; the handling of practical problems, the meetings and discussions with those by whom the ultimate decisions were made, the opportunity sometimes to carry into effect, however imperfectly, the ideas that had been worked out in the Foreign Office. He became increasingly convinced that frontiers should be drawn according to nationality. To substitute economic for strategic boundaries would be a cause of future war. The right principle was to settle the frontiers according to nationality; once that had been achieved every effort should be made to encourage the greatest amount of free commercial intercourse between the nations. Whenever possible the local population should be consulted. As late as 1 April, in a paper[4] submitted for Lloyd George's personal attention, he

[1] See letter to Edwyn Bevan, 4 April, and letter to George Saunders, 7 April 1919.
[2] P.C.M., 'The Origins and Procedure of the Conference. III The Peace Conference' Confidential 13915.
[3] P.C.M., 'The Origins and Procedure of the Conference. II From the Armistice to the Opening of the Conference', Confidential 13681.   [4] Lloyd George Papers.

suggested that Germany should cede Danzig to the Allied and Associated Powers and that the final decision should await a detailed examination on the spot. He regretted that in regard to the Saar Valley the original intention became obscured owing to the French demand for annexation on political and historical grounds. He discovered that other provisions for coal deliveries were to be made only as a result of a casual conversation with Keynes.

None the less he agreed that it was necessary to make a major exception in granting to Czechoslovakia the historic boundaries of the kingdom of Bohemia. He enjoyed a constant exchange of views with R. W. Seton-Watson and came to believe that the Czechs, under the leadership of Masaryk, could be trusted to treat their minorities justly; that a state of mixed nationality might be successfully established.[1] But if nearly three million Sudeten Germans were to be separated from Austria on grounds of geographical necessity it was all the more important to prevent the cession to Italy of the Germans in the South Tyrol – the land of Andreas Hofer. He urged the point on Lloyd George who said he could do nothing about it as he was tied by the Treaty of London. Lloyd George told him to see the President. He did in fact have a further interview with Wilson which is not recorded in the Memoir. Wilson was as always courteous and attentive but on this occasion rigid in refusal. He was having a major row with the Italians about Fiume and the Adriatic and would not be involved in further trouble over 500,000 Germans.

Headlam assumed that the League of Nations would be a permanent standing organization, not just a conference to be summoned at times of crisis. Many of his own proposals, notably in regard to the Saar Valley, Danzig and the protection of minorities, presupposed the supervision of an international administration. The League of Nations should make possible the peaceful coexistence of nations great and small.[2] The partitions of Poland had been the greatest crime against European civilization. Her restoration and the liberation of the Baltic peoples could not have been achieved by peaceful means. If war had been avoided in 1914 the aspirations of the Slav populations of the Danube Basin would in the long run have caused the forcible disruption of the Habsburg Monarchy. Now, at great cost, the 'suppressed nationalities' had won their freedom. The setting-up of independent national states from Finland to Yugoslavia might prove the one positive result of the war – the foundation of a lasting peace.

[1] P.C.M., 'The Territorial Settlement with Germany. The Southern Frontier', Confidential 13918.
[2] Draft of 'Memorandum on the League of Nations'. Not completed.

The experts in the P.I.D. sent constant reports on the disastrous consequences of the blockade. Edwyn Bevan, George Saunders and Alfred
Zimmern agreed that in Germany there had been a genuine change of
heart, a sincere response to democracy; the Spartacists and right-wing
reactionaries drew their support from people driven to despair by hunger
and privation.[1] These were all men who had given devoted service during
the war and had been opposed to a compromise peace. Their views were
endorsed in even stronger terms by officers returning from Germany.
Unless the blockade were lifted, the children fed, there would be anarchy,
and from anarchy a disillusioned people would turn to Bolshevism.[2] My
father drew hope from the appointment of Lord Robert Cecil as head of
the Supreme Economic Council.[3] But its functions were chiefly advisory
and the Americans, who had had enough of it over reparations, not unnaturally looked askance on British proposals for reconstruction. Headlam
became convinced that the most urgent necessity was to secure peace. The
territorial provisions were on the whole just, the worst parts of the
Treaty, which would break down in any case, could be amended afterwards.

The Memoir ends with the signature of the Treaty of Versailles.
Headlam stayed on in Paris until the Austrian treaty was finally drafted
at the end of August. In spite of all the difficulties – the heat, the whittling-
down of the delegation, the flagging interest of those who remained – he
enjoyed the work on the New States Committee. The Austrian treaty
drove him almost to despair. The Foreign Office had from the first
advised that a voluntary economic federation of the Danubian states would
be the best solution. Should German Austria afterwards decide to join
with Germany, she should not be prevented.[4] Headlam did his best to
introduce a measure of consistency. Austria should be established as a
new state, not as an inheritor of the rights or obligations of the Habsburg
Monarchy.[5] The economic and financial arrangements he considered
utterly unworkable. He thought the Austrian Ministers would be well
advised to reject the whole thing and throw the responsibility on to the
Allies.[6] It was not to be – the tragedy of Austria must take its course.

[1] Letters from Edwyn Bevan, 5 February and 17 March 1919. Letter from George Saunders.
[2] See report from Lieutenant Thornby Gibson on a journey through Germany 1–24 February. My father received this on 6 March and sent it straight on to Philip Kerr.
[3] Letter to Alfred Zimmern, 10 March 1919.
[4] PC 4523. Minute by Lord Hardinge on the 'French Attitude as to the Future of Germany
and German Austria', PC 65, PRO FO 371/4354.
[5] Letter to Mr Randall, 4 June 1919, and letter to George Saunders, 26 July 1919.
[6] Letter to Lewis Namier, 29 August 1919.

My father much regretted that neither Lewis Namier nor Rex Leeper were included in the British Delegation. He did manage to get Namier out for a short time in May and arranged for him to see Paderewski about the minorities treaty. (The visit had a further significance since it was the occasion of Namier's first meeting with Weizmann.) Both Namier and Leeper wrote regularly, Namier at great length, sometimes two or three times a week. They were both in their different ways anti-Polish and friendly to Russia. My father agreed that the final settlement of the borderlands should be held over until it was possible to negotiate with a Russian Government. In the meantime the *de facto* Governments should be given provisional recognition, and aid, especially food, should be sent at once.[1] He held that General Haller's army in France should be allowed to go home to Poland. Leeper, who maintained that the Bolsheviks were a small but ruthless minority, would have favoured intervention on behalf of Kolchak. Namier, who agreed with my father that intervention would be dangerous and impracticable, seems to have assumed that somehow some kind of popular government would emerge.

At my father's request Namier supplied detailed information about political personalities and trends of opinion in eastern and central Europe. He was highly critical of Dmowski, Grabski and the whole 'chauvinist gang' of the Polish National Democrats. He admired Masaryk and Otto Bauer, the Austrian Socialist leader,[2] 'one of the best men in office in Europe'.

Namier was a firm believer in nationality. The peoples of the former Habsburg Monarchy should be given full freedom to express their national aspirations. He approved the desire of the Austrian Socialists to join with Germany. As Otto Bauer pointed out, the 'French' solution of an economic union of the Danubian states was impossible without political union. It could be achieved only if there were submission to a majority decision in a common assembly: 'this cannot be expected of people who have recently gained their independence'.

In regard to Galicia, the home of his childhood, Namier's own feelings were deeply involved. West Galicia could justly be claimed by Poland, but in East Galicia there was an overwhelming majority of Ruthenians, a sturdy, self-reliant peasant people who had suffered too long under the oppression of the Polish landlords. They should be free to choose their

---

[1] Letter to Zimmern, 18 February 1919. Referring to Estonia, Courland and Lithuania: 'It seems to me appalling to have left these people all these months practically without any help.'
[2] Letters to H.–M., 1 and 3 February 1919.

own destiny – either a small independent state or union with their com-
patriots and co-religionists in the Ukraine. There was a substantial
minority of Jewish traders and intellectuals. They too had had their fill
of Polish repression and would support an independent Ukraine.[1] My
father agreed. As an authority on Germany and central Europe he had no
official standing in the matter, but he did all he could to support Namier's
view, he pressed it on Sir William Tyrrell and circulated to the conference
a number of Namier's papers. As a matter of fact Lloyd George and Balfour were remarkably well informed on the racial issues of Galicia.[2] The
P.I.D. had done its work. The French supported the most extreme Polish
claims. The Americans wavered. Namier wrote with increasing bitterness of the pogroms, the violence of the Polish forces, the exploitation of
the anti-Bolshevik bogy. Petlura, the Ukrainian leader, was fighting on
three fronts against Dennikin, against the Bolsheviks and against the Poles.[3]
My father agreed that Sir Esme Howard had fallen completely under
Polish influence. But the real trouble was the difficulty of effective
intervention in this remote area. He thought it most regrettable that no
Allied representative was sent to observe and advise the Ruthenian provisional government at Tarnopol.[4] In the end the Ruthenians were suppressed by force and the decisions taken in Paris were brushed aside. So
that spark of freedom was blown out.

In the drafting of the minorities treaties my father was much indebted
to Namier's advice and the information he supplied. On one point they
disagreed. In regard to the Polish Treaty Namier constantly referred to
'Jewish National Autonomy'; my father objected that although it was
legitimate for the Zionists to seek national independence in Palestine it
would be most dangerous for them to claim separate nationality within the
states to which they owed citizenship.[5] Namier accepted this in so far as
instead of 'national autonomy' he used the expression 'cultural autonomy'.
The assimilationist Jews, he wrote, were concerned chiefly with countries
where the Jews were a small, scattered minority. 'Every one who has
gained a foothold in another nation does not want those whom he has
abandoned to develop an individuality of their own.'[6] In Poland and in
other East European countries there were homogenous Jewish communities. 'The Polish language and Polish culture is strange to us and hostile.
It is permeated by a spirit of Roman Catholicism and by the most rampant,
aggressive, intolerant anti-Semitism, to make the Jews feed on it is the

[1] Letters from Namier, 10, 13, 14 May 1919. [2] P.C.M., East Galicia, N 4819/77/55.
[3] Letter from Namier, 16 April 1919. [4] P.C.M., East Galicia.
[5] Letter to Namier, 30 June 1919. [6] Letter from Namier, 12 July 1919.

same as to make men eat straw and wood.' Earlier he had written more generously of the 'Polish tradition which is bound up with Poland's history, and its villages and fields and its churches and the graves of their ancestors and the altars of their saints . . . We also have our traditions which are strongly national . . . which start with the prophets and will not end till the last of their prophecies comes true.'[1] In the Polish minorities treaty there is no specific reference to Hebrew or Yiddish, but my father secured a provision that Jewish committees should be appointed to administer the funds granted for Jewish schools and hospitals.[2]

Namier's reaction to politics was often emotional, sometimes inconsistent. My father was essentially rational, detached, objective. None the less they had many things in common, not least their sense of the respect due to the defeated enemy. In the German response to their humiliation Namier saw something of the Promethean spirit.

> Müsst mir meine Erde doch lassen stehen
> Und meine Hütte die du nicht gebaut
> Und meinen Herd um dessen Glut du mich beneidest.

But one could not be astonished that the French and Belgians should not feel the same since their hearths and homes were not left to them.[3]

My father set great store by Namier's knowledge and insight. He did, however, rebuke him in no measured terms for his fanatical dislike and suspicion of the Poles and for his unwarranted diatribes against Paderewski. Namier took this in good part. About Ruthenia and Haller's army he was inclined to say 'I told you so'. He did not resent criticism. He treated my father always with affection and respect, what the Germans would call *Ehrfurcht*. He was the most faithful of friends.

When he left Paris Headlam took a short, well-earned holiday. He had not lived at Whorlton since his father died, but his elder brother was generous in hospitality. Headlam and his family spent many holidays there. He loved the moors and fells of Upper Teesdale – rich in alpine flowers; the lakes and mountains of Cumberland where he enjoyed the company of his Spedding cousins; the bare limestone hills of Ribblesdale where, for a brief period before he sold the Morley estate, he was Lord of the Manor of Rathmell. He and my brother were ardent geologists; they would clamber along the bed of the Tees chopping off bits of rock to see

---

[1] Letters from Namier, 19 May to 2 July 1919.
[2] P.C.M., Minorities Treaties, Confidential 13507. He wrote a chapter on 'Treaties for the Protection of Minorities' in Temperley's *History of the Peace Conference*.
[3] Letter from Namier ,13 February 1919.

how the shale had been metamorphosed by the basalt dykes at High Force and Cauldron Snout. Sometimes I was allowed to join in searching for crystals in the old lead mines near Keswick or explore the caves at Settle where the river runs underground through a forest of stalactites and stalagmites. In the year after the conference we were taken for the first time on a climbing expedition to Switzerland.

In 1920 the P.I.D. came to an end. Headlam was then appointed historical adviser to the Foreign Office. The post was created for him and was not renewed after his retirement.[1] During the next nine years he was called upon to write memoranda giving the historical background of all manner of current problems – from China to the Rhineland. He greatly enjoyed the work. Since he was 'adviser' he did not hesitate when occasion arose to give advice. In his spare time he wrote reviews on pretty well all the significant books on international affairs, published in this country and abroad – mostly for *The Times* and the *T.L.S.*

He was much concerned at this time with the setting-up and development of the Institute of International Affairs. It started in a small way in Malet Street but soon moved to Chatham House. His work in the P.I.D. had led my father to believe that the conduct of foreign policy, which had suffered much from ignorant popular agitation, would be assisted by the informed opinion of people engaged in other branches of public life. He and Lionel Curtis had hoped that it would be possible to establish an Anglo-American foundation. This was not to be.

Headlam was from the first a member of the Council and Chairman of the Publications Committee. It was largely owing to his initiative that Arnold Toynbee was invited to produce an *Annual Survey*. At first it was a modest undertaking but under Toynbee's guidance it became, as it now is, an established classic of historical research. In the early days my father used to read through the proofs. I remember once, when the thing had outgrown the publisher's prescription of length he threw it on the lawn in despair – 'if only Toynbee did not know so much history'.

Headlam was instrumental also in setting up the Press Cutting Bureau at Chatham House. It has proved of inestimable value to those who attempt research in recent history.

It was at this time that he got to know John Wheeler-Bennett and advised him to take part in the work of the Institute. Wheeler-Bennett

---

[1] See Arnold J. Toynbee, *Acquaintances* (New York and Toronto: Oxford University Press, 1967). From time to time distinguished scholars – notably E. L. Woodward and Rohan Butler – have worked for the F.O. as historical advisers but they also held academic appointments and were not full-time Civil Servants.

was then a young man, quite unknown. The books that have made him famous were not yet written. My father treasured his friendship. He admired his individuality, his ceaseless inquiry and his generous response to every kind of human problem. Sir John writes:

> I often used to go and have tea with him at the Foreign Office, bringing him problems of my own work and research and sitting at his feet imbibing wisdom (also rather stale cake) . . . One of the important things about him from the point of view of a young man was that he never 'rebuked one's genius'. He was always evocative and stimulating. For a man of great brilliance himself, he was really very humble and he always had time to listen to the views of others. When he disagreed or could clearly show that the other person was wrong, he did so with great kindness and courtesy.

Headlam reacted strongly against Keynes's *The Economic Consequences of the Peace*.[1] He did not question the purely economic argument but he considered Keynes's account of the procedure and purposes of the conference to be a travesty of the facts. He proposed writing a series of articles which, if published in England and America, might do something to counteract the prevailing mood of cynicism.[2] This was approved by Lord Curzon. But official caution prevailed and nothing came of it. It did, however lead on to a larger project. Headlam was instructed to write an official history of the Peace Conference. This would consist partly of memoranda prepared to elucidate issues of policy; partly of research specially undertaken for the purpose. It is ironic that when he came to study reparations he produced a memorandum (1922)[3] which, although – or perhaps because – it is more moderate and detached than Keynes's book, is an even stronger indictment.

A study of the evidence then available left no doubt that the pre-armistice note of 5 November 1918 was a British draft. Germany must make compensation for all damage done to the civilian population of the Allies and their property by her aggression by land, by sea and in the air. It was not at that time questioned by the French. The Belgians wanted to include a reference to indemnities but Lloyd George opposed this since it might lead to a prolongation of the war. Afterwards the Prime Minister came to realize that the actual payment made would in all

[1] John Maynard Keynes, *The Economic Consequences of the Peace* (London: Macmillan, 1920).
[2] Letter to Philip Kerr, 23 June 1920, Lothian Papers, GD/40/17.
[3] P.C.M., Reparations, Confidential 11984.

probability be limited by Germany's capacity. This was taken as justification for the shifting of the ground to total cost of the war, which would
increase the share due to Great Britain and meet the demands of the
Dominions. The rest of the story is recounted in detail: the undermining
of Lloyd George's position by the report of the Cabinet Committee,
which at a crucial stage of the election campaign recommended that
Germany both could and should pay interest on a liability of £24 milliard
(the Treasury had calculated the liability at £4 milliard, the capacity at
about £3 milliard); the firm opposition of the Americans; Wilson's
surrender over the inclusion of pensions and separation allowances as
civilian damage (surprisingly enough on the advice of General Smuts);
finally the failure to fix a sum and the indefinite prolongation of the period
of payment. In conclusion Headlam pointed out that the Americans had
consistently refused to discuss reparations in relation to war debts. Where
their own interests were concerned they too were subject to a democratic
electorate.

The memorandum was circulated to the Cabinet in 1924. It led to an
extraordinary outburst by Sir Maurice Hankey,[1] who quite contrary to
my father's intention seems to have taken it as a personal affront. He
chastised the 'professional' historian not only for his disloyalty but for his
incapacity and dismissed much of the evidence as tittle-tattle. (Headlam
had made it clear when he was taking his facts from documents and
when he was referring to information given by people who took part in
these events, a legitimate and proper source in the writing of contemporary history. The most important of these verbal sources was a long interview with Col. House.) In his answer Headlam pointed out that he had
accused Lloyd George only of giving way to extreme pressure. Hankey
asserted that Lloyd George had always had in mind the possibility of
charging the total cost of the war. If this were true – which it was not –
the Prime Minister would be guilty of a far graver offence: deliberate
duplicity not only towards the Germans, but also towards the Americans.[2]

[1] Reparations, Confidential FO 11984, enclosed a criticism of Mr Headlam-Morley's
memorandum, 23 July 1924.
[2] Headlam-Morley, answer to Sir Maurice Hankey, enclosed with FO 11984. See also
Stephen W. Roskill, *Hankey: Man of Secrets* (London: Collins, 1972), Vol. II. In a footnote
(p. 49) referring to Hankey's appointment as Secretary to the Conference Captain Roskill
quotes one sentence from Hankey's paper which in this context is entirely irrelevant. He
does not refer to Headlam's answer (in which he paid tribute to Hankey's unique service in
his own field); Lord Hankey attacked Headlam's views on the armistice as though they were
an individual eccentricity. He does not mention the Treasury memorandum or the Foreign
Office proposals. As Hankey became ill at the time and was seriously overworked it is probable that he was genuinely unaware of the implications of the pre-armistice agreement.

In his life of Lord Balfour Mr Kenneth Young gives quotations from Hankey's correspondence which show that Balfour was partly responsible for Hankey's effort.[1] Balfour was notoriously absent-minded and by this time he may well have forgotten the part he himself played in the negotiations leading up to the armistice. My father never thought Balfour would resent criticism. Their personal relations were unaffected. Balfour took a sincere interest in my mother's music. He and my father were drawn together by the mutual affection of Balfour's niece, Mrs Dugdale.[2] Baffy, as she was called, was also a great admirer of Lewis Namier. They had a common interest in the Zionist cause. My father always maintained that the Balfour Declaration had been not just an opportunist move but a genuine expression of idealism – all the more impressive since it came from a man who was often sceptical to the point of cynicism.

Already at Paris Headlam had maintained that the more extreme demands of the French were due not to imperialist ambition but to a not unnatural sense of insecurity: 'The French are so frightened of a great Germany with nearly double the population of France that they resort to any manoeuvre or intrigue to break off a fraction of it.'[3] The French had been given no firm promise of military support; the Anglo-American guarantee had come to nothing. This had bedevilled every post-war issue, including reparations, and had made impossible the economic reconstruction of Europe.

In 1925, when Austen Chamberlain was about to reject the Geneva Protocol, Headlam wrote urging the need for an alternative European protocol. Partial alliances between individual countries were scarcely compatible with the League of Nations. But in certain geographic areas the states concerned might well undertake special obligations. Great Britain had always in her own interests been concerned in the security of western Europe. She could no longer dissociate herself from eastern Europe. (The failure to recognize this had been a fundamental cause of war in 1914.) Great Britain could not remain indifferent to a new partition of Poland or to the dismemberment of Czechoslovakia. Adjustment of frontiers would be possible once there was a firm sense of security. But in

[1] Kenneth Young, *Arthur James Balfour* (London: G. Bell, 1963), pp. 411–12. Mr Young's argument is a little difficult to follow since he refers to the 'Peace talks in Paris at the beginning of 1919' when it seems that he means the discussions leading up to the armistice in October and November 1918. He also seems not to have heard of Keynes's *Economic Consequences*.
[2] Mrs Edgar Dugdale, author of *Arthur James Balfour*, 11 vols. (London: Hutchinson, 1936).
[3] Letter to Alfred Zimmern.

its main features the territorial settlement was just, and it should be maintained. Germany should be invited to join the League of Nations. The European members should undertake special obligations towards each other. In this European protocol the British Dominions need not take part. There was every reason to suppose that Germany would prove a loyal member of the association. Given proper support the democratic government would be firmly established. Should things go wrong a clear statement of our intentions in regard to eastern Europe would be all the more essential.

> Imagine . . . that Austria rejoined Germany; that Germany using the discontented minority in Bohemia demanded a new frontier far over the mountains including Carlsbad and Pilsen, and at the same time, in alliance with Germany, the Hungarians recovered the southern slope of the Carpathians. This would be catastrophic, and, even if we neglected to interfere to prevent it happening, we should be driven to interfere, probably too late.[1]

In stressing the dangers that might arise in eastern Europe Headlam had run too far ahead. The Government were concerned with the immediate problem of French security. Sir Eyre Crowe asked for a further memorandum in which Headlam emphasized the historic continuity of British interest in the freedom of the Low Countries. In view of recent developments he suggested that Great Britain, France, Belgium and Germany should join in a mutual guarantee of their respective frontiers. It was greatly to be desired that Holland also should participate. Such a Western security pact would be a first stage in achieving the purpose of the Geneva Protocol; it would be in accordance with traditional British interests and would be confined to an area where the frontiers conformed with the wishes of the peoples concerned: 'we could therefore without misgiving ask the federated nations of the Empire to join with us in a formal guarantee'.[2] Headlam strongly supported the Locarno policy. But he was never quite happy about the British attitude in regard to eastern Europe. In a private letter to Lord D'Abernon he pointed out that if there were danger from Germany in the future this would be in the east rather than on the Rhine.

Headlam and his colleagues in the F.O. had hoped and expected that Germany would join the League of Nations at the earliest opportunity

---

[1] 'Memorandum on the History of British Policy and the Geneva Protocol', 12 February 1925, PRO FO 371/11064.
[2] 'Memorandum on the Problem of Security and the Low Countries', 10 March 1925. PRO FO 371/11065. See Sybil Eyre Crowe, 'Sir Eyre Crowe and the Locarno Pact', *English Historical Review*, January 1972. Also *Studies in Diplomatic History*.

after the ratification of the Treaty. My father held that this would be the proper occasion for revising, or at least mitigating, the effects of the punitive clauses, especially the so-called war guilt clause (art. 231). At Paris he had not been directly concerned with the matter. But it did come to his notice that the Committee on Responsibilities was about to accept a French version of the causes of war which was historically untenable.[1] In a strongly worded note he pointed out that essential facts were omitted, the Russian mobilization was not even mentioned, no notice was taken of the German contention that their purpose was to localize the conflict between Austria–Hungary and Serbia. Sir Eyre Crowe minuted that the note raised important questions which should not be overlooked;[2] it could be brought to the notice of the committee by the British representative. Sir Frederick Pollock, who in these matters was entirely ignorant, ignored the advice. Unfortunately the report leaked out. It was eventually published in the proceedings of the American Senate. The Germans used it with great skill to discredit the intentions of the conference.

Afterwards Headlam was consulted by the Attorney-General about the trial of the Emperor and the war criminals. He held that we should stick to the then established system of international law and not apply *ex post facto* rules (this also was the American view). The Emperor could in theory be charged with a flagrant breach of treaty obligations in regard to Belgium and Luxemburg. But it would be almost impossible to establish an adequate tribunal. He pointed out that the Dutch Government would in all probability refuse extradition. So indeed it turned out and we were forced into ignominious retreat after an unedifying attempt to bully and coerce a small neutral country.

At the time of Locarno Headlam once more returned to the issue in a 'Memorandum on Responsibility'.[3] There could be no doubt that at the time of the Peace Conference the Allied statesmen had been sincerely convinced of the culpability of Germany and her allies. This was no trumped-up charge invented for propaganda purposes. The Germans thought otherwise. The fault consisted in compelling them, by threat of force, to admit that they and their allies were solely responsible for the war – a statement which they, no less sincerely, believed to be untrue. The result had been an unending controversy. Volume upon volume had been written but impartial scholarship was made almost impossible by political bias. In Germany it led to bitterness and resentment which was grist to the mill of every political mischief-maker. When Germany joined the League of Nations she would undertake to abide by her treaty obligations. The

[1] P.C.M. 4471.   [2] Minute on PC 5463, 473/2/4.   [3] P.C.M. 4771.

Treaty of Versailles would be voluntarily accepted. This surely was the moment to remove the stigma of moral guilt which she had consistently rejected. It could be done by a simple statement to the effect that the Allies, whilst retaining their freedom of judgement on the subject, no longer desired officially to maintain the position taken up in 1919, still less would they expect the German Government to be bound by it. The new evidence available should be left to the normal course of historical investigation. This proposal was turned down by pretty well everyone concerned. 'It would raise a storm', 'it would spoil the prospects of real progress', 'passions would be aroused', the guilt of Germany had long since been established by the verdict of opinion, nothing would alter it.[1] Sir William Tyrrell alone showed some sympathy for the views expressed and directed that the paper be brought to the notice of the Secretary of State (Sir Eyre Crowe had died earlier that year). Austen Chamberlain minuted: 'To raise the issue now in any form is to rush upon bitter controversy.' They intended to receive Germany into the community of nations, they hoped in all sincerity to help her in overcoming the economic and financial difficulties that had resulted from the treaties. But the condemnation must stand. My father thought that things might turn out better if an attempt were made also to resolve the moral issue. Maybe he was right.

In 1926 Headlam was ill with pleurisy. At that time some doctors still thought that a warm climate would do good. (What he really needed was the mountain air of Switzerland.) His brother, the Bishop of Gloucester, who then as always was concerned with Christian reunion and the overseas missions, suggested that he should examine and report on the Church of England schools in Palestine. The following year I accompanied him on this expedition which he greatly enjoyed. We stayed in grandeur with his old friend George Lloyd at the British Residency in Cairo. After that there followed hectic weeks of travel, inspection and sight-seeing throughout Palestine, Syria and Transjordan. We visited the holy places at Jerusalem and Bethlehem. At that time Nazareth was still an unspoilt village. Standing among the fields and olive groves one could look down on the lake of Tiberias. In Jerusalem my father was greeted with warm affection by Fred Kisch and Norman Bentwich; they took great pride in showing off to him the beginnings of the Hebrew University. He was pleased to find that in the Jewish schools the children were taught Hebrew –Yiddish was dying out. His visit took place during a short period of peace under the firm but benevolent rule of Lord Plumer. My father hoped we would succeed in establishing a successful multiracial state in Palestine,

[1] Covering letter to memorandum C 13831 and 6121.

where the great religions of the world would respect and tolerate each other.

After his illness he took up his work at the F.O. with renewed energy. When he got a chance he enjoyed seeing the places and meeting the people he had come across in his work. With my brother he travelled in Poland and the Baltic states and stayed with the High Commissioner in Danzig. He derived great pleasure from a visit to Prince Max von Baden at Salem. They had much in common – their love of lakes and mountains, their concern with war and peace, their interest in education. During this time also he made friends with Winston Churchill. He had known him on and off at the time of the Peace Conference. Now Churchill asked him to help in the writing of the 'Aftermath'. I used to drive my father to Chartwell at the weekend and pick him up again on the Monday. On one occasion there was quite a large luncheon party. As my father was the chief guest I was told to sit next to Churchill's empty chair at the big round table. After a considerable interval he and my father came in. Churchill continued to talk to him across the table about some problems of international politics. He took not the slightest notice of the other people. On another occasion Churchill was laying down the law about something. My father looked up and said, 'Winston you talk more nonsense than any man I ever met.' Churchill paused, grunted and went on in a slightly subdued tone. (In my father's generation they called each other by their surnames. Churchill was the only friend, not a relative, whom he addressed by his Christian name.) The children were rather spoilt but kind and friendly. Randolph was a good-looking, talkative boy. He and the girls showed me the wild geese, the pigs and the wall their father was building.

Whenever he had time Headlam continued his historical work on the origins of the war. He had welcomed the decision of the German revolutionary Government to start producing diplomatic documents and tried in November 1919 to get permission for Bernstein and Kautzky to come to England for advice and consultation.[1] Later the Austrian and then the German Governments appointed historians who examined the archives and issued very full publications including confidential documents. He urged that we should do likewise. In 1924 Austen Chamberlain endorsed a decision to this effect which had already been taken by Ramsay MacDonald.[2] Two independent historians, G. P. Gooch and Harold Temperley, were appointed as editors. They found that Headlam had already made a

[1] Letter to Philip Kerr, November 1919.
[2] The immediate incentive came from the two historians, R. W. Seton-Watson and Sidney Lee.

complete collection of the relevant correspondence from the murder of the Archduke on 28 June until the British declaration of war on 4 August 1914. This was published first – though in subject-matter it was the last – of the series.[1] In his introduction Headlam pointed out that the opening of the archives had entirely justified the integrity of Sir Edward Grey and of the officials who at his direction had – under enormous stress – produced the White Paper of 6 August.[2] Nothing had been concealed, nothing distorted. He might have confined himself to giving an unabridged text of documents that had been paraphrased but he decided to begin his account some days earlier and to include also some background material. His most important innovation was the inclusion of private letters and of minutes written on the papers at the time. It was a regular custom for representatives abroad to send in addition to their official dispatches private accounts for the information of the Foreign Secretary. To these were added selections from the very valuable correspondence of the Permanent Under-Secretary Lord Carnock (at that time Sir Arthur Nicolson). The minutes written by officials, often briefly and in haste, show better than anything else could do the reaction of those whose duty it was to advise the Secretary of State. A study of the comments written by Sir Eyre Crowe would give to the reader some conception of the qualities which made him one of the most distinguished public servants of the time; 'the quickness and sureness of judgement, the power of bringing his exceptional knowledge and experience to bear upon the immediate problem, above all the intense feeling of responsibility and the single-minded devotion to the honour of the country'. Headlam drew special attention to the memorandum addressed to Sir Edward Grey on 31 July; should it be decided for fear of financial collapse that we could not go to war in a just quarrel we would break the moral bond that had been forged in the Entente and hazard the whole future of the country.[3] Headlam collected and assimilated pretty well all the material available, but official duties pressed hard upon him and he did not get time to write his own book. Arnold Toynbee wrote of the 'tragedy of his untimely death'; 'Headlam died without having had the chance of giving to the world the masterpiece that was in him.'[4]

He became seriously ill in the early summer of 1929. He was only sixty-five and mentally young and vigorous. He had not reached the age when

---

[1] G. P. Gooch and H. Temperley (eds.), *British Documents on the Origins of the War 1898–1914* (London: H.M.S.O., 1926), Vol. XI.
[2] Ibid., Introduction, pp. vi–vii.
[3] Ibid., No. 367, p. 226.   [4] Arnold Toynbee, *Acquaintances*.

it is natural to man to attune his thoughts to death – *memento mori*. He did towards the end realize that he had not long to live. But apart from arranging his affairs he did not seem to trouble much about it. He was interested still in this world and was prepared to take the next on trust. Two days before he said casually, 'I wonder if I shall be alive when my book comes out.'[1] He took his suffering lightly.

He died sooner than had been expected on the 6th of September. It was a beautiful day of early autumn. My brother who was working at Middlesbrough did not arrive till the next morning. I was overcome by grief. My mother, whose grief went deeper, remained calm and composed. They buried him at Whorlton. His old friend and opponent, André Tardieu, wrote of him: 'Nous n'étions pas toujours d'accord mais la magnifique droiture de son jugement et de son caractère faisait qu'on s'entendrait toujours. Il avait une nature douce, amicale et gaie.'

[1] *Studies in Diplomatic History.*

'Note on the Diary by Miss Hughes'

Mr Headlam-Morley arrived in Paris on 11 January 1919. He came over with the Prime Minister and many of the principal Delegates. The subordinate staff, including registry clerks, shorthand typists, etc., had preceded them; some had been sent out before Christmas, but another contingent, including myself, had gone out with Sir Eyre Crowe on 4 January. My instructions had been that we were to work in Sir Henry Penson's Department (the Intelligence Clearing House), and I succeeded in procuring a comfortable room on the second floor in the Astoria for Mr Headlam-Morley and a small slip room for myself, and busied myself in arranging the papers and books which I had brought with me.[1]

When Mr Headlam-Morley arrived, all this was changed. There had been some discussions between Sir Henry Penson and Mr Alwyn Parker, who was responsible for the organization of the Conference staff, as to whether he should act in conjunction with the Foreign Office staff or be entirely submerged in Sir Henry Penson's Department. The former course appears to have been determined upon, and Mr Headlam-Morley was therefore assigned a room on the third floor, next to Sir William Tyrrell. It was dreadfully cold during those first weeks, and the heating in the Astoria was very unsatisfactory. Somebody, I believe Lord Hardinge, bought a large quantity of logs, and we endeavoured to make fires on the flat hearths, without any small firewood or coal. This was sometimes successful, but I think the heating must have improved later as I do not remember battling with these fires for very long. Influenza was rampant at the time throughout the whole staff: one after another went down with it; the 'hospital' rooms on the top floor of the Majestic were full to overflowing, and Dr Beauchamp and three nurses were hard pressed to do

---

[1] For further reference to the setting-up and to the internal arrangement of the British Delegation see Harold Nicolson's *Peacemaking, 1919* (London: Constable, 1933), pp. 44–5, as well as Lord Hankey's *The Supreme Command at the Peace Conference, 1919* (London: Allen & Unwin, 1963), pp. 21–9.

what was necessary. Combined with this were food difficulties, no fresh milk, butter or fresh vegetables. This improved later on owing chiefly, I believe, to the insistence of Dr Beauchamp, who took up the question with the Manager of the Midlands Hotels (who was responsible for the catering), but it must of course be remembered that these were early days after the war and food supplies in Paris were very difficult. Mr Headlam-Morley himself escaped the influenza plague, but for some weeks suffered from a bad cold and loss of voice.

As soon as we had settled down and things began to be normal, Mr Headlam-Morley started to write a diary of the events of the Conference, and at first dictated regularly every few days. After that I was laid up with influenza, then came a rush of committee and other work, and unfortunately the diary was only written very intermittently.

I have attempted in the following pages to find sufficient material to present a detailed story of his activities during the whole period of the Conference. In order to do this, I have had to include official minutes and memoranda as well as private letters. It will be noted that he was interested in a very large number of problems and took a prominent part in the work of several committees. The private letters were generally dictated after dinner in his private sitting-room at the Majestic, and typed the following day. No one who was not present can realize the stress of work and the difficulties under which it had to be done. Consultations with members of other delegations started often at 8.30 in the morning and continued far into the night; official dinner parties, followed by long conversations, added to the pressure, and the days were taken up with meetings at the Quai d'Orsay, consultations with economic, legal and other experts, combined with the drafting of reports and clauses in preparation for the next meetings of the Committees.

It will be noted in the letters and diary, especially during the first few weeks, that special reference is often made to the work of Mr Allen Leeper and Mr Toynbee; the reason for this is that they and Mr Headlam-Morley were the three members of the Political Intelligence Department chosen to go to Paris on the permanent staff, and they had of course worked together in London for many months beforehand. Other members of the P.I.D. came over for short periods when special questions came up, including Mr Carnegie, Mr Zimmern, Mr Namier, etc.

THE MEMOIR

Letter to Mr Koppel (F.O.)   13 *January* 1919

We have been trying to start work today in the Hotel Astoria. It is quite a nice building; the rooms are small and very French, but I think they will prove quite comfortable. The F.O. have got a floor to themselves; at present I have a room next to Tyrrell's and am posing as 'Sir William Tyrrell's Assistant'. There is an acute difference of opinion between Parker and Penson whether I should remain here or go down to the second floor where Penson has got his general clearing house. Anyhow I shall remain here until Tyrrell comes and I expect that he will be called upon to decide the question. At present I think I am of most use where I am.

It is very difficult at present to see exactly what we shall have to do and how it will have to be done. I am, however, quite certain of one thing, and that is that we shall want as much information as to current events in different countries as the P.I.D.[1] are able to send us. In particular I feel very lost by not being in close touch with sources of information about Germany; Dudley Ward of the Treasury, who came over on Saturday, of course knows a good deal about it, but I have not come across anybody else who seems to have any interest in the matter at all. Will you therefore tell Saunders, Zimmern and Bevan that I hope they will send us out material either in a raw condition or in the form of memoranda or special notes whenever there is anything of importance, and I am quite sure it will be useful to have, as I suggested, a weekly summary of events. I cannot find out yet what arrangements there are for circulating telegrams; I understand that they are about somewhere, but I have not been able to get hold of any.

P.S. The whole thing is very amusing. The Hotel Majestic has a large lounge in which everyone meets and talks. One sees everyone there and it is quite useful for getting to know who is here. Armitage-Smith[2] is very

---

[1] P.I.D., Political Intelligence Department.
[2] Sydney Armitage-Smith, a member of the Financial Section of the British Delegation.

debonair; of course there are a great number of uniforms and it will be useful being able to get into touch with the military and naval people. The people who have the most work so far are the League of Nations; they have a separate flat in the Majestic where Cecil, Percy, Curtis and Baker are evolving elaborate schemes; hitherto no one else has been allowed to see what they have produced. Important people like Howard and Crowe have their own sitting-rooms in the Hotel where they can see people, in addition to their rooms in the Astoria.[1] The Treasury people, Keynes, Dudley Ward and Armitage-Smith, also have their own flat with their special sitting-room, and I expect a good number of other people will try to get the same. Harris[2] is already very busy and on the ground floor of the Astoria. When going out to lunch today, I found a large crowd of the blaggards who are generally in attendance on him in the Foreign Office. He, I think, is very much wanting Tyrrell to come out.

There is a whole floor at the top of this building given up to the registry; I am glad to say that Miss Bigby seems to have an important position there, and she was very kind to us so that I hope we shall get what we want done.

Extract from letter to Mr Namier (F.O.)   *13 January 1919*

. . . The very first thing I have done on arriving here is to begin getting in touch with the Poles. Rose[3] came to see me yesterday. He had meant to go straight on to Siberia but had found that the Polish Deputation had arrived in France and he had been to see them. He came up and had a long talk to Howard about it yesterday afternoon and has arranged for a meeting to take place today between the leader whose name I cannot possibly remember, and your friend Dmowski, and I am looking forward to hearing the result of it. I gather that the hope is to bring about a *rapprochement* so as to get a union of parties. I will let you know when I hear what has happened, but I think I can already anticipate the result.

I hope you will keep me well supplied with material; if there is anything you do not send officially, will you at any rate write to me quite freely and I shall probably be able to use any information or suggestions that you have to make.

[1] A little later on Mr Headlam-Morley had a very nice suite assigned to him, consisting of sitting-room, bedroom and bathroom. (M.H.)
[2] S. R. Harris, a member of the Political Intelligence Department.
[3] W. J. Rose, a Canadian journalist then employed by the Polish National Committee. See 'Fortnightly Report on Slavonic Affairs', prepared by the Uncommon Language Department, no. 18, 16 January 1919, FO 371/4536/79

Minute to Sir William Tyrrell   *16 January 1919*

Sir Henry Penson is now organizing the work of the Intelligence Clearing House. I feel no doubt that for the efficient working of the Delegation this is absolutely essential. Some general bureau of the kind is necessary if the different sections are to be fully informed about what the others are doing and if the Delegation as a whole is to be kept apprised of the proceedings of the Conference and Committees of the Conference.

The work of his Department so far has consisted chiefly in the answering of inquiries which have been addressed to it from the War Cabinet Secretariat. Several of these have come in and he has been enabled to supply the information wanted very rapidly. It is to be anticipated that similar enquiries will come from other external sources as for instance from Dominion Delegations or from the American Delegation and from other countries. This in itself is a considerable piece of work as it implies rapid communication with sections here and eventually in many cases will require communication with London. If further information is required from London, it is essential that there should be some authority who is to determine by whom the reference to London is to be made.

Again, Sir Henry Penson is proposing to issue a daily bulletin which will contain first the notices of Committee meetings, whether sectional or inter-sectional, which are to take place, and also the meetings of the Conference and Committees of the Conference with the subjects that are to be discussed. In this way each section will know beforehand whether any matter is coming up for discussion in which they are interested. The bulletin will also contain information as to the results of these meetings so that the conclusions arrived at in the Conference itself will be automatically brought to the knowledge of members of the Delegation, and also resolutions arrived at in the Delegation itself will be automatically circulated.

Thirdly, a list is being prepared of official documents which have been prepared by the various sections. This will be classified so that everyone will be able to find out quickly what information on any particular point is available. I need not point out how much we suffered in London from the want of some such method of finding out what had been and was being done by other Departments.

It will be necessary for the working of this scheme that there should be for each Department one officer in that Department to whom inquiries may be addressed from the Central Clearing House, and also an officer in the Central Clearing House representing that Department. The duty of the latter officer could be, among other things, to read the information which comes in from the point of view of the Department he represents.

Originally it was determined that I should be attached to the Clearing House, with Mr Toynbee and Mr Leeper. Mr Toynbee and Mr Leeper are already fully occupied with important work on the matters on which they have special knowledge, and I think it would be most undesirable to take them away from this for more general work. I find that I have been assigned a room, not on the second floor where the Clearing House is situated, but on the fourth floor with the rest of the Foreign Office Staff. The question then arises as to Foreign Office representation in the Clearing House. Personally I think that I could probably be of more use where I am; I should then become the channel of communication on the Foreign Office Staff with the Clearing House. Sir Henry Penson suggests that Mr McKinnon Wood, who has been working at the War Trade Intelligence Department, should be appointed as the political officer there. I should suggest that this arrangement will be the best, at any rate for starting, if Lord Hardinge approves.

I should like to add that the other Departments, the War Office, the Admiralty, the Board of Trade, the Treasury, are all most anxious to co-operate in this scheme, and it is clearly very desirable that there should not be any suggestion that the Foreign Office is holding aloof. There was, I believe, some apprehension that this might be the case, but I have assured Sir Henry Penson that there is no foundation for this at all, and that the Foreign Office will co-operate with it fully.

The original suggestion was that I should be in charge of the whole of the political section downstairs, Mr Carless Davis taking the economic section, and I understand that the War Office and Admiralty representatives had agreed to this.

Extract from diary   *19 January 1919*

We have been here for a week and everyone is settling down to work. The conditions remain, however, in all essential things as unsatisfactory as they were in London. While all subordinate officials are producing their material and are ready to take up and to bring to a practical solution the matters with which they are charged, there remains as before a complete absence of leadership, statesmanship, decision and, apparently, of any sense of responsibility above. It may be useful to mention illustrations of this. I was talking last night to Sir Erle Richards, who has just been summoned from

London to assist in preparing the British case. The two principal points in which he was interested were Western Asia and the Colonies. On both matters he has already apparently drawn up for General Smuts a statement of our case; this, however, was for the confidential use of our own Cabinet. Now it has been determined that each of the Allies shall lay their case upon the table. Of course the statement which would do for our own people would not be suitable for communication to other nations. He finds himself, therefore, in the difficult position that he can get no decision of any kind from the Government as to what our policy is; as he says, he is like a solicitor who cannot get any instructions from his clients. In regard to the Colonies, the major point to be determined is whether we propose to take the Colonies avowedly as the natural fruits of victory after a successful war, or to base our claim on the principles of the League of Nations and the welfare of the natives. This course would imply that we should undertake to accept certain restrictions upon our sovereignty; these restrictions would in reality imply little, if any, change in our established methods of administration. There have been discussions on this matter in the War Cabinet, but they are quite inconclusive and apparently the problem has not been seriously faced. As Sir Erle Richards says, we should be in a stronger position if from the beginning we definitely put forward our acceptance of the new principles on condition that the other colonial states are prepared to do the same. If then these proposals broke down owing to the resistance of the French and other nations, we should be able to adopt the alternative policy with a much better face; but he is completely handicapped until he can get definite instructions. It is to be hoped that the substitution of Lord Milner for Walter Long[1] at the Colonial Office will remove the obstruction which has hitherto come from there.

Sir Erle Richards is confronted by a similar difficulty with regard to the Sykes-Picot Agreement.[2] Concerning this also, no definite decision has been made as to the attitude which we are to assume towards the French.

He talked at length about the question of indemnities and the Fourteen Points. He said he had always taken the view that we were bound by the

[1] Walter Long, Milner's predecessor as Colonial Secretary. In January 1919 he became the new First Lord of the Admiralty.

[2] Secret agreement signed on 16 May 1916 by Sir Mark Sykes and George Picot for the partition of the Ottoman Empire after the War. France was to acquire Syria, the Lebanon, Cilicia and Mosul; Britain was to obtain Transjordan, Iraq and northern Palestine. The rest of Palestine was to have an international regime. Some sort of Arab state was to be established.

Fourteen Points and much regretted that we should in any way give ground for the suggestion that we wished to treat our engagements as a scrap of paper. A short time ago he had been talking to the Attorney-General[1] about it, who said that he and the Government had always held that they were not bound by the Fourteen Points. Sir Erle Richards expressed much concern on hearing this and had asked him whether he had gone into the case carefully; he said that he had not done so. Three days afterwards he came back much concerned, saying that he found on looking through the documents that there seemed no ground for doubt of any kind that we were completely pledged; but apparently the Government does not in the least realize how serious the situation is.

Two days ago Lord Hardinge stopped me in the Hall and started conversation. He said that he had noticed that I was always recurring to the point. I am not sure whether he did this as an expression of approval or of warning. He implied that he did not entirely agree with my view and said that he understood that President Wilson was changing his attitude on the matter. This is inconsistent with what I hear from other sources, and that is that Wilson becomes quite furious when anyone mentions the word 'indemnity' to him and says he will hear of nothing of the kind. But it is perfectly clear that people in authority are not in the least prepared to face the consequences of their own actions in this matter.

A few days ago Mr Dresel, a quasi-American diplomatist, who had just returned from Berlin, was lunching with me. Among other Germans he had seen Rantzau, who said that they were quite prepared to accept the consequences of defeat, but that if the Allies tried to impose upon them unjust terms, inconsistent with the Fourteen Points, they would refuse to accept them and adopt a policy of passive resistance. I mentioned this to Lord Hardinge and pointed out that this would imply the postponement of demobilization; he said it would mean continued occupation of Germany; obviously the total result would be disastrous.

The first formal meeting of the Conference took place yesterday; probably the date was fixed so as to coincide with the anniversary of the proclamation of the German Empire at Versailles. It was characteristic that the days immediately preceding were chiefly occupied with getting out of a very undignified controversy with the press. Wilson and Lloyd George, indignant at an untrue statement made in an American newspaper, had agreed that the proceedings of the Conference should be secret and

[1] Presumably Richards is referring to the previous Attorney-General, F. E. Smith, who had recently become Lord Chancellor, and not to Smith's successor, Sir Gordon Hewart, the former Solicitor-General.

that nothing should be allowed to be published except a single official communiqué. This aroused a storm of indignation. As a *Daily Mail* correspondent, talking to me, said, the democratic countries were not going to stand being treated in this way. The Americans apparently hold that they had come over to sweep away secret diplomacy and bring life and light into the obscurantism of the incompetent old world. The real truth probably is that all the newspapers have spent a great deal of money in sending excessive numbers of correspondents to Paris, and that they naturally want them to get something for their money. The result of the whole thing is that the Conference has been completely beaten; there have been indignation meetings of the press; they have been obliged to assent that all meetings of the Conference shall be public. The only result of this will be that no business at all will be done at the Plenary Sessions and it will probably meet very seldom.

The proceedings at the opening Conference seem from all accounts to have been very undignified. The press could not get any information as to the rules for admission until nearly 2 o'clock; it was then determined that all who had a press pass should be present during Poincaré's speech and fifteen, three from each of the principal Allies and three from the others, should be present during the rest of the proceedings. As a matter of fact, that part of the room reserved for the press was overcrowded and some of them pushed their way forward into the actual Conference room itself, and even began talking to some of the Delegates. There are a great number of press men about, and the Americans appear to be incredibly ignorant.

A similar blunder was made about the representation of the smaller nations at the Conference. President Wilson, for some reason, pressed very strongly the claims of Brazil to three representatives; his avowed reason seems to have been that there were so many Germans in Brazil that if they were allowed a larger representation, they would be won over to the right side. The real reason presumably was that he wanted to counter our move in appointing an ambassador to Brazil. As a result Brazil got three members, Portugal and Serbia, and even Belgium, only two each. This decision was very badly received and had immediately to be reversed. In the first list Arabia, though it had been recognized as a sovereign belligerent Power, was entirely excluded; it is said that the reason was that Mr Balfour forgot all about it.

The treatment of Russia is equally unsatisfactory. In the discussions everything inevitably leads up to Russia. Then there is a discursive discussion; it is agreed that the point at issue cannot be determined until the

D

general policy towards Russia has been settled; having agreed on this, instead of settling it, they pass on to some other subject.

The whole difficulty arises from the fact that neither the British nor the Americans have any competent diplomatist among the plenipotentiaries. They are all amateurs, and especially the Prime Minister, who will not even read the documents put before him. The question of the British representation on the Secretariat of the Conference has just come up. Lord Hardinge was to have been appointed. At the last moment the decision was altered and Sir Maurice Hankey put in his place. He is an admirable Secretary, but with no diplomatic experience and no knowledge of Europe, and it is apparently regarded as a very grave slight to the Foreign Office and to Lord Hardinge, and may lead to his going back to London.[1]

More satisfactory is the result of a Mission to Trèves [Trier] to discuss the terms of the renewal of the Armistice.[2] Keynes and Dudley Ward went as financial experts. It was the first time that there had been any serious meeting for discussion with the Germans. Apparently British and Germans got on well together. They observed the utmost propriety of demeanour, but, as they said, it was impossible not to recognize the fact that they looked on things from the same point of view and understood one another, while the French, who from time to time made impassioned speeches, represented a completely different atmosphere. All the Germans present were apparently ordinary officials of the old stamp; there did not seem to be a single Socialist among them. They were old corps students with the customary slashes on their faces. They were pleased when they began to recognize that the English wanted a serious discussion and were gratified with the prospect which was opened as to food being allowed to get into Germany. Keynes took the view that the distribution should be done by the Germans themselves. In a conversation with him I suggested the importance of making a condition that food should only be given to those who were working so as to avoid the danger of subsidizing unemployment. The matter was, he said, mentioned at the Conference and the Germans said that it might quite conceivably strengthen their hands. They

---

[1] Lord Hardinge did not return to London but, as Headlam-Morley suggests on page 33, he lost interest in the negotiations.

[2] At Trier on 16 and 17 January the Allies and the Germans negotiated the second extension of the Armistice. In return for placing the German merchant fleet in Allied hands for the duration of the Armistice, the latter agreed to allow the importation of certain food commodities into Germany. See H. W. V. Temperley's *A History of the Peace Conference of Paris*, 6 vols. (London: Oxford University Press, 1920), I, pp. 313, 477–81. The day-to-day negotiations with the Germans for the implementation of the Armistice were not carried out at Trier, however, but at Spa.

would say if they thought it would be desirable. Keynes, who is extremely sensible and open-minded, was anxious to leave the responsibility for such matters to the Germans, but to meet their wishes. He wanted to do away with the blockade and meanwhile to let as much as possible get into Germany surreptitiously through neutral countries. As he said, this would be better than keeping the whole control in the hands of the Government, which would involve far too much work and, in addition, individual Germans would be able to make their own arrangements. No doubt some of the neutrals would be willing to take the risk, giving of course usurious terms. This the Governments of the Allies could not do and it would therefore be better to leave a good deal to private enterprise.

The Germans looked worried and depressed; on the other hand, the administration is continuing; all the Delegates were accredited by the Central Government and when necessary telegraphed to Berlin where the Council of Ministers was called to answer their inquiries. The Stock Exchange continues open and the banks are functioning. There is great financial depression but at present no breakdown of the administration.

The League of Nations people have been working hard at their schemes; I have not yet seen the results. All accounts say that they are becoming less visionary; Lord Robert Cecil has been warned by the very impracticable nature of the French League of Nations people. Apparently the Conference have now decided that one of the first things they are going to take up is international labour legislation. No doubt they have been driven to this by political pressure at home. In consequence, the Ministry of Labour must at once produce their scheme, and Butler, who is now in England, is to be recalled immediately. So far as I understand it, their scheme is to be a general conference consisting of three representatives of every State, one for the Government, one for labour and one for the employers; they will not have any legislative authority, but if resolutions are carried by a sufficient majority, the delegates will be pledged to bring them officially before their own parliaments. This is all right so far as it goes, for it maintains the principle of the authority of national parliaments.

Memorandum of interview with
Mr Posner   *22 January 1919*

Mr Posner came to see me today; he had a personal introduction to me from Mr Namier. I thought it better to see him alone for the first time in order to find out what sort of person he was. He has been resident in Paris throughout the war; his sympathies are with the Socialist Left though he is not in any way a Bolshevik. He seemed intelligent and talked to me very freely for over an hour and a half. I said nothing except to ask questions. I think he would be useful if we want to get the point of view of his party, but he was very frank in explaining that as he had not been in Poland since 1913, he could of course not speak with the same confidence that he otherwise could have done.

He began by talking about the political events of the last few weeks. His view was frankly that of one who was opposed to the National Democrats and he was very critical of Monsieur Pichon's[1] action in recognizing them as a Polish Government. Entirely without any suggestion from myself, he referred to the difference between the action of the British and the French Governments and said that sending Colonel Wade to Warsaw was an action which showed genuine political insight. Those who had done it obviously wanted to find out the truth on the spot. He regretted that this action had not been followed up, and spoke very critically of Monsieur Paderewski's arrival on a British cruiser.[2]

He said that Monsieur Dmowski was very unpopular in Poland and any authority that he had there was derived entirely from the fact that people in Poland had been led to believe that no help, and especially no food, would be forthcoming except through National Democratic influence. The people were starving and this had been used by the National Democrats. He stated that this point of view had been very strongly pressed in Poland and it was for this reason alone that the former Ministry fell and that Monsieur Paderewski had come into office. I asked him whether Monsieur Paderewski would be able to maintain himself in power. He seemed to think that he might do so; he laid great stress on the fact that he had declared a state of siege and thereby got the power of sending his

[1] Stephen Pichon, the French Foreign Minister and one of France's five plenipotentiary Delegates.
[2] Since the Armistice there had been acute division between the Polish National Committee in Paris, headed by Roman Dmowski and the *de facto* Government established by General Pilsudski in Warsaw. The French and British Foreign Ministries recognized the urgent need to get the Poles to form a unified Government, but they pursued different policies. On 29 December 1918 Monsieur Pichon recognized the Polish National Committee as the 'regular Government of Poland'. Meanwhile, Mr Balfour, who had already ordered the sending of a military mission to Warsaw under Colonel H. H. Wade to gather information on the domestic situation, now decided to invite the Polish pianist, Jan Paderewski, to accompany the mission. Paderewski's arrival in Warsaw led to the timely formation of a coalition on the eve of the opening of the Conference. Paderewski served as Prime Minister and Polish representative at the Conference; Pilsudski as Chief of State; and Dmowski as Chief Polish Delegate at Paris. The bitterness between the two groups, however, continued. Their hostility is the key to Polish political life in the inter-war period. See Hans Roos, *History of Modern Poland* (London, 1967).

opponents to prison. He thought it was quite possible that partly for this reason, partly owing to the belief that if he failed, the supplies and support from the Entente would be cut off, and partly through the influence of the Church, there might be a majority in the Constituent Assembly to support the present Government, but any such majority would not really represent the opinion of the people. I asked whether, supposing the present administration got a majority in the Assembly, the people would obey, or whether there would be revolts. He seemed to think that probably there would not be any immediate outbreak of violence, but in regard to this he said that he did not know how far the mentality of the Poles had changed during the war. It was quite possible that revolutionary influences had produced an important change in their outlook. He stressed the fact that the peasants in Poland were very different from those in Russia. They were like Western Europeans, strongly individualistic, and had not been influenced by communal conditions in Russia. They wanted the land and wanted large portions of the land, but they wanted it in secure private ownership. For this reason they would not accept it as a free gift, but would prefer to pay for it. They had for long been saving in order to buy land and were prepared to pay for it by instalments. They feared that if it was given to them gratuitously it would at any time be taken away as freely as it had been given. For this reason the peasants were a conservative element as against Bolshevism. Even the Conservatives really recognized this and it was common ground of all parties that the agrarian question must be settled.

On the other hand, there was great danger from the large number of Poles returning, 700,000 from Germany and 1,500,000 from Russia and Galicia; both of these classes had been demoralized and impregnated with revolutionary sentiments. It was quite essential that Pilsudski should be supported. He was the only person who could keep things together. If he fell there would be revolutionary outbreaks at once. He spoke repeatedly, with great admiration, of Pilsudski as a national hero. He compared Monsieur Paderewski with Orpheus; as Orpheus was torn in pieces by the Bacchae, so Paderewski would perhaps be torn in pieces by the Bolsheviks, although he was popular in Poland owing to his great personal generosity.

He said he looked forward to the future with pessimism. I pressed him what he meant by this. His answers were not very clear, but it seemed to come to this, that he had looked forward to an independent Poland starting in line with the Western Democracies, whereas it seemed as though it would begin its new life in slavery to a reactionary Government imposed on it from outside. I suggested that after all this would not matter much;

the great thing was to get the new State going and there would be plenty of time for democratic evolution later.

The practical conclusion I should draw from the conversation is the immense importance of seeing to it that it should not be allowed to be thought in Poland that Allied support and intervention is the prerogative of the Right, and especially of supporting Pilsudski. This clearly implies strong British representation on the spot and frank and sympathetic communication with the parties of the Left. I hope that this may be secured by the personality of Colonel Wade's mission. It would be fatal to allow things to be managed so that the Left were deprived of all influence on the Government. With this proviso, the conversation left in my mind the feeling that there was some hope that the coalition Government might maintain itself. I should add that Mr Posner entirely confirmed Mr Namier's observations with regard to the personalities of the present Government; he said that all the members of the Government who had political experience and capacity were National Democrats and that the others, who did not belong to that party, were men, so far as his knowledge went, entirely without political experience or influence.

Extract from letter to Mr Namier (F.O.)   22 January 1919

I wrote and asked Mr Posner to come and see me and have just had a talk with him which lasted about an hour and a half. He is an interesting person and explained everything most clearly, and I hope it will be useful. I will write a note of the interview, which I will send you.

The situation is obviously very difficult. It seems to me that the best thing to do is to accept what has been done; at present to refrain from anything in the nature of criticism about what has happened, but to do all that is possible to prevent things taking a bad turn; especially to get strong and wise British influence in Poland itself so as to prevent allied intervention having the influence which you seem to anticipate that it will have. I hope that Kenney[1] will have got there by now and that when he and Wade get together they will be really useful. I wish something could be done to get a clear intimation put out from the Allies that if in the course of any military operations which may take place, the Poles occupy Russian or

---

[1] Rowland Kenney, at this time a temporary clerk in the Foreign Office. He went to Warsaw in late December with Wade's mission. When on 23 January hostilities broke out in Teschen (see p. 19, footnote 3), Wade despatched him there to gather information and then to Paris where to Headlam-Morley's surprise (see p. 19) he appeared in early February. At the request of Sir Esme Howard, Kenney was promptly appointed to the Inter-Allied Commission to Warsaw and left again for Warsaw before mid-February.

Lithuanian territory, this temporary military occupation does not in itself constitute any claim to permanent possession by Poland.[1] Of course this ought to be done, not for Poland alone, but for all the districts in dispute; it will, however, be easier to get it done if one refrains from criticism and pinpricks.

[There follows a résumé of the previous document.]

24 January 1919

I kept this letter to see how things got on. While I am quite prepared to accept your criticisms as to the events connected with the establishment of the Paderewski Government, I think that now this has been done, the only practicable policy to pursue is to do everything possible to support it, though of course I agree with you that the support ought to be based not merely on the principle that we are supporting Paderewski, but that Pilsudski should be put much more in the foreground than he has been.

I do not know whether you see the official reports of the conversations between the plenipotentiaries. The results of that on Poland seems to me most unsatisfactory. Foch argued strongly for intervention and seemed to be carrying the day, when Wilson interposed and raised the point that the Poles might use the forces supplied to them for illegitimate objects. Confronted with this problem, the meeting characteristically put off any further immediate action and determined to send an Allied Commission to investigate on the spot.[2] This seems of course a fresh postponement, refusal to recognize that some definite line of action must be agreed upon. However, I understand that something is to be done with regard to food. Very confidentially, you may be interested that Howard has been asked to go on this new Commission; I had a few words with him about it this morning. I hope myself, as I told him, that he will not go, for it would be

---

[1] The territory in question had belonged to Poland up to the second partition of 1793. It was claimed for outright annexation by Dmowski, while Pilsudski envisaged federation. Both believed it to be strategically necessary for defence against Russia. Ethnically the Poles were in the minority, forming the landed and educated class. The majority of the population consisted of Lithuanians and Belorussians; see ethnic map by Burky in G. R. Gayre, *Teuton and Slav on the Polish Frontier* (London, 1944), folder, map 3. For the political and strategic significance of these territories, see Piotr S. Wandycz, *Polish-Soviet Relations 1917–1921* (Harvard, 1970). For Pilsudski's federal policy, see M. K. Dziewanowski, *Joseph Pilsudski: A European Federalist, 1918–1921* (Stanford, 1970).

[2] On 12 January the Supreme Council turned down Foch's proposal for returning the Polish army in France under General Joseph Haller in favour of sending an Inter-Allied Commission to Warsaw. Its purpose was to gather information on the domestic situation. See P.P.C. III, 471–2.

serious if he were taken away from here, and I think that when he got there he would find the position almost impossibly difficult . . .[1]

Note of an interview with Professor Herron

23 January 1919

Professor Herron, who has been resident in Switzerland during the war, came to see me today. Among other matters he mentioned the Ukrainian Delegates who had come to see him; they have apparently been sent by the Ukrainian people and Government in order to have an opportunity of presenting their case at Paris.[2] They have, however, been refused permission to proceed, by the French Government. He spoke well of them and said they seemed intelligent. Apparently what they want is the temporary recognition of the Ukraine as an autonomous state, the future relations to Russia to be postponed for the reconstitution of Russia. Like all people whom he has seen who have come from eastern Europe, they show great bitterness against the French, whom they suspect, among other things, of wishing to restore the Romanoffs.

It seems rather a remarkable and unfortunate condition of things that apparently the determination as to whether a particular people should have an opportunity of coming to the seat of the Peace Conference and making their case heard, if not as recognized Delegates, at least as authorized spokesmen, should be made by the French Government alone. I should have thought it was eminently desirable that these people should have the opportunity of coming to Paris so that those who are interested in these matters should be enabled to learn their views and desires at first hand. Presumably the Ukraine would be represented at the forthcoming Russian Conference, but even this does not seem a sufficient reason for refusing them access to Paris. They are neither enemies nor are they Bolsheviks.

---

[1] In his reply Namier said: 'I do not understand what fault you find with Wilson's objection to Foch's scheme. I agree with every word of it and think inaction and delay better than playing into the hands of the bandits.' (M.H.)

[2] The West Ukrainian Republic, proclaimed in East Galicia in November 1918, voted for union with the Ukrainian National Republic in Kiev on 4 January 1919. The Act of Union was proclaimed on 22 January when the West Ukrainian Republic took the name of the Western Province of the Ukrainian National Republic but kept full territorial autonomy. The first head of the Ukrainian Delegation to the Paris Peace Conference was G. Sydorenko, who was replaced at the end of July 1919 by M. Tyskevich. For the Delegation's notes to the President of the Conference, see *Notes présentées par la Délégation de la République Ukrainienne à la Conférence de la Paix à Paris*, I, février–avril 1919; II, avril–juillet 1919 (Paris, 1919).

Extract from diary   *25 January 1919*

Professor Herron came to dine last night; I asked Sir Esme Howard and Mr Maclagan[1] to meet him. He took a very serious view of the whole situation; we prided ourselves too much upon our civilization which was like an iron chain round the world, but it would all be destroyed in six months when Europe would again become a jumble, and this would happen unless the right thing was done now.

The Congress have decided to invite representatives of all Russian Governments to meet on an island in the Sea of Marmora. This proposal was made by Mr Lloyd George and President Wilson. It has been very badly received, but on the whole it seems a wise one; at any rate, if it is clearly understood that there shall be an armistice during the meeting of the Congress, this will stop the immediate danger of an invasion of Poland and the Baltic Provinces and give time for help to be sent out to Poland. They made the mistake, however, of not sounding the Russians in Paris first as to how such a proposal would be received and Monsieur Sazanoff has definitely refused to have any part in it. Sir Esme Howard went to see him last night and pressed him to reconsider his determination. He said nothing in the world would make him do so; two members of his family, his brother-in-law and his nephew had been murdered by the Bolsheviks and he would rather die than sit at the same table with them. Sir Esme Howard was asked by the Prime Minister to go as the British representative; he refused because if his instructions were to try and bring about an understanding with the Bolsheviks, he could not undertake the duty. He is therefore going to be sent to Poland on a new Allied Mission. The history of this is characteristic. There was a discussion about sending immediate help to Poland, which Foch strongly pressed; Wilson pointed out the difficulties that might arise from the Poles using force and material supplied against the Germans or the Lithuanians or the Ruthenians.[2] One would have thought that this difficulty could easily have been got over, but the result was that they simply decided on sending another mission, which means more time wasted.

Today is published the general warning to all nations to refrain from resort to force in order to secure control over debatable territory. This was drafted in the Foreign Office by Sir Esme Howard about a month ago, was

[1] Eric Maclagan, Comptroller for France at the Ministry of Information; a member of the Press Section of the British Delegation.
[2] The term Ruthenian was at this time used to denote the Ukrainians, including those of Galicia.

accepted by France and England, but for some reason has been hung up ever since.[1]

There was a long discussion at our dinner party last night as to the Italians. Professor Herron had been lunching with the Italian Delegation. He said that they were in a very dangerous state of mind. They considered they were not being treated as equals by the other Powers; they were attacked and criticized on all sides; they were told what was good for them, but not taken into the real discussions. He pointed out that Italy, who had done and suffered much during the war would, according to the present principles, gain very little from it.[2] Leeper, who was there, put the case against the Italians, which is in fact unanswerable, but it seems as if there must have been some serious want of tact and discretion in dealing with them. Herron said that if care were not taken they would simply leave the conference and go home.

Professor Herron talked a good deal about the French. He said that extreme animosity was being aroused against them in every country in the world, particularly in eastern Europe. All their agents are apparently working deliberately and under instructions to upset the League of Nations, to overthrow Anglo-Saxon predominance, and are sowing discord wherever they go. They are universally hated and distrusted.

President Wilson says that Lord Robert Cecil is the greatest man in Europe – the greatest man he has ever met.

Sir Frederick Maurice came to see me in the afternoon. He said that as far as he could make out from his investigations in France, what was really concerning French politics was the succession to Clemenceau. He would probably retire as soon as peace was made. The French Colonial party were asking for a combination with Briand and somebody else whose name I have forgotten; what they really cared for was Morocco; they did not attach much importance to Syria. This would all be in our interests, as if they choose Morocco as the place from which they are to get their compensation, it would bring them in conflict with no one except the Spaniards. In order to get the Spaniards out of Morocco, however, it would be necessary for us to give up Gibraltar. He wanted to know the present Admiralty view with regard to this. The military were, as he knew, in favour of it. He much regretted the general trend of the discussions which

---

[1] See P.P.C. III, 715, for the actual draft. It was presented to the Supreme Council by Wilson and, despite Headlam-Morley's remarks, evidently emanated from the American Delegation.

[2] A reference to the Italian claims to Fiume and the Dalmatian coast which were opposed by President Wilson.

was apparently based merely on the principle of bargaining and compensation. He urgently pressed that the general principle should be laid down strongly and instructions given to all committees to work in accordance with these principles. Everybody agrees about this, but no one seems to do it.

Extract from letter to Mr J. W. Phillips
(Board of Education)   *31 January 1919*

. . . It is very interesting and also amusing here. On the whole I am coming to have much higher respect for the Congress of Vienna than I used to have.

Extract from letter to
Mr A. E. Zimmern (F.O.)   *3 February 1919*

I have been having conversations with the other sections here with special reference to the general labour situations abroad and the Berne Conference. We have had suggestions coming in from various sources that we may have to meet a rather dangerous move on the part of the Germans. Herron was here last week and took a very pessimistic view of the whole situation. The idea seems to be that there are secret meetings going on in Germany between big industrialists on the one side, and the talkers – especially Erzberger and Naumann – on the other; the Germans have not changed their mentality, but are still concocting large schemes for the reassertion of German influence. It is whispered that they are hoping to depend for this upon business and financial interests in America. They are in fact profiting by the long and what seems to me very unfortunate delay in approaching the German question. Meanwhile, they are also elaborating a new propaganda scheme; the obvious line for them to take in this is to appeal to idealistic labour and pacific opinion among the Allies so as to break down the harmony and the combined will and cut away the ground from under the Allied Governments. All this is rather vague and it is not corroborated by the reports I have seen and the conversations I have had with those who have returned from Germany; they represent the people as conscious of defeat, crushed and humble. However, there are certainly possibilities of danger in the situation and we must be on the look-out.

It appeared as though the storm centre would be the Berne Conference. The last I have heard of it is, however, that it is likely to be a washout; hardly anyone is going to attend and it is to adjourn after two or three days. I was rather alarmed by the prospect, for so far as I could understand, our people were going with a sober and businesslike programme of international labour legislation, and in view of the character of the British representatives, they might easily have found themselves at a disadvantage if the Germans seized the opportunity for bringing up larger political problems.

Extract from letter to
Mr John Bailey (F.O.)   *3 February 1919*

The situation here at first was so difficult and the ground so uncertain that I really did not know quite what to write. . . . For the first fortnight the Conference did practically nothing; they did not seem to be even approaching the territorial questions in which we are particularly interested. My own position was very obscure; I did not know whether I was working in what is called the Intelligence Clearing House or if I was part of the Foreign Office Staff. . . . If I had written at all fully, the letter might have appeared querulous. This I wished to avoid. The situation changed very rapidly. Last week the Conference suddenly turned its attention on to the territorial claims in Europe and they have been hearing the representatives of Romania, Czechoslovakia, Yugoslavia and Greece. Allen Leeper, Nicolson and Toynbee have been present at the different meetings. . . . The representatives of each country stated their case; a few questions were addressed to them, but that was all. This, however, is being followed by the establishment of inter-allied committees to discuss all these different claims, and they will be getting to work at once.

We have also received instructions to have a free interchange of views with the Americans (this must be kept very confidential[1]) and therefore we are at once immersed in all the questions which we were writing about at the end of last year. I am going down this afternoon with Crowe and Akers-Douglas[2] to the American Delegation to discuss all questions connected with the western frontier of Germany, which of course includes

[1] Headlam-Morley's remarks here are among the most important in his diary. Little is known about the secret Anglo-American talks and their scope. The minutes of two meetings have been found in Headlam-Morley's papers. One of the American participants, Charles Seymour, alludes to them in his *Letters from the Paris Peace Conference of 1919* (New Haven, Connecticut: Yale University Press, 1965), pp. 148, 152–4, 156–7. Harold Nelson in his *Land and Power* (London: Routledge & Kegan Paul, 1963), pp. 147–51, briefly mentions them.

[2] The Hon. A. Akers-Douglas, a member of the Political Intelligence Department as well as adviser on German affairs to the British Delegation.

French claims in which you are particularly interested. At the same time Howard is discussing the German–Polish frontier with them. . . .[1]

The most interesting thing which has happened so far has been in regard to Poland and the Czechs. As you know, the Conference decided that instead of sending out the Polish army or material assistance to the Poles, they should send another Commission. Howard, who has been appointed, will be leaving at the end of this week. Meanwhile, the conflict between the Czechs and Poles has brought up in a rather acute form the whole question of these debatable frontiers.[2] Howard has been occupied during these last few days in trying to bring about a provisional agreement. I do not know the precise arrangement which has been come to, but I understand that the Czechs, and especially Krammarsch, were very difficult. They have, I think, lost ground very seriously during the last week or so owing to the excessive nature of their demands, and the rather arrogant manner in which they are put forward.[3] The result is that sympathy seems to be going round to the Poles. Yesterday afternoon in the Majestic, to my surprise, I came across Kenney. He had come straight from Teschen. Wade had said that the best thing he could do would be to come straight back and report here; he is at this moment discussing matters with Howard. I have not seen much of him, but from his account the Czechs behaved very badly; curiously enough the Czech army was in its advance accompanied by officers of the Allies, whose position and attitude seems to have been curious and irregular.[4]

---

[1] In his memoirs *Theatre of Life*, Howard refers briefly to his meetings with his American counterpart, Robert H. Lord (II, 307–10).

[2] The Duchy of Teschen was a former possession of the Habsburgs lying in south-eastern Silesia. Three of its four districts contained Polish majorities; the fourth, a Czech. The duchy was highly industrialized, oriented towards and important to the economy of the new Czech republic. Fearing its loss following the announcement of Poland's intention to hold elections in her districts, the Czechs on 23 January invaded them. In the hopes of eliminating Polish opposition, they carried out their operation under the guise of Allied authority. Not taken in, however, the Poles counter-attacked and hostilities commenced. See Dagmar Perman's *The Shaping of the Czech State* (Leiden: E. J. Brill, 1962). For a different view see Piotr Wandycz, *France and her Eastern Allies, 1919–22* (University of Minneapolis Press, 1962).

[3] On 29 January the Council of Ten had taken up the dispute and instructed the Inter-Allied Commission to Moscow to negotiate a cease-fire. See P.P.C. III, 772–83, 820–2 and 836–7.

[4] Since one of the Allied officers was a member of the United States army, the American Delegation ordered an investigation. The report can be found in Box 69 of the Tasker Bliss Papers, Library of Congress, Washington, D.C.

Extract from letter to Mr Namier (F.O.)   *3 February 1919*

. . . I have not had any full talk yet with Kenney; what he came here particularly about was the situation which had arisen in Teschen. There seems no doubt from his and all other accounts that the Czechs have behaved very foolishly. He had seen Pilsudski about a week ago; he said that he was apparently a good deal broken by his imprisonment; his lungs were affected. He said that the conversation was very pathetic. The great difficulty he suffers from is the want of provisions, clothing and material of every kind. It seems to me a very grave error that the Allies should not have sent help more rapidly, and I am not at all convinced that they ought not to have allowed the Polish army to go long before this. Rose has just been on a visit to the Polish army in France and draws a lamentable picture of the conditions among them. I will confess that I am not entirely convinced by your apprehensions of the danger of Polish imperialism. I do not deny that they exist, but I should have thought that an alternative danger of a complete collapse in Poland itself would be greater, and that we should do all we could to support any administration which would keep things together during the crisis. The actual situation is that the Poles have, as you quite rightly say, accepted a Paderewski Government contrary to their inclinations, because they were led to believe that if they did that they would get help from the Allies; they have done it and no help is forthcoming. Pilsudski said to Kenney that they were beginning to wonder whether after all the Germans were not better.

I am not going to attempt to discuss the justice of your reading of the Polish character, but I am quite sure that we ought not to let ourselves be too much influenced in our policy by this kind of thing. Most of us, I suppose, are quite prepared to dislike and distrust many of the nations with whom we have to deal; none the less, the only possible practical policy is to make the best of the situation and to enable each one of them to establish a firm Government. If you will not mind my saying so, I know that nothing interferes so much with the value of your work as the feeling which you allow to appear that you have no sympathy with Poland at all. After all, you are charged with Polish affairs and what people look to you for is not merely criticisms of Poland, but sympathetic advice as to how the Poles can best be helped. You are quite right in saying that the greatest kindness we can do them is to avoid encouragement of their chauvinistic schemes, but the value of this is easily discounted if it is accompanied by a general polemic against the nation as a whole. This makes it impossible to put forward some of your letters, for I am sure they would do more harm than good, just for this reason.

I am very much concerned about the want here of someone with actual knowledge of the Galician question.[1] Whether Wade was wise or not in the suggestions that he made, I cannot say, but after all, he is on the spot; all that he is attempting to do is to make a provisional arrangement which would stop the continuation of warfare, and it is a very serious responsibility under the present condition not to counter the advice of the man who has the immediate responsibility on the spot.

Extract from letter to Mr Koppel (F.O.)   5 February 1919

. . . We are getting down much more to work now than we did during the first fortnight. Leeper and Toynbee are very busy as they have been going to Conference meetings in connection with Romania, Greece and other small states; they are both being put on the Inter-Allied Commissions, so that they are really getting quite important work to do and seem to be enjoying themselves greatly. . . . My work here is miscellaneous and disjointed. There falls to me a good deal rather similar to what you and Carnegie have to do, that is, distributing papers; I find it very boring and do it very badly, but I hope that they sometimes get to their proper destination. . . .

Memorandum   6 February 1919[2]

I have just seen a copy of the proposed Polish frontier on the west and north-west, which has been agreed upon in consultation with the Americans.[3] This raises serious problems of policy.

The frontier as agreed upon is so drawn as to assign Danzig to Poland and to leave a strip of territory in Polish hands intervening between Pomerania and East Prussia. This problem is of course one of the most difficult which the Peace Conference will have to meet. In the original

[1] East Galicia was annexed by Austria from Poland in 1772. The landowners and the urban population in Lemberg were predominantly Polish. But the peasants who formed the bulk of the population were Ukrainian. Namier strongly urged the right of the Ukrainians of Galicia to join in the Ukrainian National Republic. See page 14, note 2. There was sporadic fighting from November till June when the Poles conquered and annexed the territory. See Headlam-Morley, P.C.M. N4819/77/55.

[2] A copy of this document can be found in FO 608/66/20216.

[3] This is known as the Howard–Lord agreement. See H. I. Nelson, *Land and Power*, pp. 148–50.

proposals put forward from the Foreign Office the suggestion was that Danzig should be left to Germany, and that access to the sea for the Poles should be provided by free navigation on the Vistula and a railway which, though running across German territory, should be in Polish hands, and that either Danzig should be made a free port under the guarantee of the League of Nations, though under German sovereignty, or that the Poles should receive in full sovereignty a port at Neufahrwasser to the north-west of Danzig. This was the solution suggested by Sir Esme Howard, who minutes: 'I agree that it would be a mistake to cut off East from West Prussia'; and Lord Robert Cecil minutes: 'To cut off East from West Prussia seems to me an impossible policy, at any rate at present, and will only create a sore place which will never heal. The Poles must be content with the free use of Danzig and the approaches to it, with a provision that at the end of ten years the matter shall be reconsidered by the League of Nations.'[1]

The whole matter will clearly have to be considered in connection with the other demands to be made upon Germany when the preliminaries of peace are drafted. I should venture to suggest the following points for consideration:

It is for political reasons of the highest importance that the concessions of territory demanded from Germany, which will necessarily be great, should not go beyond that point at which a strong justification can be put forward which will appeal to the German Liberal and Socialist opinion. The cessions required are: first, Alsace-Lorraine; secondly, it has been proposed that the French demands for the Saar Valley shall be supported with the proviso that this is to be justified as part of the indemnity exacted from Germany for the destruction of the mining district in the north of France; thirdly, it is, I imagine, generally agreed that an important strip of territory running along the Polish frontier, including part of the mining district of Silesia, the towns of Posen and Thorn, and probably a strip on the southern frontier of East Prussia, shall be ceded. This can be abundantly justified on grounds of ethnology and presumably also on the wishes of the population.

These cessions mean in fact taking from Germany large and important districts, portions of which happen to be of great industrial importance. This is, I should venture to suggest, a cession of territory so great that it will leave no doubt in the minds of the Germans that, having embarked on an unjust war, they must pay the penalty, but all of these cessions can be abundantly justified on the general principles.

[1] These minutes were made in November 1918 and can be found in FO 371/4354, pp. 110–13.

In addition to this the question of the German frontier as regards Bohemia will have to be considered. The Germans will undoubtedly desire to bring it about that the northern frontiers of Bohemia and Moravia, which are German-speaking, shall be attached to Germany. I hope that it will be possible to bring it about that these Germans shall agree to remain in the new Bohemian state; this, however, will be undoubtedly interpreted in Germany as a direct violation of the principle of nationality, and an attempt will be made to set up a strong opposition to it. Under these circumstances, to assign to Poland a town such as Danzig, which is almost purely German in population, which was founded by Germans and has a long history quite unconnected with Prussian aggression, will undoubtedly arouse the most bitter animosity, not only among the Prussian military party and the chauvinists, but among the whole of the commercial community, and will be interpreted as the bitterest affront to old-established, just national feeling which is quite different from the imperialistic feeling of the last two generations.

I venture to urge, therefore, that this decision should be seriously reviewed and considered, not only in connection with the Polish question, but with the general question of the treatment of Germany.

Even as regards Poland, it seems very doubtful whether the interests in the future security of the Polish state will be furthered by an arrangement which we may almost certainly predict will not be accepted by Germany.

This paper is different in form to the others which are being drawn up in that it traces the boundary in great detail but omits any statement of the reasons for the boundary chosen. Surely it might be unwise for either the British or the Americans to commit themselves to the details in a much disputed frontier. All that we can depend upon are language statistics, which are often disputed and unreliable; ultimately we must leave an opportunity in the disputed districts for some consultation of the inhabitants.[1]

Extract from letter to
Mr Hurst (Legal Adviser, Paris)   *7 February 1919*

. . . I have been asked if it is possible to devise any scheme by which the French would get the control and exploitation of the coal mines without complete annexation [of the Saar]. Could you give me any help? Are there any precedents? It is clear that under any such system the French

---

[1] The views expressed by Headlam-Morley were shared by Sir Eyre Crowe, Lord Hardinge and Lord Milner as shown by their minutes. See FO 608/66/2216.

E

would have to have in fact complete control and the Germans no executive or administrative power, but I suppose that certain restrictions might be placed on the French; but as soon as one begins to analyse this one gets into great difficulty. There could of course be a clause forbidding them to fortify the district; the French certainly would not agree to any such clause unless the Germans were forbidden to fortify the whole of the left bank of the Rhine; this would probably be required.

There could, and I think there should, be a clause that the inhabitants of the district should not be subject to French military service, but of course in this case it is necessary to guard against the difficulty of Frenchmen deliberately migrating into the district in order to avoid military service.

There would have to be security for the use of the German language both in schools and in courts of justice and public administration.

The district would have to be included within the French commercial frontier. Would it be possible to exclude it from the legal and administrative system? The inhabitants clearly would not be able to send representatives to the German Reichstag; I think they ought also not to send representatives to the Chamber in Paris. It would probably have to be governed by administrative authority with the help of a local council. Perhaps the precedent of Bosnia and Herzegovina under Austrian occupation is the nearest.

Extract from letter to Mr Philip Kerr (Paris)   *7 February 1919*

. . . In regard to the Saar: I have been trying to think out a scheme by which the French would get the administration and exploitation of the mines without formal annexation. It is not easy, as of course any kind of co-ordination would be absolutely excluded. There would have to be full control by the French subject to certain restrictions, but as soon as I begin to try and work out a scheme, the technical difficulties seem almost insuperable.

Extract from letter to Mr Namier (F.O.)   *10 February 1919*

I saw Kenney yesterday on his way through to Russia. He told me what I expected to be the case, that you were very much dispirited and felt that all of your work was in vain. I can quite understand this, but I am sure that it is not the case. There can be no doubt that the work that you have been doing in the last two years has had an important and permanent effect and that it has done much to open people's eyes as to the true character of the National Democrats. None the less, at this moment the practical position is a very difficult one. I have been doing what I can to get your points attended to, but it has been extremely difficult for me to interfere at all as I have no official *locus standi*. What we both anticipated has in fact, I think, undoubtedly happened, and Howard has been more and more falling under the influences of Paris and drifting away. Kerr is most sensible and open-minded and fully recognizes the importance of what you say. There is indeed a clear difference between you and me on the best method of action at the moment. Even assuming that everything you say is completely true, I still feel that in the present emergency, a compromise is essential. Whatever one may think of the course of events which led up to the establishment of the Paderewski Government, the fact still remains that it is the only Government existing at this moment in Poland, and I should have thought that our only policy was on the one side to support it, on the other to use all the influence we can to persuade them to keep the balance between parties and make it a real coalition Government. This is the line on which I have been going. Whether it is the right one or not, it is, I am sure, the only way in which anything at all can be done.

I went down last night to see the Polish Mission off;[1] they had a beautiful train, Paris to Warsaw, the first time such a train has left Paris; each of the nations had its own car; our people were Howard, Leveson-Gower,[2] Carton de Wiart and some other soldiers whom I did not know. Kenney was going with them and I am sure that his influence will be useful. He said that his talk with you in London had been very valuable to him. The worst thing in the situation is, I think, the treatment of the Ukrainian question; I made attempts to talk about it to Howard, but I found it did more harm than good. On this point he is completely under Polish influence and will scarcely listen to the opposed view. He was very much interested in the controversy between the Poles and the Czechs in which the Czechs had put themselves in the wrong, but would not acknowledge that the Poles were equally wrong in the Lemburg point. There is no one else here that I can find who takes the slightest interest in the matter. How things will work out now, I do not know. It was said that Tyrrell was going to take on Howard's work; if he would do it and really apply himself, he might do good. It is more probable that things will really be neglected. Of course, as far as Poland goes, everything will depend on the

[1] This was the Inter-Allied Commission referred to on p. 13 above.
[2] Captain C. E. G. Leveson-Gower, Howard's personal secretary on the Inter-Allied Commission to Warsaw.

reports of the Commission, which means again a long delay. As to Russia, there is no provision to have the matter properly watched. I hear from every side stories of the very deep bitterness which was felt by the Russians in Paris, as well as in London.

Of course, as you know, Spicer, who has now come back to the Foreign Office, is going to be acting Assistant Secretary, looking after Russian affairs. You are very lucky to have him. He frankly knows nothing about Russia and Poland; he comes to the whole thing with quite a fresh mind, but he is a first-rate person, simple, straightforward and open, and only desires to get at the truth. I had a long talk to him before he left and explained the situation to him so far as I was capable of doing so, and you may be sure that he will see to it that you have full opportunity of seeing the papers and putting down your observations. I think you will find that his appointment will materially help matters.

P.S. Howard has changed his view completely about Danzig and has committed himself to proposing that it should be given to Poland. This seems to me absolutely fatal; however, I do not think that this view will receive any support.

Extract from a minute to Sir Eyre Crowe   *11 February 1919*

. . . [With reference to the Czechoslovak case.][1] There are two points raised to which I should like to be allowed to draw attention.

The cultural rights of minorities. As to the Germans in Bohemia, we find the words 'it is obvious that they must be guaranteed cultural, linguistic and equal political rights'. On p. 3 again, 'the Viennese Czechs can be assured of their minority rights', and also of the Lusatian Serbs, 'they should be assured of their minority rights on the same footing as the Germans of Bohemia'. Has the question as to what this expression 'the guarantee of minority rights' really means been worked out in detail? I assume that it implies definite clauses to be entered in the treaties, by which the new states are recognized, and that if the substance of these clauses is not observed, there will be a right of appeal to the League of Nations, by whom the treaty will be guaranteed. Would it not be a good thing to ask the Legal Section to draft clauses so that we might know more

[1] This refers to Memorandum No. 31 issued by the Political Section of the British Delegation, 3 February 1919, 'The Czechoslovak Case' (FO 374/20/P117). The report advocated the cession of the predominantly German mountain fringes of Bohemia. It is interesting that Headlam-Morley brought forward the minority question so early. The New States Committee was not set up till 1 May. See p. 91 below.

precisely to what we are committing ourselves? As I have before pointed out, the whole subject is one which might become extremely dangerous.

With regard to the case of the Germans in Bohemia, no doubt there is a strong case to be made out for special exceptional treatment just as there would be with regard to the Magyars who are apparently to be included in the Romanian state. I much regret to see the suggestion that the Czechs in Vienna should be treated in a similar manner. Surely the case is completely different. In German districts of Bohemia we have a large indigenous population which at any rate in some parts comprises the great majority of the inhabitants. In Vienna we have to deal with a condition of things where large numbers of individuals and families have migrated to a large city in order to find work either as officials, clerks, etc., tradesmen or workmen. Surely when people of one nationality, for private reasons of this kind, choose to take up their residence in a foreign city, there is no claim of any kind to receive special exceptional treatment. It seems to me an intolerable thing that the Czechs should first of all claim complete separation from Austria and at the same time special privileges to those of their countrymen who happen to have gone to live in Vienna at a time when it was the seat of the Government for Bohemia. On this principle Chinese washermen in Liverpool would be able to claim guaranteed privileges as a cultural minority. I should be inclined strongly to demur to any international recognition being extended to the Serbs in Lusatia. Is it not much wiser to leave these things alone unless a very special and exceptional case can be made out for them?

. . . It is stated with regard to Western Silesia[1] that 'the Czechs' case on economic grounds, however, is very good. The Poles have already more than adequate supplies of coal which the Czechs lack and to the latter the coalfields of Karvin are essential.' This seems to mean that if in the territory which belongs on ethnographic grounds to one nation, there are mineral resources the use of which would be very convenient to another nation, the latter is justified in pressing for the annexation on this ground. Surely this is quite inadmissible. The only principle on which we can get this frontier question permanently settled is that each nation should occupy in secure possession territory which it inhabits with such natural wealth as is included in it. The Germans claimed Briey and Longwy because the mineral wealth there would be useful to them. The claim was rightly repudiated by everyone. The Czechs are now doing precisely the same thing towards the Poles. If we adopt this principle we shall be laying the foundation of future wars which would be fought not as in the past for

[1] The western part of Teschen in Silesia.

strategic, but for economic frontiers. Surely the right principle is, having got the frontiers settled on national grounds, that everything should be done to encourage the greatest amount of free commercial intercourse between the nations. Of course it would be more convenient for the Czechs themselves to own Polish minefields and not to have to buy coal from the Poles, but to give official support to this is in fact simply to base the settlement on the right of that nation which at this moment happens to be the stronger, to take such goods of its neighbours as it covets.

It may be said that the use of the coal which cannot be got elsewhere is essential to the Czechs, and that the Poles might refuse to sell. It is, I presume, to prevent this sort of thing that among the proposals of the League of Nations is the adoption of the principle that there shall be no special differential tariffs as against one particular nation; the Poles, therefore, would be unable to refuse to export all coal to Bohemia unless they acted on the same principle towards all the nations by which they were surrounded. If special differentiation of this kind is forbidden and the Polish coalfields are the nearest to Bohemia and Moravia, then in the natural course of trade, an important export trade will arise. This will encourage the free commercial intercourse and the consciousness that the nations contiguous to one another depend for their prosperity on mutual business dealings. This is what we want to encourage.

Extract from letter to Mr Namier (F.O.)   *12 February 1919*

I read your letter with great interest and I hope you will believe, not without sympathy. My letter of two days ago will perhaps have explained to you rather more clearly my position. I think ultimately the difference between us is that while your attention is quite naturally concentrated on the Poles and the fatal faults of their politicians, as I watch what is going on in almost every country, not only on the Continent of Europe, it seems to me that the Poles have no special monopoly of vice. Assuming that your picture of them is on the whole true, I should be inclined to answer that this is just the sort of thing which I should expect and that much of the blame belongs not to them, but to the Allies who, by their extraordinary weakness and vacillation, have allowed all the influence and power which they might have exercised to drift out of their hands. If one sees a child growing up in vicious habits, it is not always the child that one has to blame; it is the parents or the school.

As it seems to me, we cannot exercise authority over the Poles except by giving them help; what I hoped, or I will not say hoped – for I have given up any hope – but what I should like to have seen is that weeks, if not months, ago, the nature of the help required should be carefully considered and that it should have been provided with the strongest guarantees which could be devised against its misuse. This, I think, could have been done. But if help is refused or postponed, then we cease to have the influence over Poland which we ought to have exercised. We are making precisely the same blunder with regard to the Germans. It is our weakness and in-action which allows all the bad elements to grow like rank weeds. Merely as a matter of tactics it seems to me that the only possibility of getting the kind of action which was required was to press for it on the lines of sympathy and help for Poland. The situation here was as bad as it could possibly be, worse than I like to explain in a letter. I had officially no justification for interfering; I found that unofficial suggestions were not well received and in fact had the result that I entirely ceased to know what was going on.

Paton has just arrived, I can quite understand your feeling that he should not have been asked to come out, but I think it will be really useful having him here.[1] With him here and Spicer in London, there will be some hope of getting people at the top to listen.

Have you been following the events in Posen? I am very anxious about the situation there as it affects Germany. There is a great gap in my knowledge for the period after Christmas. What I never can get quite clear from such things as I see is the extent and nature of action by Poles from Congress Poland in Posnania, or other territories, which are still technic-ally under German sovereignty. It is extremely important that we should know what amount of justification the Germans have for maintaining that the Poles from over the frontier have interfered. Technically speaking, under the terms of the armistice, they have no right at all to intervene. Telegrams and other accounts are always obscure because when they use the word Poles, one does not know whether they are referring to the Poles of Posen or Poles of the Kingdom. I should be very much obliged for any definite facts with chapter and verse, preferably in the form of a chrono-logical summary. The matter is one of extreme importance because it is quite possible that there may be something like an open breach with the Germans about it and I do not know if we are well informed here, and I

---

[1] As a result of his criticism of the Polish National Committee and in particular of Dmowski, Namier had aroused too much Polish as well as French enmity to replace Howard in Paris. Disappointed and annoyed, he wrote that 'the fact that Paton has been summoned and I have been passed over will be exploited by my enemies'.

am quite sure that the Council of Ten have not really thought about the matter.[1]

Note. The first Committee on which Mr Headlam-Morley was appointed to serve was the Committee on Belgian and Danish Affairs. On 12 February the Supreme Council, on a resolution by Mr Balfour, agreed to appoint an expert Commission, composed of two representatives each of the United States of America, the British Empire, France, Italy and Japan, to consider and advise on the following questions arising out of the statement made at the Quai d'Orsay on 11 February by the Belgian Minister for Foreign Affairs on the claims of Belgium: (1) the proposed transfer of the town and district of Malmedy to Belgium; (2) the definite incorporation in Belgium of the town of Moresnet; (3) the possible rectification in favour of Holland of the German–Dutch frontier on the lower Ems, as a compensation to Holland for meeting Belgian claims in regard to sovereignty over the mouth of the Scheldt and the southern part of Dutch Limburg.[2] The members of the Committee were: Sir Eyre Crowe and Mr Headlam-Morley for Great Britain, Monsieur Tardieu and Monsieur Laroche for France, Signor Ricci Busatti and Comte Vannutelli Rey for Italy, Dr Haskins and Col. Embick for the United States, and Monsieur Kato for Japan.[3]

Extract from letter to Mr John Bailey (F.O.)   *15 February 1919*

I have now been put on an Inter-Allied Commission to settle the Belgian frontier, but we have not yet got our terms of reference and I do not know quite what it will involve.

. . . Feisal,[4] who is here, attended by Col. Lawrence, has made a very great impression; he is much the most dignified figure at the Conference

[1] After the rising in Posen at the end of December 1918, and the formation of a local Polish National Committee, the situation became tense. According to the terms of the Armistice the Germans were to remain in former Prussian Poland so long as the Allies thought fit. The Poles extended the rising to the whole of Prussian Poland and fighting went on till March 1919.
[2] For the details of the Belgian presentation of their territorial claims on 11 February, see P.P.C. III, 958–69, and for the Supreme Council's discussions of them on 12 February see pp. 1006–7.
[3] The minutes of the Commission on Belgian and Danish Affairs can be found in *Recueil des Actes de la Conférence de la Paix, 1919–1920*, 36 vols. (Paris: Imprimerie Nationale, 1924–34), IV, C. 6.
[4] His Royal Highness Emir Feisal, son of the King of the Hedjaz and one of her two plenipotentiary Delegates at the Conference.

and has put forward strongly the Arab claim to some sort of sovereignty over the whole of Syria. The French see that this means that Syria and Arabia will have to have the same mandatory, which will obviously be Great Britain. Hence we get the strong press in the *Temps* and other papers, which you have no doubt seen, on Feisal and his claims. I have been trying to find out how much real genuine feeling this represents; the serious thing about it is that there can be no doubt that the French press would not have taken the line that they have been doing unless they were acting in accordance with instructions and suggestions from their own Government. There are two interpretations; one is that the French really intend to press the matter and to insist on their control over Syria; the other that they are putting it up as part of their case, but will be willing to withdraw if they can get sufficient compensation elsewhere. Compensation could be got partly in Morocco; they want to keep the Spanish out of Morocco altogether and some people suggest that this can be done if we give up Gibraltar. . . . It seems to me that the best solution would be to give the French control of Constantinople and make them the mandatory power of Turkey; this would please their pride and no doubt they would make it a very profitable business; it would clearly be a great advantage if we could get complete control of Syria and Arabia and leave the Straits and Turkey in French hands. I do not know how far this idea receives support in higher quarters. Another point of view is that the French are using the Syrian question in order to force us to support their claims as against Germany on the left bank of the Rhine. Whatever the truth may be, the situation is certainly an awkward one.

I think it is a good thing that Wilson has gone away;[1] it is extraordinary to hear from those who have heard his speeches at the Conference how very strong a feeling of distrust and opposition he creates. . . . There is no doubt a very nasty feeling arising between the French and the Americans, and there have been awkward incidents which of course are kept very secret. The League of Nations scheme, which is now public, derives all the merit which is in it from our people, starting with Zimmern and Percy, and carried on with great energy by Cecil.

Of course one sympathizes very much with France but I cannot feel that they are well advised in all that they are doing.

---

[1] Wilson had sailed for the United States on 14 February.

Extract from letter to
Mr A. E. Zimmern (F.O.)   *18 February 1919*

. . . I read the different memoranda which have come over about events
in Russia with great interest; the situation seems to get more and more
hopeless, both there and here. Everyone says that they ought to have a
policy, but they never seem to succeed in approaching within a hundred
miles of having one.

My own feeling is that we ought to begin by really taking vigorous and
active steps to free from Bolshevism the outlying districts. We have in
Esthonia, Courland and Lithuania, together with Poland, territories in
which, according to all accounts, a moderate amount of assistance in arms
and material of different kinds would enable an indigenous force to be
organized which would be quite capable of fighting effectively against
Bolshevik intervention. It seems to me an appalling thing that we should
have left these peoples for all these months almost entirely without any
kind of help and, in the case of Lithuania, without any kind of encouragement. Here is something which can be done which does not involve the
very serious military difficulties of actual intervention in Russia and
against which I do not think that even the Labour Party could raise any
outcry. We could always base intervention here on the ground that the
Peace Conference are willing to award provisional recognition to the *de
facto* Governments established in these countries, and that, therefore, they
are justified in helping them to defend themselves against an external invasion. It does not matter in the least whether the people who invade them
from the East are Bolshevists or any other kind of military aggressive
force; we have the plain fact that people from one country are attack-
ing another country; we have responsibilities towards the other countries, or can assume them, and this is nothing at all to do with the
theoretical principles of Bolshevism or struggle between capitalism and
socialism.

If we did this, then we could begin by getting the establishment of
healthy conditions which might possibly spread to Russia; even if they did
not, a barrier would be interposed between western Europe and Russia,
but I am quite sure that the general moral effect would be good. What we
are suffering from is the inexcusable neglect to give the help that we could
give to all these peoples who are begging for assistance. As to actual intervention in Russia, I am much more doubtful; it is a very big proposition
involving both political and military difficulties, but I suppose, as soon as
the spring comes, it would be comparatively easy to occupy Petrograd . . .

I wonder what you think of the League of Nations scheme.[1] It has obviously been very carefully drafted, and a good deal of it shows very sound workmanship, but it is not an interesting scheme; it will not arouse popular enthusiasm. I rather fear that the interest will quickly wane, especially as Wilson has left and apparently Cecil is going off to other jobs. . . .

Note. At the beginning of February a good deal of time was taken up with consultations between the representatives of the American and British Delegations and, in exchange for their 'Black Book' containing an 'Outline of tentative Report and Recommendations prepared in the Intelligence Section, in accordance with instructions, for the President and Plenipotentiaries',[2] Mr Headlam-Morley received permission to communicate to the American Delegation certain memoranda which had been prepared in the Political Intelligence Department immediately after the Armistice in preparation for the Peace Conference. These meetings were very secret, and among the papers there is only a record of one of them, held on 21 February. This was attended by Mr Akers Douglas, Colonel Cornwall,[3] Mr Headlam-Morley and Mr Paton, of the British Delegation, and Mr Bowman, Dr Haskins, Major Johnson, Dr Mezes and Mr Seymour of the American Delegation. It is recorded that the meeting had not been informed as to the procedure which it was proposed to follow, whether the terms of peace would be simply communicated to and imposed upon Germany, or whether opportunity would be given to the Germans for discussion and negotiation. It was agreed, therefore, that the territorial proposals which they drew up should be maximum terms so that if negotiations took place the amount of territory to be ceded by Germany might be reduced rather than increased. They then proceeded to discuss certain cessions demanded by France and included the proposals that to France should be transferred full and complete right to the management, administration, exploitation and ownership of the Saar coalfield, as a compensation for the destruction by Germany of the French coal mines

---

[1] See 'Draft Resolution Relative to the League of Nations' dated 25 January 1919 in P.P.C. III, 201.

[2] For the Black Book, see the Woodrow Wilson Papers (Library of Congress, Manuscript Division), Series V-A, Box 9. In late February it was superseded by the Inquiry's final recommendations, the Red Book. For details see Shotwell, *At the Paris Peace Conference* (New York, 1937), p. 134, in whose papers at Columbia University (Butler Memorial Library, Box 1) a copy can be found.

[3] Lt.-Col. J. H. M. Cornwall, a member of the Military Intelligence Branch of the British Delegation concerned with Austria–Hungary and Czechoslovakia.

in the neighbourhood of Lens and Valenciennes. The Belgian and Danish frontiers were next considered and much time was given to a discussion of the provisional frontier on the east of Germany, which had been proposed by the Howard–Lord agreement, and which included the cession of Danzig to Poland.[1]

21 February 1919

Note. On 21 February it was decided by the Supreme Council that the questions raised in Monsieur Bernhoft's[2] statement on the Danish territorial interests in the Peace Settlement should be referred for examination, in the first instance, to the Committee which was examining the Belgian problems. It should be the duty of the Committee to reduce the questions for decision within the narrowest possible limits and to make recommendations for a just settlement. The Committee should be authorized to consult the representatives of the peoples concerned.

A few days later, on 26 February, the terms of reference to the Committee were extended and it was decided that the Belgian Committee should examine the question of the neutral status of Belgium as established by the Treaty of 1839, and make recommendations to the Council concerning modifications of that status.[3]

Minute addressed to Sir William Tyrrell   *24 February 1919*

Mr Seton-Watson, who came across to Paris for the British War Mission, finds that his work in connection with that has now ceased. It has been suggested that he should go to Prague to watch the political situation there and also to help Lady Muriel Paget's mission for the relief of the people. I understand that the Czech Government is anxious that he should be allowed to go. We have had many complaints as to the absence of British representatives in addition to the official mission at Prague, and I am sure that it would be of the greatest use to us if Mr Seton-Watson was there; he would of course communicate freely with us. There are many matters on which we should be glad to have further knowledge.

Mr Seton-Watson was, as you know, called up for military service; the Army Council ordered his discharge previous to the Armistice, but owing

[1] A partial résumé of the meeting is to be found in FO 608/66/20216, as well as in Nelson, op. cit., p. 150.
[2] M. H. A. Bernhoft, the Danish Minister in Paris.
[3] See P.P.C. IV, 65–6, 141–4.

to various delays and the fact that he has been obliged to be absent from England on an official mission, the final stage of discharge has not been completed. All the papers are, I understand, in London, but it would be necessary for him to return to London for the process to be completed. This would cause unnecessary delay.[1]

Minute addressed to Sir William Tyrrell   26 February 1919

I am a little anxious as to the situation with regard to the method by which a provisional boundary is being established between the Poles and the Ruthenians. It is, I think, unfortunate that as would appear from the available information, the only representatives of the Allies who are in charge of the matter are those who are in a position to hear the Polish side of the case. I do not understand that we have any representative who is in close touch with the population and such provisional government as exists in Eastern Galicia. It appears that the Ukrainians are inclined to reject the proposals which have been put forward,[2] and one cannot but fear that they will feel that they have not had a sufficient opportunity of stating their own point of view. I do not know whether there is any British or Allied representative at present in East Galicia, or if it would be possible to order one of the representatives who is in that part of the world to get in touch with the Ukrainians. What I fear is that it may appear as though the Allies are allowing themselves to become merely the spokesmen of the Poles; this would inevitably tend to an unfortunate result and make it more difficult to bring about the cessation of hostilities.[3]

Extract from letter to Mr Namier (F.O.)   27 February 1919

I enclose for your information a copy of a minute[4] I wrote to show that I am not entirely neglectful of your warnings, and you will see that the

[1] Permission was granted and Mr Seton-Watson left for Czechoslovakia on or about 2 May. (M.H.)

[2] In fact the Ruthenians on 24 February had accepted unfavourable armistice terms proposed by the Inter-Allied Commission to Warsaw but repudiated them four days later. As a result the hostilities resumed.

[3] This was sent to the Military Section. Lt.-Col. F. H. Kisch minuted: 'I do not think Mr Headlam-Morley need be anxious. General Carton de Wiart has proceeded to Lemberg to endeavour to arrange an armistice line between the Poles and Ukrainians. He can be relied upon to listen to the delegates of the rival groups with complete impartiality. Further, it has been made abundantly clear to all concerned that any settlement now reached in order to bring about a cessation of hostilities will in no way prejudice the final determination of the frontiers.' (M.H.)

[4] See immediately preceding document. (M.H.)

result is one which I fear will not remove your apprehensions. Carton de Wiart is, I believe, a very good man, at any rate he is a very good soldier; whether he will be able to maintain his equilibrium after being exposed to Polish influences is perhaps doubtful.

I do not think that I look on this matter in quite such a gloomy way as you do; I suspect that when one is in Warsaw, then one finds that the Poles are much better than one would be led to think by what is said and done by their representatives abroad. They are certainly to some extent influenced by this *mégalomanie de grandeur*, but I do not see that they are any worse than any of the other small nations, Czechoslovakia, Yugoslavia, Greece or Romania. Anyhow, unsatisfactory though they may be, we must take them as they are and try to build up as sound a condition as possible. I am quite sure that it is essential to give them help in food and do all we can to get work restarted and the factories opened. Letters from Howard and others give a terrible picture of the material condition of the country. If we can do this and at the same time let the Polish army go back to Poland, we ought to be strong enough to keep them in check. Where I think we differ is that you on the whole are inclined to regard Bolshevism as a lesser evil than Polish imperialism;[1] in this I cannot follow you; I suppose the difference springs from ultimate causes and our whole attitude of mind towards political affairs, but in the long run if they can get the Polish State started on a liberal basis with the necessary agrarian reform, then in the long run I should not be frightened of Polish imperialism. This is a disease which we know all about and I think will soon tend to ebb away if the people can be brought face to face with problems of administration and government. What has produced much of the evils of Poland is I imagine that they have no responsibility of government, they have been nourished on dreams, and dreams are often unhealthy. My remedy for this would be, as I say, the hard work of building up a State, but it is impossible to expect them to apply themselves to this so long as they are deprived of the absolute necessities of life and until the material necessary for the restarting of industry is available.

[1] Namier referred to Polish claims to territory east of ethnic Poland, including East Galicia, as 'Polish imperialism'. See his 'Report on Poland', 3 December 1918, FO 371/4354/P.I.D., f. 46, pc. 73. In 1918–20 the Foreign Office supported the Ukrainian objective of including East Galicia in a Ukrainian state federated with a non-Bolshevik Russia. The British General Staff preferred its incorporation in Poland so as to prevent giving Russia a gateway into the Balkans. See 'Russia and the Ukraine', General Staff, War Office, 29 October 1918, FO 371/4355, f. 100, pc, 100. Also Headlam-Morley, P.C.M. 11836.

Extract from letter to Mr Rex Leeper (F.O.)   *27 February 1919*

I was very much interested in your letter about Russia and Poland and I will do what I can to get your points attended to here. I will do this, although, quite frankly, I do not agree with you on many points and, in particular, about military intervention in Russia. I quite agree that an army say of 50,000 supported by a fleet could, as soon as spring comes on, take Petrograd, and it is quite possible that it would be welcomed there. Indeed to judge from the accounts, anyone would be welcomed there who could bring a breath of the open air to Petrograd. But I cannot close my eyes to the fact that the occupation of Petrograd is something very different from the occupation of Russia. I suppose that if this were done, the Bolsheviks would fall back upon Moscow and would at once appeal to Russian national sentiment against the Allies. To advance beyond Petrograd would be a most dangerous undertaking; even if there was no hostility from the peasants, it would require a much larger army than 50,000 men, and I cannot ignore the possibility that the Bolsheviks would be successful in appealing to peasant feelings; they would say that the Allies were coming to restore the old regime and might easily bring about a rising of the whole population, which would make occupation of the country a most hazardous undertaking.

Are you also not too prejudiced against Poland? . . . Even if it is true, and I am not entirely convinced, that the Poles are incompetent and are 'indulging in a mad wave of imperialism and chauvinism', they are not, as far as I can see, any worse than the other minor states which are being created.

With regard to the situation in Germany, you say that Bolshevism is not a disease arising from hunger; I am not quite sure what this means; I do not think that we can ignore the evidence that even if hunger is not the cause of Bolshevism, people in a state of starvation are much more liable to the infection than those who are living a normal, cheerful and prosperous life. I have recently seen a number of officers who have come back from Germany; they have been working separately; they have been to different parts of the country, but they are unanimous that unless food is supplied there will be a collapse of social order which will take the form of Bolshevism. Of course the Bolshevik influence is spread by paid emissaries who are in most cases deliberately misleading the people; a meeting at Berlin was described to me by a man who had been present at it, in the course of which the speaker said: 'Our Government is no good, not even the Allies trust it; if they did, they would give food', and then he pointed out to them the alternative of turning for help to Russia who would bring food.

If we can get first of all the food question dealt with and quickly get peace with Germany, then normal business life ought to begin again; with that the minds of men would turn to work, comfort, making money, all the ordinary motives of life; as soon as their individual interests are directed in this way, then the Bolshevik propaganda will begin to lose its attractiveness. It thrives on the present abnormal condition of the world. It is, as the Bolsheviks themselves have always seen, a creed which will find assent only in a country which has been defeated and is in the state of depression which follows defeat. What I should do, therefore, is to concentrate attention on central and eastern Europe, and try to build this up again. I attach the greatest importance to giving help to Poland and the Baltic Provinces. It seems to me that we think much too much about what at present is rather an academic question, whether at some future period the Baltic Provinces are to be restored to Russia; I am quite prepared to leave this point, but I am not prepared to continue our present policy of neglect to give them the help they demand, simply because by so doing we may be offending the Russian exiles in Paris and London.

This is as much and more than we can do during the ensuing year. It is, however, a definite scheme of work; if we do not do it, I am sure that disaster will follow. We have not resources, men or money enough to do this and intervene in Russia as well. I should therefore be prepared to leave Russia alone. This will sound to you callous and brutal; I do not see how it can be helped. I should like to do all that is possible to help the Russians, but I am not convinced that we can really do anything, and I am afraid that if we attempt to do it we shall be dissipating energy which is even more necessary for other purposes.

Memorandum   3 March 1919

I have had more than one conversation lately with Professor Shotwell of the American Delegation.[1] Professor Shotwell emphasizes the immense importance of bringing about a permanent better understanding between America and Great Britain; this, as he says, is essential for the future welfare of both nations. He foresees, however, that on the American side there is likely to be some reaction. He anticipates a revival of the distrust with which Great Britain is traditionally regarded and thinks that the pro-

[1] An account of one of these meetings is given in Shotwell, *At the Paris Peace Conference* (New York, 1937), p. 191.

German feeling which was strong in large sections of the population before the war will revive, and the fact that Germany has been defeated and that, having been defeated, has overthrown the Emperor and established a democratic form of Government, is important. There will be many people in America who will incline to the view that Germany has been purified, but that England has not been. The traditional republican feeling – I do not refer to the Republican Party – is very strong and American sympathy will tend to drift towards a republic in Germany.

In this connection he attributed the greatest importance to spreading a better knowledge, not so much of the events accompanying the outbreak of war, but the history of the preceding fifteen years. There would be a very strong feeling in America that after all England was not so innocent as she professed to be, what had happened was merely an instance of the extraordinary Machiavellian cunning of secret British diplomacy, which was infinitely cleverer than the Germans, and really beguiled them into the war. He thought that it was of real importance that the case should be put before the Americans and at as early a date as possible.

I said that, speaking personally, I quite agreed as to the extreme importance of a full publication explaining British policy before the war. He said that to carry conviction in America it would be of very great service if some well-known American scholar could himself be allowed access to the Foreign Office records. He said that he would not himself do for this object as he was Canadian born and would therefore not be trusted, but he mentioned the names of two or three well-known American historians. I said that I would put forward the suggestion, which is I think an important one. The whole question of the publication of records between 1900 and 1914 has been obliged to stand over owing to great pressure of other work, but if, as I hope will be the case, it could be put in hand very shortly, it would be necessary that more than one person should be associated with it and, if so, I should like to suggest for consideration that some American scholar should be invited to take part in the work.[1]

Minute   *3 March 1919*

I think Mr Paton makes out a very strong case.[2] As to West Prussia, I am inclined to agree, always with the proviso that a clause should be inserted

---

[1] The original is in FO 371/4378/P.I.D. 196/pp. 209–11. The proposal was not favourably received. It was strongly criticized by Lord Hardinge and Lord Curzon.
[2] The reference is to a long memorandum by Mr H. J. Paton dated 27 February 1919 entitled 'The Polish Claims to Danzig and West Prussia', FO 608/66/20216. Paton argued that

in the treaty that, before the boundaries are fixed and the cession takes place, an opportunity should be given to the inhabitants of any district, if they ask for it, to express their own preference.

As to Danzig, it is not really a matter merely of German sentiment but of principle. After all that has been said I cannot reconcile myself to the policy of handing over a city such as Danzig to an alien Power, completely disregarding the wishes of the inhabitants, and this is all the more important when the transference is to be to a state which is only now in process of formation, and as to the character and government of which we are still completely in the dark. It is certainly true that the commercial interests of Danzig are entirely identified with Poland, and that the comparatively slow growth of the population is a result of the political separation from the natural hinterland.

I still believe that the right solution is to be found in the conception of the autonomous and, perhaps, semi-independent city-state. We want to shake ourselves free of the obsessions of the unified and centralized national state which is the growth of the period since the French Revolution. It is the exaggeration of this which is the cause not only of the war, but of the difficulties with the peace. We are still under the obsession of the political ideas which created Pan-Germanism and threaten to bring about an equally aggressive and uncompromising spirit among the new nationalities.

If we leave Danzig autonomous, revoke the annexation to Prussia assure to it the full control of its own government, free it from the apprehension that it shall become a subject for Polish national propaganda, do not subject its citizens to compulsory service in the Polish army – possibly for a war against Germany – then we can be sure that the commercial advantages of co-operation with Poland will soon do their work. There are many forms in which this could be brought about. It is proposed, I believe, to establish some separate regime for the German territory on the left bank of the Rhine; in Danzig, again, we could have a separate regime. It might be either complete independence, or it might be a position such

---

Poland should have direct access to the sea because West Prussia had a preponderantly Polish population according to the German census of 1910. He held that Danzig should also belong to Poland because it lay at the mouth of her chief river, the Vistula, and was the only port which Poland could have, if she were to have one at all. He thought that the German population, which had originally settled there for trade, would remain there for the same reason as long as its rights were safeguarded by some kind of autonomy such as that it enjoyed under the Polish Crown before 1793. If, on the other hand, Germany were allowed to keep Danzig and West Prussia, he thought that she would then have a stranglehold on Poland and reduce the latter to vassal status. For Germany, Paton argued, there were questions of sentiment, while for Poland they were a vital necessity.

as that which Hamburg held before it joined the German Customs Union, or it might be incorporation with Poland, but as a free autonomous state under international guarantees. What I maintain we cannot do is simply to annex Danzig to Poland without consulting the inhabitants, in such a way as to make the German population subject to Polish compulsory military service, religious and educational legislation.

Extract from letter to
Sir Esme Howard (Warsaw)   4 March 1919

. . . As you know, an Inter-Allied Committee has been appointed, of which Tyrrell is a member, to receive and act on your reports. My own information of what is going on is really very scrappy, as I do not see all the papers. I have, however, been attending as a listener one or two meetings with the Americans, to come to a final decision as to the frontier. The frontier which you and Lord drew up appears to have held its own very well, and I gather that the final recommendations, which I think have been agreed upon by Tyrrell's Committee, follow it very closely.[1] There has been much discussion about Danzig and many minutes and memoranda written upon it. The situation seems to be working out that there is an increasing preponderance of opinion for giving Danzig to the Poles.[2] I am afraid I am not entirely convinced and have been trying to device some kind of compromise; I am sure that if it is given it will be the most essential to secure that neither the Polish language should be forced upon the people of Danzig, nor that they should be subjected to forcible service in the Polish army. I quite see that the natural future of Danzig is with Poland, and if we go slowly, carefully and prudently, I should hope that eventually the recognition of the enormous advantages which would come to the place from the development of Polish commerce will outweigh national feeling, but I feel convinced that this will be brought about all the more easily if we carefully avoid the mistakes which the Germans made in Alsace-Lorraine. From the point of view of Poland, it would be worth an enormous amount to get Danzig to come in to the Polish system willingly . . .

I know you think that I am a very impatient person, but I cannot help

[1] See 'Report No. 1 of the Commission on Polish affairs', 12 March 1919. *Recueil*, IV, C (2), 53–73.
[2] On 24 February the Supreme Council had agreed that all territorial commissions set up before 15 February to deal with the German settlement should submit their recommendations not later than 8 March. See P.P.C. IV, 102–4, 108–9, as well as Hankey's *The Supreme Control at the Paris Peace Conference, 1919*, pp. 76–80.

but feel that all that is happening now confirms the impatience which I have felt and often expressed during the last few months. The parole now is to speed up and to get the Preliminaries of Peace settled with Germany, but I cannot see why that was not begun long ago, for until we get peace assured with Germany, the world will not begin to settle down. But even more important than peace is food, manufactures and employment. The reports from Germany during the last few days have been very bad, and it looks as if the second revolution, which has been so often foretold, is on the point of breaking out. If it does, the consequences, not only in Germany but throughout central Europe, will be very serious. All the countries seem to me to have held together better than one could have anticipated under the enormous strains of the last few months, but I cannot help asking myself whether the strain might not have been relieved before now. A little food, but not much, has got into Vienna, but with this exception, as far as I can make out, practically nothing has been done in all the time which has elapsed since the armistice . . .[1]

Extract from letter to Mr Philip Kerr   5 March 1919[2]

. . . At this moment the thing that matters is to get some food into Germany and to give what support can be given to the Government in getting work restarted. The situation there is an impossible one. The shortage of coal, the difficulties of locomotion, created partly by the excessive demands for locomotives made in the Armistice and enforced with excessive severity by the French, and the uncertainty as to the future, make it impossible for productive work to be carried on. The blockade has been increased in stringency since the Armistice. The Government are helpless and the people are being driven to Bolshevism. It is no good discussing terms of peace with Germany when too probably there will be no Germany left to make peace with.

For weeks and weeks discussion and talk about food has continued. Nothing has happened and I see little prospect that anything will happen. The only possible chance of saving the situation is that those in the highest authority should intervene and force a solution. To this everything else is subordinated. If there is difficulty about getting food in to otherparts, why

[1] Food supplies for Germany were delayed first by French insistence that the blockade be maintained as a means of pressure, and secondly by the German Government's procrastination in agreeing to deliver merchant ships to the Allies. Agreement on this point was reached on 15 March. But in fact supplies did not reach Germany till June.
[2] The original is in the Philip Kerr Papers, GD 40/17/71 p. 27.

not send some through Emden, whence communication is easy to Westphalia and Hanover?

Extract from letter to Mr Namier (F.O.)   5 March 1919

Monsieur Filipowicz came to see me today with an introduction from
Zaleski. He is going to London at the end of the week and I advised him
to come and see you. I told him that he would not agree with you about
the Ukraine; he of course supports the extreme Polish view. He seemed,
however, a very reasonable sort of person to talk to and quite recognized
that there was another point of view to his own. I understand from Tyrrell that he is not one of the National Democrat set – in fact Tyrrell said
that it looked as if he was being sent to London as a compliment to you!
I do not know what this means, you probably will.[1]

Extract from letter to Mr Edwyn Bevan (F.O.)   5 March 1919

I quite agree with you and Saunders and Zimmern about Germany. The
whole treatment strikes me as having been as unwise as possible. The origin
appears to have been that we depended far too much on French opinion
and whatever merits the French may have, that of understanding Germany
does not seem to be included among them. It is curious to see how suddenly the press is beginning to swing round and is becoming aware of the
real truth; the misfortune is that this is happening so late, but it seems to
me that with wiser action, we could have done almost anything we wanted
to with Germany. Now things appear to be going very badly. The great
mistake has been the delay in getting the food question settled. Of course
there were enormous difficulties to be overcome, but many of them were,
as far as I can make out, of our own making. The origin of half the difficulty is that we have scrupulously insisted on refusing all communications
with Germany except through Spa[2] and thereby left things much too
much in the hands of the soldiers. The idea that there should be no conversation with the Germans except on military lines is, I should have
thought, quite unnecessary and it is an idea which I think has no precedent
in the past.

[1] Namier regarded Filipowicz as an extreme Polish imperialist and therefore was not flattered
by the suggestion that he would welcome Filipowicz's visit simply because the latter was
also a bitter enemy of Dmowski and the National Democrats. See also p. 13, note 2 above.
(M.H.)
[2] The Armistice Commission was still sitting at Spa and was the main channel of communication between the Allied Governments and the new Government of Germany. See
p. 8, note 2 above.

Everything here is being speeded up as much as possible so as to get an early Peace; much of the merit of this seems to me to be Balfour's;[1] he has been taking a much more prominent part since Lloyd George went away.[2] The frontier questions are getting on pretty well; on the other hand, I do not know, and nobody seems to know, what the French proposals are for dealing with the left bank of the Rhine; a great deal depends upon them.[3] Philip Kerr came to me last night and asked if I could give him any information; I could only answer that this was the kind of thing on which we looked to him for information.[4] I think there is every desire here to deal with the Germans fairly on the Polish question, but Danzig remains a difficulty; I have practically no doubt that it will have to go to Poland, but I hope that some securities for local autonomy will be insisted upon.

Even the French are beginning to realize that if German–Austria wishes, it will have to be allowed to go to Germany, but the line about that is that the decision must be deferred until after the Peace. It would not do to allow them to join Germany until the whole peace settlement had been concluded even if they desired. This will give time, which is much wanted, for them to see how things are developing in Germany and to make up their minds at leisure. Most of the frontier questions are in a fair way towards settlement, except those between Italy and Austria. When one says 'settlement', however, one only means that people in a room here or at the Crillon or at the Quai d'Orsay have come to an agreement; I sometimes ask whether the people on the spot are ever to be consulted, but I am always told that this is out of the question. Self-determination is quite démodé. Leeper and Nicolson determine for them what they ought to wish, but they do it very well.

What makes one most anxious, apart from the food question, is that of reparation. I gather that the bill to be presented to Germany will be an enormous one – I fear so great that it will be quite out of the question for

---

[1] Balfour's proposals for speeding up the Conference are described by Hankey in two letters to Lloyd George of 20 and 23 February. See the Lloyd George Papers, F/3/4/13 and F/23/4/22 respectively. The latter is partly quoted in Thomas Jones's *Whitehall Diary*, 3 vols. (London: Oxford University Press, 1969), I, 78–9.

[2] Lloyd George left Paris on 10 February and returned in early March.

[3] Not until 25 February did the French formally indicate their proposals for the Rhineland. On that date one of the five French plenipotentiary Delegates, André Tardieu, presented to the British and American Delegations a memorandum which proposed the partial dismemberment of Germany by detaching the left bank of the Rhine and creating a buffer state. See Tardieu's *The Truth about the Treaty* (Indianapolis: Bobbs-Merrill, 1921), pp. 147–70.

[4] Headlam-Morley evidently gave advice to Kerr, as several of his arguments were used during the course of secret meetings between Tardieu, Mezes and Kerr on 11 and 12 March. Minutes in the Lloyd George Papers, F/89/2/40.

the Germans to pay. In that case they may either simply refuse, saying that it cannot be done, and leave us to take what steps we like, which would be very inconvenient, or they may promise to pay and then after the Peace is made point out that it is impossible for them to carry out their engagements.

Note on the proposal for the control of the navigation of the Rhine made by the French Delegation 7 *March 1919*

This proposal is open to the most serious objections. France apparently proposes to insert in the Treaty of Peace with Germany clauses affecting the Treaty of Mannheim,[1] to which Holland, a neutral Power, is a party, without consulting Holland. This in itself is a serious breach of the most ordinary rules of international courtesy, and she is asking the other Allies to make themselves partners to it. The proposal by which Germany is to bind herself to adhere 'to any other alterations in the agreement which France may, within a period of five years, consider it desirable to make' is one which is quite unjustifiable, even in a treaty imposed on a defeated state.

The whole scheme is fundamentally vicious. France starts from the Treaty of Mannheim in which France, Germany and Holland were alone represented, binds Germany by those clauses inserted in the Treaty of Peace to agree to everything which she, France, may suggest, without consulting Holland, and thereby in practice gives France the complete and absolute control over the whole navigation of the Rhine. The interests of Switzerland in the Rhine are completely ignored and the powers which France claims for abstracting water from the Rhine are so extensive as to make it probable that she intends to refuse to render the river navigable between Strasbourg and Basle. It is of course for British interests to secure that the river should be fully open to traffic up to Basle.

For the Rhine, as for other rivers, there should be established a completely new convention, a commission which will control and manage the waterways; on this commission should be represented the riparian states, viz: Switzerland, Holland, Germany, France and also Belgium, in proportion to their interests. In addition to this it is clearly essential that Great

---

[1] Signed by Baden, Bavaria, France, Hesse-Darmstadt, the Netherlands and Prussia on 17 October 1868, the Convention of Mannheim removed all remaining river tolls on the Rhine, opened that river to traffic without restrictions and created a Central Commission for the management of navigation.

Britain should be represented and perhaps one or two other non-riparian states. It must be remembered that in this matter French interests are not identical with those of Great Britain and it is clear that France is using the opportunity under cover of imposing fresh terms on Germany, of establishing so complete a control over the navigation as may be used to interfere with just British interests. We have no interest in refusing to Germany that share of the navigation of the Rhine which accrues to her from her predominant position as a riparian state.

For these reasons I should suggest that at a meeting of the Inter-Allied Commission, the British Delegates should begin by stating that the draft is fundamentally vicious; no good can come from discussing a draft drawn up on these lines. The French ought to be asked to withdraw it. In addition to this, I may point out that certain of the clauses are of such a nature that they could not with any propriety, even under the present circumstances, be imposed upon Germany for they deprive her of sovereignty over her own territory; no peace in which such conditions are inserted could be permanent. The only result would be to provide a constant and increasing cause of friction and political unrest.

Memorandum   *8 March 1919*

At a Departmental Committee to consider proposals for International Waterways, two points came up on which the opinion of the Political Department is required. The present suggestion is that the existing international Commission for the control of the Danube as far as the Iron Gates should continue, and that a new international commission should be appointed to deal with the upper waters of the Danube and its tributaries. It is proposed that the existing Commission for the lower waters should be continued with the same membership as it has hitherto had, with the sole exception that all enemy states should be removed from it. In discussion the position of Bulgaria was raised. It was pointed out that as a riparian state she was in a different position from other enemy states. It was, however, stated that she has hitherto not been on the Commission and there seems no reason for putting her on now. No doubt the time would come when she should apply to be admitted and the matter might then be considered. The point for decision is whether in reconstituting the Commission, Bulgaria should be entirely ignored, or whether a clause should be inserted under which she would have a right to become a member after some fixed period. This is a matter on which the opinion of those dealing with the political settlement of the Balkans is desired.

With regard to the new Commission to be appointed for the upper waters of the Danube, it is proposed that all riparian states should be members, i.e. Yugoslavia, Hungary, Czechoslovakia, Austria, Germany; the present proposal is, however, that the enemy states should for the present, though members of the Commission, not have the right of voting. The wisdom of this decision was called in question and it was suggested that the position of at least Hungary, and also German-Austria, if it were not united with Germany, might be unduly prejudiced by this arrangement and that it was not desirable to put them in a position of such marked inferiority as regards Yugoslavia and Czechoslovakia. It was suggested, therefore, that they should be admitted with full rights to vote at some definite and early date. On this point also an opinion is desired.

I may add that it was generally agreed that it would be desirable to appoint on this Commission for the upper waters of the river at least one non-riparian state, presumably one of the Allied Great Powers.

Extract from letter to Mr John Bailey (F.O.)   8 March 1919

It is very hard to get time to write to you as I am rather busy just at present with Commissions. We have been dealing with the Saar Valley and also with the revision of Belgian neutrality. On the latter point the Inter-Allied Commission has adopted a report which I think is on the whole quite satisfactory; it is devised so as to bring Holland into a general revision of all the treaties. Of course the Belgians want to use this to get not only Limburg but also South Limburg. I think they are quite right, but I see little probability that they will succeed. At present it looks as if they will get nothing but Moresnet and Malmédy, which will not satisfy them.

As to the Saar Valley, we have worked out a scheme by which, as reparation for the destruction of the French coalfields, the French will get complete control over the mining district in the Saar Valley, but the sovereignty will be limited by clauses protecting the inhabitants, who will not have to serve in the French army and will not be regarded as a part of France; for instance, they will not send deputies to the Chamber of Deputies. We do not propose to give them Landau. So far this is only an informal arrangement arrived at by conversations with the Americans, and I do not know whether it will be accepted; yet there are signs that the French themselves are prepared to accept something of the kind if they cannot get the 1814 frontier in the Saar Valley in full sovereignty. It is drawn up on the hypothesis that the left bank of the Rhine shall be sterilized from the military point of view, but it is impossible to find out among all the French schemes put forward for dealing with this district what the Government itself is going to adopt.

We have also been dealing with the Slesvig question. A Deputation attended the Commission yesterday,[1] representatives of Slesvig and Denmark, and I think that this will be settled pretty easily on quite reasonable lines. There will be one plebiscite in north Slesvig and another plebiscite in mid-Slesvig.

The Polish business is also getting on fairly quickly. The great problem has of course been how to deal with Danzig. I gather that it has been determined to give Danzig to Poland without conditions or reservations;[2] this I think is a mistake; they might have secured to the city of Danzig full privileges of local autonomy so as to safeguard it from unreasonable Polish propaganda and penalization of German language, etc. I am sure that people are going too far in ignoring the just German feeling, and I fear that the eventual result will be very disadvantageous, especially to France.

Extract from letter to Mr Koppel (F.O.)   10 March 1919

. . . Everything is being speeded up with the object of getting peace with Germany as soon as possible; that means that all the reports of the Committees have to be got out and then drafts have to be made of clauses to be put into the treaty, all the work in fact which ought to have been done well ahead weeks ago has to be compressed into a few days. Whether they will be able to get this treaty as soon as they think seems to me very doubtful. Everything depends really upon reparation; this is an awful mess and I do not find that anyone has any suggestion for a way out.[3]

Extract from letter to Mr G. Saunders (F.O.)   13 March 1919

I think we have got the Slesvig question fairly well settled; the account in *The Times* today (Wednesday), though brief, is pretty accurate. A plebiscite in north Slesvig taken *en bloc*, central Slesvig to be divided into two zones in each of which there is to be a plebiscite taken by districts. The

---

[1] See P.P.C. IV, 195.
[2] See P.P.C. IV and p. 51.
[3] There were differences of view between the British and American Delegations as well as differences between the French and British. See Headlam-Morley's Memorandum on Reparations (11984).

arrangement is unnecessarily complicated, but this will not do much harm . . .[1]

Wilson is arriving tonight or tomorrow and as soon as he comes no doubt we shall get a decision about the left bank of the Rhine, which is holding everything up; I have not the slightest idea what it will be; the French are sure to put forward very exaggerated proposals, and I expect there will be rather a fight about it between them and the Americans.

Memorandum   *14 March 1919*

General Mance mentioned to me today certain points of difficulty and importance which have arisen during the discussions of the Inter-Allied Commission on Waterways, etc., and he is anxious that he should have authoritative guidance as to the attitude to be adopted with regard to certain general principles on which an immediate decision must be taken.

The particular points he mentioned are:

(1) Is the British Delegation to insist that they can impose clauses relating to the freedom of transit and liberty of navigation and movement on enemy states and on territories the sovereignty of which has been changed by the treaties of peace, even if no general agreement is arrived at to impose such conditions throughout the world?

(2) What principles should regulate the imposition on the enemy of terms which are penal in nature in the sense of their not being reciprocal, and which therefore cannot presumably be indefinitely imposed? For how long should such clauses be applicable?

The British Delegation have with regard to freedom of inland transit suggested a clause to the following effect:

> The above obligations shall take effect immediately on the ratification of the Treaty of Peace; they may be modified by the Council of the League of Nations on application by any of the [Central Powers] made not less than five years after the ratification of the Treaty of Peace.

It is clearly desirable that the wording of any such clause should be uniform throughout the treaty; this is a political matter with which the technical commissions are not qualified to deal.

Points have come up on which there is acute difference between some of the Allies, and it seems therefore extremely desirable that the British

---

[1] The Committee's report on Slesvig was presented to the Council of Foreign Ministers on 28 March, see P.P.C. IV, 529–32.

representatives on the different technical committees should meet in order that they may be able to acquaint one another with such differences as have come up, and that the general scope of these differences should be considered and their relation to one another, so that the British representatives on the Commissions should not act in isolation. The time seems now to have come when it would be advantageous that, in order to facilitate co-ordination, the draft clauses of the treaty prepared in these separate Commissions should be sent to some central body, who could compare them and draw attention to any points as to which revision or reconsideration seems desirable.

To a large extent the matters which come before the Commission on Waterways are most closely connected with those discussed by the Reparation Commission, the Financial Section who are presumably responsible for the financial clauses of the treaty, and those which presumably fall under the purview of the Supreme Economic Council. To some extent also they seem to require closer co-operation than has hitherto existed with the Political Section. As an illustration of the points, I may mention the proposals made by France for the future control of the navigation and waters of the Rhine. Some of these proposals obviously entrench on the functions of the Reparation Committee; others are of such a nature that they would probably be more properly dealt with in connection with the transference of sovereignty over Alsace-Lorraine from Germany to France. Others, which affect neutral countries, viz: Holland and Switzerland, require consideration from the political point of view and seem to raise important points as to the general attitude which should be adopted by the British Government towards the future relations between France and Germany.

Extract from letter to Mr Koppel (F.O.)   *14 March 1919*

. . . We have now finished our Committee on Belgium and Slesvig but Carnegie is still struggling with proofs and translations. All the English versions have been brought out by the Americans and that causes a good deal of extra trouble, as we have to fight to get as much English instead of American as we can, both in language and in spelling, and then they are rather apt to rush off to print before their proofs have been properly revised; they are, however, very pleasant to deal with. Most of the Committees are now getting to the end of their work and the next thing will be to see what the Supreme Council make of all the reports that are sent up to them; there is a Co-ordinating Committee, on which

Crowe is the British representative, through whose hands they have to pass . . .

The most busy people at present are Hurst and Malkin[1] as they are drafting clauses of treaties as hard as they can.

Extract from letter to
Mr John Bailey (F.O.)   *17 March 1919*

We have lately seen a good deal of the Danes as a deputation came to present their views about Slesvig; the French were very insistent that all the Danes were Germanophil and it is quite certain that they were asking the least possible amount of territory. The main thing in their minds was to avoid trouble with Germany by annexing anyone who might be found a crypto-German. Frankly, I was rather pleased to find a small nation that was asking for less rather than more than belonged to it and I think everyone would have welcomed a little more of the same spirit among the Italians, Poles, Romanians, Czechoslovaks, Greeks and Lithuanians. However, we have been doing our work bravely and insisting on a plebiscite being taken far south of the line for which they asked. We have also had representatives of Slesvig itself and of the Danish chauvinists, who warn us against the timidity of the Danish Government. But the Danish chauvinist is a very mild sort of person; I have just been lunching with him; he would rank as a pacifist anywhere else.

With regard to Germany, I do not suppose we really differ so much as may appear. . . . The last thing I should wish to do is to spare the Germans the consequences of their defeat or to remit any part of the penalty which they have justly incurred. In particular, it is quite obvious that if there is a shortage of food, it is the Germans who ought to be fed last. My real complaint is that by worrying the Germans about small and unessential matters, which do them more harm than they do good to any of the Allies, we distract attention from the great essential point; just because I wish them to feel, in such a way that there can be no mistake about it, that what they have to undergo is the necessary and just retribution for what they have done, it seems to me all the more important that we should not in any way give them grievances which might appear to be just. This I think we have done by such measures as forbidding them to fish in the North Sea during the continuance of the blockade, extending the blockade

[1] H. W. Malkin, Sir Cecil Hurst's assistant at the Foreign Office as well as adviser to the British Delegation on legal affairs.

to the Baltic and making it absolute there, enforcing with meticulous and unnecessary severity the cession of locomotives and, in particular, the long delay in settling the terms of peace. It is this, combined, as you say, with the want of frank and open statement on the part of the Allies, which is doing so much harm; but of course there is behind a spirit which is I think absolutely bad, and which one sees in such matters as the French proposals for the navigation of the Rhine, which would have made it quite impossible to publish the motives by which the Allies were influenced. I think that there are signs now that the French are getting a good deal more sensible . . .

Ultimately the problem is not so much a question of what Germany deserves, but of what it is in accordance with our own respect and honour to do; and moreover, after all, the Germans have done more than anybody anticipated they ever would to dissociate themselves from their former Government, although they may have done this with characteristic awkwardness and the appearance of duplicity. But the fact remains that they have overthrown the old Government and nothing but extreme stupidity on our part could make them wish to have it back again. Finally, there are certain elementary principles of humanity and christianity which seem to me too much forgotten.

Now the press and the Governments are suddenly getting into a panic as to the consequences of their attitude towards Germany; with a little foresight they could have acted months sooner and I think many of our present difficulties would have been avoided. People complain that the Germans do not realize that they have been defeated. It seems to me that the Germans are not the only people of whom this may be said. The Germany of which we were justly in dread was the Germany with all its powers of organization backed by a powerful military force. The military force has been crushed and dissipated. German *Kultur* has lost whatever charm it had and I see no reason why we should continue to be in constant dread of the German power of organization. In a Germany humbled as she must inevitably be, it may be a quality which we shall gladly make use of.

Extract from letter to Mr Namier (F.O.)   *20 March 1919*

It seems a long time since I have heard from you, but I understand that you are very busy and have plenty do to. I have really very little news to give about Polish affairs. Your prognostications have come quite true and I understand that the members of the Mission to Warsaw have all become pure Poles.[1] Polish affairs are now practically in the hands of Kisch; Tyrrell is away, Carr is in bed, Paton looks after the Polish frontier, but Kisch is the English member of the Polish Committee. He has certainly great intelligence and ability and I should think pretty good judgement. The chief subject of interest today is the action of the Council of Ten, who have turned down the report on the frontiers of Poland, although the report had been signed by all the members of the Commission.[2] I am inclined to think that as a matter of fact they were right although I understand from Paton, who was present at the meeting, that they were wrong in the reasons which they gave. The Polish Committee had another meeting this morning and agreed to stand to their guns.[3] It is an interesting situation, for this is the first one of the frontier Commissions which has reported, and if the Council of Ten are going to review all these detailed recommendations, we shall certainly be a long time before we get to peace. I do not like the report altogether, but I think the right thing would be to accept it on the condition that the territories were ceded in the first instance by Germany to the Allies, and not direct to Poland; this would give plenty of time to deal with all sorts of difficult problems which must inevitably come up; however, the lawyers make an objection to this that it would be very difficult to draft the treaty; my view is that it is the duty of the lawyers to draft treaties, however difficult, in accordance with the wishes of the political people, and of course the French have seized hold of this objection and are delighted with it.

I have just been lunching with Bojanczyk and Sokolnicki; I do not think that I got anything important out of them but I took the opportunity of suggesting that there were objections of principle to the Polish claims in the Ukraine.[4] They are sensible people, with whom one can talk, and quite took the point, but I find that such Poles as I have seen are very strong about the Ukraine, even when they placidly acquiesce in the objection that there is no foundation for their demands except the convenience of Poland. I think that the Council of Ten are beginning to realize the importance of the Ukrainian question and are trying to find out some means

[1] Headlam-Morley's remark is no exaggeration. Largely as a result of the French members, the Commission, especially over the issue of Eastern Galicia, lost all semblance of objectivity. Upon return to Paris in April, its mandate was terminated and its request for amalgamation with the Polish Commission rejected. For information on the activities of the Commission and its French members, see the official dispatches of the American military representative, General F. J. Kernan, found in the Parker Bliss Papers, Manuscript Division, Library of Congress, Box 72.

[2] See P.P.C. IV, 414–19.

[3] See *Recueil*, IV, C (2), 98–9, P.P.C. IV, 452–4.

[4] i.e. Eastern Galicia.

of bringing about a real understanding, and that they feel that for t hi purpose they must have more direct communication with the Ruthenians. I imagine that Carton de Wiart's visit here did good.

In one of your letters you refer to a certain Gielgud who, it was said, had gone to Poland with Carton de Wiart. I understand that this is not the case and that he was not taken.

Minute addressed to Sir H. Llewellyn Smith   23 March 1919

I had an interview today in Sir William Tyrrell's absence with a Mr Schill, who brought an introduction from the Foreign Office. He presented that he was by origin a Romanian from the Bukowina,[1] who had been living in America, and had there been in the service of M.I.5.

Mr Schill was much interested in the possible commercial developments in the Bukowina and drew attention particularly to the potential importance of the timber trade. He stated that the French and the Americans were already aware of this and were proposing to send agents to enter into contracts with private proprietors of the forests; in general he was concerned about the activity which the Americans especially are showing, with regard to commercial opportunities in eastern Europe. He represented that it was of great importance that the possibilities should not be neglected by our people. The particular object of his visit was that he might personally be authorized to go immediately to the Bukowina with powers either on behalf of the British Government or of British firms to get options or contracts for the purchase of timber.

I promised to let him know whether it was a matter in which interest was taken and should be glad to be told what I ought to say to him. I do not quite know why he should have come to Paris, for it seems to me that this is a matter which could more conveniently be dealt with in London.

Extract from letter to Mr Namier (F.O.)   24 March 1919

I am much obliged for the material you have sent me during the last two or three days. I have sent it on and hope that it will do good, though I do not expect that it will. However, it is now becoming clear that at least the British representatives at the Conference are waking up to the fact that

---

[1] This province of the former Austro-Hungarian Empire was claimed by the Romanians who, despite the Supreme Council's objections, occupied it in February 1919. The Supreme Council withdrew its objection in mid-March, however, in the hopes that the Romanian presence might prevent the Bolshevik infiltration into Hungary. See David S. Spector, *Rumania at the Peace Conference* (New York: Twayne, 1962).

we have got into a mess in the Ukraine and are doing their best to get a more impartial judgement on the matter. This is what always happens. They refuse to listen to advice for weeks and months and then take up the problem when the mischief has been done and it is probably too late. The only thing to do is to go on and try to get the mess cleared up.

I do not think that I quite agree with you about the Jews in Poland. It seems to me a mistake, certainly in tactics, to talk about national autonomy. So far as I understand it, the Jews ask for two separate things: first of all that they should not be murdered promiscuously and that they should have the full protection of the law; to this they are absolutely entitled. Secondly, they ask that they should have their own schools, but I do not know whether this applies to all grades of education or only to primary schools. In this too they ought clearly to have – subject to the conditions they have accepted – the right to have Polish taught in the schools. Is there anything more which they really want? If not, why use the expression 'national autonomy', which is open to all sorts of different interpretations and makes it appear that they are asking for a privileged position which would prevent them from identifying themselves with the country in which they live? You will say, I know, that the Jews feel themselves as a nation. That may be the case, but what we are concerned with practically is not their racial or national feeling, but the positive guarantees which they wish to have. If the educational liberty is all that is necessary to them, it is not wise to stress the other point.

The Polish Commission has now got on to the eastern frontiers of Poland; Paton is very sensible on the matter and I think we may be assured that he will do his best to get a just result; it is rather a serious responsibility to put on someone with so little experience. I am of the opinion, however, that things will be better in his hands than in those of anyone who is not equally honest and scientific in spirit.

The man I lunched with was Bojanczyk; he seems to be staying on in Paris. I am going to a Polish dinner tomorrow night; I am told by Carr and Paton that it is all right, but I will try and be very prudent and not drink too much wine!

Memorandum   *28 March 1919*

I enclose with this a copy of the draft of clauses to be inserted in the treaty with Germany, adopted by the Sub-Committee on Ports, Waterways and Railways, together with criticisms and observations.[1]

[1] See *Recueil*, IV, B (5).

G

I venture to suggest that the adoption of this report entirely substantiates the minute which, at General Mance's request, I put forward some days ago, pointing out the necessity of better opportunities for discussion and co-operation.[1] In particular it seems to me of the greatest importance that the British representatives on these technical Inter-Allied Committees should receive more help than has hitherto been given to them on the political questions which inevitably come up.

The history of this particular proposal, so far as I understand, is as follows: The French put in a draft series of articles which contained many clauses which were extremely objectionable. When I saw them I suggested that the whole structure was so fundamentally faulty that the British representatives should take the line that it was impossible to accept this even as a draft proposal for discussion. However, they were taken as a basis for discussion and General Mance succeeded, after vigorous discussion, in getting very important modifications introduced. I still think that the faults are so fundamental that no good can be made out of this draft at all. Quite apart from the points I have raised in my memorandum, there is the essential point that the French are trying to embody in what is intended to be a permanent Convention clauses and conditions which are in the nature of penal conditions imposed on Germany and not arising directly out of the war. Surely we ought to refuse to be a party to any such procedure.

The first thing to be done is to decide whether the new Rhine Convention ought to take the form of a revision of the Treaty of Mannheim, or whether the Treaty of Mannheim should be denounced and a completely new Convention made. For reasons which I have given in my memorandum, there seems no doubt that the latter would be the most convenient form. There then has to be discussed the proper means for gaining the consent first of Holland and secondly of Switzerland, and any other neutral who might be interested. Thirdly it must be determined how much is to be inserted in the Treaty of Peace with Germany. Is the general Convention on Waterways to be appended to the treaty and made an integral part of it, or is the final agreement as to this to be reserved till the League of Nations has become a working body?

I had always thought that the best procedure in the Treaty of Peace would be simply to require from Germany that she would assent to the principle that certain specified rivers, including the Rhine, should be regarded as international waterways, and should be subjected to such rules as might eventually be agreed upon by the League of Nations. In the case

[1] See Memorandum of 14 March, p. 49 above.

of the Rhine there would have to be added the special clause that Germany agreed to the denunciation of the Treaty of Mannheim. In the case of the Rhine, and perhaps in that of other rivers, it may also be desirable to insert certain conditions as to the constitution of the Commission which is to control the waterway. Anyhow, the important thing at this moment is that these political questions should receive adequate consideration.

Fortunately in this case there appears to be an opportunity for reconsideration of the whole matter, as I understand that this report from the sub-Committee has never received the approval of the main Committee, and has been sent up to the Supreme Council prematurely. This is to be discussed at a meeting tomorrow.

Extract from letter to Mr John Bailey (F.O.)   30 March 1919

We have been rather busy this last week as the Council of Four are now really trying to get on with peace with Germany. As you will have seen, there is, instead of the Ten, sitting in formal session with all their secretaries, etc., the four big people, who meet quite alone and I presume have a heart-to-heart talk.[1] From time to time they put out a statement in the press to say that they are getting on beautifully. I regret to say that the better opinion seems to be that they are not very much further than they were when they began under the new procedure.

The chief thing I have been interested in is the Saar Valley problem. The other day I got a message to go and see Lloyd George; I went to his flat in the Rue Nitot, and found him and Balfour alone, and we had quite a long conversation about that and other things. I explained the project which I have written to you about before, and they seemed quite attracted by it; curiously enough it appeared to be quite new to them. As you know, the idea is that instead of giving France the 1814 frontier, which seems to me for many reasons to be very objectionable, they should be given the whole of the Saar Valley, including all the mining district, with complete administrative control and ownership of all the coal mines; this would be justified as reparation for the destruction of the French mines; but they should not have complete sovereignty, and there should be strict arrangements to guard the interests of the inhabitants. In the afternoon I had to go

[1] Headlam-Morley noted in 'The Eastern Frontiers of Germany' (FO 13917) that, as a result of the leakage to the French press of Lloyd George's opposition to the report of the Commission on Polish Affairs, and of the Prime Minister's vehement protest on this point, the Council of Ten was reduced to a Council of Four. For Lloyd George's protest, see P.P.C. IV, 444–7. The first meeting of the Council of Four took place on 24 March. See Mantoux, Vol. I.

to Wilson's house, where the Four were sitting in case I might be wanted. After sitting there for two and a half hours with Maurice Hankey, Philip Kerr and one or two other people, nothing happened. However, it was interesting going to the place and we had a very comfortable room to sit in where there was a nice collection of beautifully bound books. It was very difficult to get into the house as the police stopped one as soon as one got that side of the street, and we had to make our way between cordons of police and sentries. No doubt they have to be careful as Clemenceau was there.[1] Yesterday I had to go again to discuss the thing with Lloyd George; Balfour was to have been there but he was in bed; the reason officially given was that he was not very well, but I suspect that the real reason was that it was at 10.30 a.m.! The Prime Minister was very alert and quick, though he did not seem to start with much previous knowledge; for instance, he asked what was the status of Luxembourg. In the afternoon I went down again, this time to the Ministry of War, where the same thing happened as the day before. After I had waited one and a half hours Foch and some soldiers came out. Then they took some financial questions. After another hour, they sent out for the papers about the Saar Valley. We sent in alternative drafts of treaties which Hurst had drafted with extra-ordinary rapidity, but after five minutes they had made up their minds that the matter was too difficult and complicated and they all came out, so we had to go away again. Lloyd George and Orlando seemed very vigorous and were talking and chaffing one another. I thought Clemenceau whom I had never seen before, looked very old and worn; his face is quite yellow, and he gave one the impression that he was rather worn out. I noticed a curious little scene; he went up to Lloyd George, apparently to press some point upon him; I thought Lloyd George's whole attitude and manner of answering was almost brutal.

The whole thing is I think rather characteristic of the way in which our business is done. Notwithstanding the change of procedure, they still have on their hands very much more than anyone can possibly get through; the result is that they never really know what they are going to discuss any day, and things do not get finished off.

The Belgian Commission, on which I was sitting, had also the Slesvig question referred to them. We produced a report which we expected would be adopted almost at once, as, though it was possible to criticize it, it was carefully devised so as to give the Danes all and more than all that they had asked for, and at the same time to do justice to the Germans.

[1] An attempt had been made in February to assassinate Clemenceau and he had been wounded.

However, when it came up before the Big Ten,[1] they talked round the subject; obviously the whole thing came to them quite fresh; Balfour especially had not taken the trouble to be coached beforehand by Crowe, who knew all about it, and the result was that, after spending a considerable amount of time, the whole thing was postponed. Here there was a matter on which a definite decision could quite easily have been made.

Another matter I have been interested in lately is the Rhine problem . . . The French put up a preposterous scheme; General Mance, who is dealing with it, fought them very vigorously on the Committee for four hours and got some of the most objectionable features cut out, but it still remains in what is I think a quite impossible form. Here the difficulty arose from the fact that the matter was left by our people entirely in the hands of the technical authorities, who know all about railways and canals, but they do not receive sufficient instructions as to the political questions which are inevitably involved. Luckily the treaty is so badly drafted that it cannot possibly stand as it is, and no doubt some means of revising it will be discovered.

Note in regard to the Saar Valley problem   *1 April 1919*

The attached note has just been handed to me by Dr Haskins of the United States Commission. It contains suggested heads of agreement for the settlement of the Saar Valley problem. They are based on a discussion which took place at the Hotel Crillon between him, Monsieur Tardieu and myself yesterday, and are the modification of a proposal which was sent to us last night by Monsieur Tardieu. Copy of the French proposal will be forwarded as soon as it has been translated and copied. I understand that Dr Haskins has forwarded a copy of this to the President. It seems to me very well devised and one that might be supported.

Enclosure

Saar Basin: United States Proposals.

(1) France to have permanent ownership of the mines, with full facilities for their exploitation.

(2) The mining area to be held for a period of fifteen years by the League of Nations, which will hold a plebiscite at the end of this period, either *en bloc* or by communes, and will thereupon hand over the area or the respective parts to Germany or France, according as the vote shall determine.

[1] The Council of Foreign Ministers, see P.P.C. IV, 529–32.

(3) During this interval France to administer the territory under a mandate from the League of Nations. By the terms of the mandate France shall be charged with the maintenance of order, including the appointment of such officers as are now named by the Prussian or Bavarian Governments. There shall be no fortifications or military establishments within the territory. The inhabitants shall retain their German citizenship (except that any individuals so desiring may be free to acquire French citizenship), their local representative assemblies, religious arrangements, law, language and schools, and shall be exempt from military service. They shall not be entitled to vote for representatives in either the German Reichstag or the French Chambers. Any who desire to leave the district shall have full opportunity to dispose of their property on equitable terms.

Notes on the Report of the Polish Commission[1]   1 April 1919

The objections raised to the Report of the Polish Commission seem to be based on the following points:

(1) The large number of Germans included in the proposed Polish State.

(2) The severance of East Prussia from Germany by the interposition of a Polish corridor. This may be called the West Prussian question.

(3) The assignation to Poland of Danzig and the immediately contiguous territory on the west bank of the Vistula with a predominant German population of over 200,000.

(4) The attribution to Poland of predominantly German areas on the east bank of the Vistula, from Graudenz northwards.

In a general way the apportionment of a large number of Germans to Poland is inevitable and just. Inevitable, because in many districts the population is very mixed; just because a considerable number of the Germans residing in the territory assigned to Poland have been deliberately introduced by the action of the German Government in order to Germanize the country. While points (2), (3) and (4) must to some extent be dealt with together, it is very important to begin by envisaging the points at issue in each one of these districts separately. A good deal of confusion

---

[1] This report had been considered by the Supreme Council on 19 March. As the result of a long discussion, when Mr Lloyd George pointed out that if the report were accepted over two million Germans would be included in the Polish State, it was agreed to refer the report back to the Polish Commission for reconsideration. On the 22nd Monsieur Cambon reported that, after a careful reconsideration of the problem, the Commission had decided to maintain its previous proposals.

seems to have arisen from a confusion between the question of Danzig and that of West Prussia.

West Prussia. It seems clear that West Prussia north of the Thorn–Bromberg line is predominantly Polish, and that on ethnographic grounds it would naturally go to Poland. As regards this district, the only objection seems to be that it is a surgical operation cutting East Prussia from Germany. The objections to this are, first, strategic. It puts Germany, from the military point of view, at a great disadvantage as against Poland. This, I suggest, should not carry any weight. Germany will, in virtue of her much larger population, her older civilization and her great resources, always be in a position of great advantage as against Poland. The other criticism is what may be called convenience. German communications with an important German province will have to pass through Polish territory. It is suggested that this could and should be met by giving to Germany ample securities for full control over the main line of railways by Konitz and Dirschau, which connects Berlin and Königsberg. This is dealt with in the second clause of Article 7 of the draft treaty. It is suggested that this clause should be greatly strengthened: the security given to Germany here is not sufficient.

Danzig. The proposal to transfer to Poland a city such as Danzig, with a population of nearly 200,000, naturally arouses grave misgivings. On the other hand, it has, I venture to suggest, been shown that as this will be the one Polish port through which the whole of Polish trade goes, it is essential to Poland that she should have full facilities for developing the port, facilities of such a kind as cannot be provided if Danzig is separated from the Polish state, whether as a free and sovereign state or on any other basis. If, however, the sovereignty over Danzig is ceded to Poland, it seems to me absolutely essential that, before the cession takes place, there should be secured to Danzig full municipal autonomy in a very wide sense of the word. In the case of a city with its municipal institutions, which has, in fact, during the whole of its existence to 1792 been a quasi-independent state, this is much easier than when we want to get local autonomy for scattered country districts without coherence or administrative conditions. The clauses of the treaty seem to me to be very defective in this matter, and security of this kind should be inserted.

The Right Bank of the Vistula. It seems generally agreed upon, even by the British members of the Polish Commission, that the arrangements here are open to serious criticism in that they assign predominantly German territory to Poland, including a town such as Marienburg, which is in a way the symbol of German civilization in these parts. It is understood that the decisive reason for the proposal is that it is essential to secure to Poland full railway facilities between Warsaw and Danzig, and also the undivided control over the waterway of the Vistula. The latter is, it is represented, a matter not merely of convenience, but also of Polish national sentiment. On this point I should suggest that a revision of the frontier might with advantage be made:

(a) The proposed frontier from Marienburg to the sea goes further east than is necessary. I do not see why it should go beyond what is necessary to include the piece of railway between Marienburg and Dirschau.

(b) The district from Graudenz to Marienburg, including Marienwerder. The frontier is drawn with the sole intention of including the railway from Deutsch Eyleu to Marienburg in Poland. It seems to me open to reconsideration whether it might not be sufficient to give to the Poles full and complete control over the traffic on the railway in a manner similar to that which it is suggested should be given to the Germans for the railway across West Prussia.

I should suggest also that the argument about the Vistula has been pressed too far. It would be quite possible, if for other reasons it was considered desirable to make the Vistula the frontier, to secure to the Poles full control over navigation.

The best practical suggestion I can put forward would be that, while the other proposals of the Commission should be accepted with regard to the districts (3) and (4), a modification should be made to the effect that this territory should be ceded, not to Poland, but to the Allies. The Allies would undertake to transfer Danzig and the district from Danzig to Dirschau to the Poles, after making such arrangements as they think fit to secure local autonomy to the population. As to (4), the treaty might be so drafted as to leave to the Allies free power to determine the final frontier; they would hand over to Poland such part as might be decided upon, and return the rest to Germany. This procedure would avoid further delay while, before the final decision was made, it would give an opportunity for consultation with the municipality of Danzig, which is, I think, desirable, and would give time for further consideration on the spot as to the frontier of (4).

I do not think that we can really make a final decision as to these matters in Paris. We want to be able to make investigations on the spot with more leisure and under more auspicious circumstances than those of the moment.

This would no doubt throw upon the Allies the obligation of maintaining order in the district which was left doubtful, but as it is easily accessible from the sea and the whole area is not large, this is in this case not a fatal objection.

Note from Sir M. Hankey to Lord Hardinge   2 April 1919

At a meeting of the Prime Ministers which took place on 1 April, it was agreed in regard to Danzig that 'a draft clause should be prepared on the basis of the creation of a free autonomous port and city of Danzig, with a High Commissioner appointed by the League of Nations, and with a Customs Union with Poland. The district of Marienwerder would be included in the scheme for a plebiscite.'

President Wilson undertook that Dr Haskins[1] should prepare a draft and confer with Mr Headlam-Morley on the subject. The Prime Minister would be glad if you would give Mr Headlam-Morley the necessary authority.[2]

Memorandum of interview with
President Wilson   2 April 1919

With Dr Mezes and Mr Bowman, of the American Commission, I went by appointment today to see President Wilson in order to discuss the Polish question.

He explained to us the project agreed upon yesterday at the Council of Four, viz: that Danzig with the adjacent territory should be established under its own Government. I asked whether it was to be a sovereign state or under the League of Nations with any kind of mandate. Of his own accord, President Wilson said that he did not like mandates for Europe; in this I concurred. The written note of the resolutions made by the Americans referred to a High Commissioner; I raised the question as to what his powers and duties were to be; it was agreed that his functions would be rather in the nature of a representative on the spot of the League of Nations to settle the difficulties which undoubtedly would arise both as to the relations between Danzig and Poland and as to the free right of transit to be accorded respectively to Poles and Germans over German and Polish territory. I said that this seemed satisfactory.

[1] This was a mistake; it should have been Dr Mezes; Dr Haskins dealt specially with the western frontiers of Germany. (M.H.)
[2] This was minuted by Lord Hardinge 'Mr Headlam-Morley act accordingly'. (M.H.)

There was some discussion as to the limits of the territory to be assigned to Danzig. The map he had before him included an area of some extent to the west; Dr Mezes, Mr Bowman and myself all suggested that this might perhaps be larger than was necessary; he said that the frontier to the west of the Vistula should extend 'so far west as is necessary to include any genuine German majority'. It was agreed that the local details as to population should be investigated. With regard to the frontier on the east, he seemed prepared to accept modifications, if they were desirable, of the frontier he had traced on the map.

He agreed that the city of Danzig should be within the Polish customs barrier and accepted the corollary that this would prevent it being a 'free port' in the commercial sense; he also agreed that the relations between Danzig and Poland should be regulated by a treaty made under the auspices of the League of Nations which should secure to Poland full facilities for commercial development.

The other matter discussed was the extension of the plebiscite area to the German-speaking populations of the east of the Vistula, which, according to the plan of the Commission, were to be included in Poland. There was some discussion as to the precise limits of the area to which this should apply; it was agreed that this should be referred to the frontier experts, and President Wilson agreed that we might accept the formula of the Slesvig Report giving the Commission, which eventually determined the frontier after the plebiscite had been held, the right to take into consideration matters of local convenience. It was agreed that the frontier should be so drawn as to give the Poles complete control over the navigation of the Vistula; it should, that is, be on the right bank of the stream and not in the centre of the stream. (This would probably imply that the Polish frontier should include the actual margin of the river on the right bank, probably as far as the dykes, which presumably have been made to stop floods.) He laid stress on the point that the plebiscite in this area would have to be distinct from the plebiscite in other parts of East Prussia.

Unfortunately I was not able to put down a note of the interview immediately, but I think this represents it fairly correctly.

After leaving the President, Dr Mezes came to my room with Mr Bowman, and we drafted together very hastily the attached note giving the heads to be worked out more fully afterwards.[1] Mr Bowman and Mr Paton meanwhile drafted a proposal as to the respective frontiers.

[1] Printed in Headlam-Morley, P.C.M. Danzig (12760).

Memorandum respecting the Saar Valley   2 April 1919

I have put together the following papers in order that there may be some record on the different stages through which the discussion on the Saar Valley has passed.

On Friday, 28 March, I was sent for by the Prime Minister and laid before him and Mr Balfour a paper containing proposals arrived at at the Crillon with the Americans.[1]

On the morning of Saturday the 29th, the Prime Minister saw Mr Hurst, Mr Akers Douglas and myself, and instructed Mr Hurst to draw up alternative schemes for carrying into effect these proposals. These schemes were sent into the Prime Minister that afternoon while he was in the Conference.

On Sunday morning Dr Haskins and Major Johnson came to see me, and drafted in my room a note which at their request I sent at once to the Prime Minister.

On Monday, 1 April, I attended a meeting at the Crillon in the morning, at which there were present Dr Haskins and also Monsieur Tardieu and Monsieur Aubert.[2] I communicated to them Mr Hurst's drafts. As a result of this meeting I received two fresh proposals: first, that from Monsieur Tardieu and secondly that from Dr Haskins, both of which I communicated to the Prime Minister.[3]

On Tuesday, 2 April, the matter was discussed by the Council of Four,[4] and I received a telephone message from Sir Maurice Hankey to the effect that they had adopted the United States proposal and referred it to Monsieur Tardieu, Dr Haskins and myself. I had assumed that the United States proposal adopted was that sent in on Monday; on further inquiry it appeared, however, that what had been done was to adopt the original United States proposal. This creates rather a curious situation for, as will be seen, this first United States proposal was meant not to be a solution of the problem, but was only intended as a record of those points on which all were agreed, and which could be a starting-point for discussion as to the actual solution to be adopted. It appears, therefore, that in fact no progress has been made up to the present towards a decision as to the various alternative projects which have been handed in.

[1] See p. 57 above.
[2] L. Aubert, one of the French Delegation's technical experts on ethnographic questions.
[3] See Nelson, op. cit., pp. 260–3.
[4] There is no record of such a meeting in either P.P.C. or Mantoux.

Extract from letter to Mr Rex Leeper (F.O.)   *2 April 1919*

... I have just been having an interesting conversation with President Wilson about Poland. He was very agreeable and quite intelligent. He was quite quiet and displayed a great virtue for a man in his position, in that he gave me plenty of time and did not allow any sense of hurry or of impatience to appear; he did not monopolize the conversation but allowed me and the two Americans who were there to say what we wanted, although it was at times very critical of his proposals. His patience was all the more admirable as Mrs Wilson came in and was trying to persuade him to go out for a walk, a project in which she eventually succeeded.

Note on railway facilities for Danzig   *4 April 1919*

Under the proposed arrangement East Prussia will be separated from Germany by a stretch of Polish territory. In the same way it may be presumed that the result of the plebiscite will be to interpose German territory over a considerable section of the railway running from Warsaw by Mlawa to Danzig. It will be necessary to arrange in both cases that there shall be full facilities for communication across the alien territory.

It has been suggested that in both cases the security for freedom of transit which will eventually be provided in the International Railway Convention, will be sufficient. I venture to differ from this view. The conditions which can justly be required in cases such as this are of a nature quite different to those which are necessary for the ordinary free intercourse between civilized states. What is wanted is that Germans, whether private travellers or officials, travelling for instance between Berlin and Königsberg, should have full security that they would be able to reach their destination without any impediment, stoppage or interference of any kind in their passage over Polish territory; more than this, the whole timetable of the railway should be primarily arranged for the convenience of this German traffic. In the same way passengers and goods travelling from Warsaw to Danzig should be able to go with exactly the same freedom as if no German territory was interposed.

This requires not merely an ordinary railway agreement between two states, but that the respective railways should be under the sole control and management of the State, the purposes of which they have to serve. We want a German railway running across Polish territory and a Polish railway running across German territory. The management, the regulations, the personnel being in accordance with the rules of the State to which the railway belongs.

A special reciprocal convention will have then to be arranged under the auspices of the High Commissioner of Danzig to provide for this. It does not seem necessary to draft this convention at the present moment, for it need not be entered in the treaty with Germany. All that need be entered in this treaty is the obligation to conclude such a convention.

Covering note to Council of Four
re Saar Valley   5 April 1919[1]

I attach a report on the Saar Valley which has been agreed upon by Monsieur Tardieu, Dr Haskins and myself.

As will be seen, the object of this report is to investigate precisely the requirements which would be necessary in order to assure to the French the full advantages of the ownership and right of exploitation of the coal-mines in the Saar Valley. The project is, as explained, one drawn up by Monsieur Tardieu. I believe with the advice of the French technical experts; Dr Haskins and I made numerous suggestions, practically all of which he adopted, which were directed towards limiting the requirements. It may therefore be taken that the final result is the minimum of what the French would consider necessary.

I should like to express more strongly than is done in the agreed report my conviction that the system hereby suggested would be one quite impossible in practice. It would inevitably involve constant and serious controversy with the German administration of the district and would, I am convinced, prove unworkable. The only result of our work so far is, I think, to show that it is impossible to secure to the French that which they may reasonably demand without introducing a much more ex-tended political control. We have therefore, in fact, come back to the situation of a week ago when, as will be remembered, I sent up alternative schemes for the establishment of a special regime which, under different forms, would give the French complete political control. The result goes to show that the adoption of some one of these alternative schemes, or something else of the same nature, is inevitable.

Monsieur Tardieu has already handed in two proposals based to a large extent on those which have been submitted to the Council of Four, which we shall be considering on Monday, and on which we shall no doubt, at the beginning of next week, present a further report.[2]

[1] See P.P.C. V, 66–70.
[2] This was minuted by Sir Eyre Crowe and Mr Balfour who agree that it was an 'impossible scheme'. See Headlam-Morley's 'The Saar Valley', P.C.M. (12150).

Extract from letter to Mr Koppel (F.O.)   *7 April 1919*

I am sorry for not writing more frequently but really this last week it has been rather difficult to get time; I have been very much rushed and work is complicated when one has to deal not only with our people here, but with French and Americans as well. We hoped that our Belgian Commission was finished, then suddenly we had to have two or three additional meetings and new points were brought up about Slesvig. At the same time I had to try to get a solution of the Saar Valley, together with the French and Americans; we are not quite sure yet how the thing will work out, but as I have been interested in it for some time, it was satisfactory to have a hand in what perhaps will be the final stages. Then I have had a good deal of bother about the navigation of the Rhine, which is an extraordinarily complicated business and has involved not only political and legal, but also very technical points about river navigation, of which I am particularly ignorant. Finally I have had a good deal to do with Danzig, which is at this moment much the most difficult outstanding question. Howard and Kenney have just come back from Warsaw. I have been having long conversations with them today; this of course does not simplify matters as they bring with them a point of view which is very likely a correct one, but which would not be altogether agreeable.[1]

8 April 1919

Note. At a meeting of the Council of Four Mr Lloyd George said that the report prepared by the Saar Valley Committee was to the effect that no really workable scheme could be drawn upon the basis that they had been given. He thought, therefore, that it would be necessary to adopt some other scheme. He then read extracts from three alternative schemes which had been submitted to him at an earlier stage by Mr Headlam-Morley. The scheme which attracted him most was one which would create a new state in the Saar Valley, somewhat larger than had hitherto been proposed, in customs union with France and for which France would have a mandate from the League of Nations. He handed copies of these schemes to Monsieur Clemenceau (who undertook to consult Monsieur Tardieu about it),

---

[1] Sir Esme Howard reported that all Polish political parties believed Danzig to be vital to the future economic life of Poland. If it were not given to Poland, he feared 'an explosion of feeling' with consequences difficult to predict. See 'Esme Howard to Prime Minister', 10 April 1919, Lloyd George Papers, F/57/6/1.

and to Colonel House. He also promised to send a copy to Monsieur Orlando.[1]

8 April 1919

Note. In their draft report, it has been proposed by Dr Mezes and Mr Headlam-Morley that the title to be given to the Free City of Danzig should be *Freie Hansastadt Danzig.* In reply to an objection raised by Sir Esme Howard to this title and also a suggestion in regard to the conduct of the docks, Mr Headlam-Morley wrote as follows:[2]

We introduced the word 'Hansastadt' because we thought it would appeal to a certain historical sentiment among the people of Danzig; it seemed to us that it would do no harm and might serve as an indication that we were taking into account their feelings and so ease the transition to the new state of things. As regards the political associations of the word it was meant to draw attention to the history of the town before it became incorporated in Prussia or in modern Germany. I speak with some diffidence on the matter, but my impression is that for long periods, from the end of the Middle Ages onwards, Danzig was as a matter of fact subjected to the Polish Crown, but enjoyed very considerable autonomy. It was thought that the title of 'Hansastadt' would remind people of this and help to suggest that the city of Danzig would be in fact reverting to something like the position which it had held in former days when it was, according to the standard of those times, an important and prosperous city. A German Merchants' Community might have in the future, as such communities have had in the past, a very prosperous existence while closely associated with a foreign Power. I will confess that I looked on the word as a complete repudiation of the associations of a German National State which have been so predominant during the last century, and it is certainly directly opposed to the whole of the Prussian idea. I discussed the matter with Mr W. H. Dawson and it appealed to him, but of course it is not at all essential, and even if omitted in the present treaty might, if it was thought desirable, be inserted later, but I believe we were right.

It seems difficult at this stage to undertake to give the Polish State 'control' of the docks, etc.[3] Our information is very defective as to the

1 See P.P.C. V, 60–1; Mantoux, I, 181–3, 193–4.
2 Printed in Headlam-Morley, P.C.M. Danzig (12760).
3 Howard had made the suggestion. Paton and Bourdillon also pressed for Polish control of the port as well as the right to build fortifications and have a naval base. Headlam-Morley, however, hoped Danzig would be left undefended. See P.C.M. Danzig as well as FO 608/66/20216.

present system of ownership and control; we do not know how much of the docks belong to the city of Danzig, to companies, to Prussia or to the Empire. I think the wording of the draft treaty does not exclude the insertion of Polish control later if that seemed desirable, but I thought that this was one of the matters which could be best settled after discussion with the people of Danzig themselves.

Extract from letter to Mr Namier (F.O.)   *9 April 1919*

I got yesterday your letter containing Zaleski's telegram and passed it on to Tyrrell. Zaleski came to see me yesterday, but I was unfortunately out; I just got him for five minutes this morning and he is coming again this afternoon. I think it is a very good thing that he has come and it may help things materially. You will be amused to hear that I have just been lunching with the Prime Minister and Paderewski; the conversation turned on a great number of subjects and I felt that we much wanted your knowledge in order to be able to check the truth of much Paderewski said. On the other hand, I must say that he made a very good impression; he talked well and clearly. Zaleski is coming again this afternoon and as he is specially attached to Paderewski, I see some hope that we may have found a channel by which to approach what the diplomatists call 'Counsels of Moderation'.

   I would rather not write any more at this moment as first of all I am very sleepy as I was up late last night doing the Saar Valley, and secondly, the whole thing is so complicated and so delicate that I do not feel capable of putting down anything on paper at this moment . . .[1]

9 April 1919

Note. The Report prepared by Dr Mezes and Mr Headlam-Morley in regard to Danzig, including draft clauses for insertion in the treaty with Germany, was discussed by the Council of Four on 9 April.[2]

9 April 1919

Note. Mr Headlam-Morley and Monsieur Tardieu attended a meeting of the Council of Four on 9 April, when they were instructed to work out

[1] In reply to this letter Mr Namier wrote that 'Paderewski is a fantastic liar, if anything worse than Dmowski. . . . Moreover he has brazen cheek . . .' (M.H.)
[2] See Mantoux, I, 197–202.

a new project for the Saar Valley on the basis of its being placed under a Commission directly under the League of Nations.[1]

10 April 1919

Note. The Saar Valley Committee submitted a scheme, which was approved subject to a reservation by Monsieur Clemenceau, who wished for twenty-four hours in which to consider the period subsequent to the plebiscite.[2]

Extract from letter to
Mr Edwyn Bevan (F.O.)   *10 April 1919*

... I have been dealing with the Saar Valley, and this has enabled me to get rather more behind the scenes than I have done hitherto. I was very much struck with the clearness and precision with which the President stated his own position: he left no opportunity for doubt that whether for good or evil he was pledged to the fourteen points and was determined to keep his word, both in letter and in spirit. As far as I can make out he is being supported from our side. Of course this makes very real the difficulties with France and the whole situation no doubt has been extremely delicate. Personally, as far as my experience goes, the French have been much more accommodating than I had expected; this is perhaps the result of much which has been going on behind the scenes and of which we have little knowledge.

11 April 1919

Note. The latest schemes for the disposal of the Saar Valley were again discussed by the Council of Four, and generally agreed to; two new proposals were referred to a Committee composed of Monsieur Tardieu, Monsieur Loucheur, Mr Headlam-Morley, Colonel Cornwall, Dr Haskins and one other American representative.[3]

[1] Tardieu, in *The Truth about the Treaty*, wrote that on 9 April the Committee met at 5 o'clock in the afternoon and worked until 3 o'clock the next morning in order to be able to submit the text of the articles to the Council of Four on the 10th (pp. 276–7). The recollection of Miss Hughes was that they adjourned for a short time for dinner, then reassembled. She remained in attendance in the next room during the whole time and was kept busy typing out drafts and redrafts of the different clauses. The meeting was held in Sir William Tyrrell's room at the Astoria, which adjoined Headlam-Morley's. See also Nelson, op. cit., pp. 276–8.

[2] See Mantoux, I, 209–13.   [3] See Mantoux, I, 224–8.

H

Extract from letter to Mr Philip Kerr (Paris)   12 *April 1919*

I saw Zaleski yesterday with Tyrrell and Esme Howard. I think that all seemed to accept the proposal for Danzig as a sovereign state under Polish protection and suzerainty. It was agreed that a matter of great importance is Polish feeling on the subject, and this has been excited because of the incorrect statements which have been published in the press. I was asked, therefore, to draft a communiqué which would put the whole situation in a more correct light. I enclose a copy of this and should be glad to know if it may be issued.[1] If the last sentence is included, it ought to be submitted to Monsieur Paderewski first: perhaps this would be best done by my sending it to Monsieur Zaleski.

I am a little in the dark as to the attitude of the Council of Four with regard to Danzig;[2] we were practically agreed with the Americans, but I do not know whether the President has given his approval to the scheme, and it seems to me rather unfortunate that the French have been entirely left out. It is, I think, very important that if this resolution is to be accepted, we should definitely get French adherence as soon as possible.

Extract from letter to Mr Namier (F.O.)   13 *April 1919*

Many thanks for your letter, much of which is very useful; I will have extracts made with judicious omissions as I am sure that what you say about eastern frontiers will be most useful. Frankly I differ with you about Paderewski. I am not thinking merely of the personal impression he made upon me, but Paton, who heard him before the Polish Commission, says also that he made on them the impression of a man who was at any rate in big things thoroughly sincere. They have also heard Dmowski and many other Poles and are therefore not speaking without experience. I think that probably he is not really very clever on many of these political matters; he is after all an artist, untrained in politics, with no great knowledge, and it is therefore not in the least improbable that he may have been guilty of inconsistencies; I think it might also be quite easy to entangle him so that he might appear insincere and dishonest. The impression he certainly makes is that he is trying to take a large view of things, that he genuinely only wants to get for Poland what Poland ought to have, and

[1] Not reproduced.
[2] At the Council of Four on 12 April, Clemenceau made a last unsuccessful attempt to gain Marienwerder for Poland. See Mantoux, I, 231. The Council had agreed on establishing a free city of Danzig on 1 April.

I suspect that he would be prepared to give up even too much. What I mean is that probably if we came to an agreement with him here, he would find when he got back to Poland that he had given up more than the nation of Poland itself would approve of.[1]

The idea now seems to be to get conversations here between the Poles and the Lithuanians[2] and also between the Poles and the Ruthenians. They may come to nothing, but at any rate it is a mode of procedure which ought to have been tried long ago. You know I always felt that the right method would have been from the beginning to throw the onus of the negotiations between all these nations on them themselves; the Allies would only have come in at the end either to ratify the agreement or to arbitrate when there was an irreconcileable difference. I do not like the procedure of our making all of the treaties on paper here in Paris and then imposing them upon the parties. As in all other things, our difficulties now arise from want of foresight three months ago. This is true not only of Poland and the neighbouring countries, but also of all the old Austrian territories; people are now waking up to the fact that we must try to get conversations between them. Smuts's mission, though it may appear to have been a fiasco for the moment, was I think in principle right, and I hope it will bear fruit.[3] Of course it broke down for the time because the people at the top had no clear conception of what they wanted; as always, they are being driven by events and do not foresee them.

13 April 1919

Note. At about 7.50 p.m. Monsieur Tardieu, Mr Headlam-Morley and Dr Haskins were introduced into the meeting of the Council of Four. They stated that they had agreed on a formula covering the first of the points referred to them concerning the Saar Valley, but not on the second. Their proposals were approved.[4]

1 In reply to this Mr Namier said: 'I am prepared to accept your estimate of him [Paderewski]. . . . There are people who are better than their reputation and I am quite prepared to believe that Paderewski is personally sincere. . . .' (M.H.)
2 Polish and Lithuanian forces seeking to capture Vilna were within a day's march of each other.
3 In late March the Supreme Council despatched to Budapest an Allied mission headed by Smuts to discuss possible peace terms with the recently installed Communist Head of State, Bela Kun. The mission spent two days in Budapest while Smuts conducted negotiations with Kun. The former readily concluded that Kun was a passing phenomenon and broke off the talks at the earliest possible moment. As a result, the mission returned to Paris without having accomplished anything. See W. K. Hancock, *Smuts: The Sanguine Years, 1870–1919*, pp. 515–17; Thompson, op. cit., pp. 208–9; as well as Nicolson, op. cit., pp. 292 ff. Nicolson accompanied Smuts on the mission.   4 See Mantoux, I, 224–8.

Extract from letter to Mr G. Saunders (F.O.)   *13 April 1919*

... At this moment I am rather tied up in details about the Saar Basin
which leave little time for looking at things from outside. I have been
seeing a good deal of Tardieu; I know you do not think well of him, but
I have found him personally very good to deal with and he takes opposition
well. I believe there has been acute friction behind the scenes, and I suspect,
though I do not know, that there was a serious struggle about a week ago
about this and other matters. One hears that Clemenceau is very bitter
with Wilson.[1] Whatever the truth about this may be, the result is that I
think we shall get a solution of the Saar Basin problem which, as far as
general principle goes, will be satisfactory. The French will get complete
ownership of all the coal under the title of reparation, and in order to
insure them security in working it, for fifteen years the district will be
put under a Commission responsible to the League of Nations. The natural
criticism is that the system is a complicated one and may not work. From
the political point of view the French are, by accepting this, definitely
and finally giving up their claim to the 1814 frontier; this is I believe very
bitter to them, but externally they accept it with a good grace and I think
that, as they have done so, we should be as generous as possible to them in
the details. There will probably be a plebiscite at the end of the fifteen
years taken area by area, which will determine the future destiny of the
country, so that any part of it may return to Germany or go to France,
according to the wishes of the inhabitants. This, I think, is as satisfactory
as anything that could have been devised.

My own experience is that the difficulties in dealing with the French
arise not so much from the people at the top, but from the technical
experts, who deal with matters of finance and mining and such things;
they bargain like Jews and they generally are Jews, and it is they who try
to insert all these intolerable petty conditions; they try to foresee and
guard against any possible claim which Germany might make in the
smallest matter which would be to the disadvantage of France, and to
secure for themselves every little point to the disadvantage of Germany. As
soon as we get to these experts then all conception of a broad statesmanship disappears.

I do not know what the arrangements are for the left bank of the Rhine,

[1] There had been a clash between Wilson and Clemenceau on 28 March. In a letter to his
Conservative party colleague in the Coalition, Andrew Bonar Law, Lloyd George wrote on
31 March: 'There was quite an unpleasant passage between Wilson and Clemenceau on
Friday evening.' See Lloyd George Papers, F/30/3/40, as well as Nelson, op. cit., pp. 231–2,

but I think that this will be treated merely as a military question and that there will not be any attempt to separate it from Germany.[1]

I hope the Danzig thing will come off all right, Danzig being given to Poland,[2] but with really adequate securities, which may do something to satisfy Danzig local feeling and to show that there has been a real attempt not to put the city and surrounding districts entirely under Polish rule without protection. I think Paderewski's presence here will be a help in this.

Minute to Mr Hurst   14 April 1919

I am afraid that the objections I have urged against the proposals for the navigation of the Rhine still stand almost in their entirety. As to the larger political questions, something has been done by hearing the representatives of Holland and Switzerland before the Commission. I still think, however, that the whole scheme of a revision of the Treaty of Mannheim is very awkward. In addition to the points I have mentioned above, I may illustrate this by difficulties which will arise concerning the Commission which is to be established under Article 35. The Treaty of Mannheim provides for a Commission to regulate the river; there is no explanation as to whether the new Commission is to supersede the old; I assume that this is meant. If so, there will have to be a very radical revision of these clauses of the Treaty of Mannheim which define the constitution and functions of the Commission. As I see the matter there will have now to be incorporated in the Treaty of Mannheim two different sets of emendations, those embodied in the present treaty and those in the general convention when it comes into being.

My other objections still stand. For instance, with regard to Article 40, I found when I was at a Committee meeting in the Astoria that no one had the slightest idea what these agreements might be. It is surely impossible for the Allies to assent to such a clause which gives France rights, the extent of which are quite unknown.

---

[1] At this point both Wilson and Lloyd George were insisting on a demilitarized Rhineland under German sovereignty. On 15 April, however, Wilson accepted a French occupation of Coblenz, Metz and a third zone close to the French frontier for varying lengths of time. See Nelson, op. cit., pp. 238–40, and Headlam-Morley, P.C.M. Left Bank of the Rhine (12347).

[2] It is strange that Headlam-Morley should write of 'Danzig being given to Poland'. On 1 April the Council of Four decided that it should be a free city united to Poland by a customs union. On 5 April, Lloyd George's instructions to Headlam-Morley specified that Polish sovereignty was out of the question. See P.C.M. Danzig (12760).

Memorandum   *15 April 1919*[1]

May I be allowed to draw attention to the extreme necessity and urgency
of a final revision of all the different chapters which are now coming in
for inclusion in the treaty of peace with Germany. As far as I can understand, they all go to the Jurists for review, but they of course only deal
with the matter from the legal and rather technical point of view; they
are not empowered, and it is not their function to deal with matters of
substance. If, however, we are to be sure that the different chapters when
put together in the form of a single treaty will produce a coherent, consistent and workable scheme, it is surely necessary that there should be a
final revision from the political point of view. This applies especially to
those matters of a more technical nature which have been dealt with, for
instance, by the Economic and Financial Sections. Many of these chapters
have, I understand, not yet been submitted either to the Council of Ten
or to the Council of Four, and if any alterations have to be made, it is
clear that there is very little time indeed to deal with them.

The sort of points which I have in mind are the different arrangements
for the plebiscites in different areas; it is not in the least necessary that
all should be identical, but it is I think necessary that if different schemes
are to be adopted for different areas, there should be on record some
precise statement of the reasons why different schemes have in fact been
adopted. We have again the question to what extent clauses securing such
points as commercial privileges and railway facilities should be reciprocal,
or if they are imposed in the form of penalties on Germany, whether there
should be any definite limit. Again, there will be many points which will
require very careful consideration in the references to the future action of
the League of Nations. Another point is the stage at which there should
be introduced a guarantee for minority rights in such cases as the transference of population (outside Danzig) to Poland or the recognition by
Germany of the present frontiers of Bohemia, including as they do large
numbers of Germans. These are matters to which the Germans will certainly
call attention and we must be fully prepared for dealing with them.

Another point which I should like to suggest is whether it would not
be desirable that there should be drawn up some kind of explanatory
memorandum to the treaty stating clearly the reasons for some of the
decisions. We have to remember that it will be subjected to the criticism
not only of Germany, but to public opinion in all countries, and a *mémoire
explicatif* would for this reason, I think, be very useful.

[1] The original is found in the Lothian Papers, GD 40/17/59 pp. 9–14..

Extract from letter to Mr G. Saunders (F.O.)   *16 April 1919*

. . . One thing which would be useful to us here would be any information or suggestions you can give as to indications of the points which the Germans are likely to bring up with regard to the treaty; I want to get quite prepared and warn the people above.

I doubt whether they will be able, when it comes to the point, to object to the Saar Valley arrangement; as to Danzig the proposal is to make it a free city, but that it should be compelled to enter into a close alliance with Poland giving Poland full commercial control, use of ports and control of the foreign relations. This of course will not satisfy the Poles in their present mood, but will, I think, give them all that they have a just right to expect. It will also be a great blow to German national sentiment, but the idea is to make it evident that we have taken into consideration the just claims of the people of Danzig; this is to be considered and I want as much propaganda as possible both by articles and in other ways, to point out that really this solution would put Danzig in a relation towards Poland not dissimilar to what it had while it was under the Polish crown. Of course in the present excited condition of public opinion all these attempts to get a reasonable settlement may fail, but a great deal will depend upon the way in which they are put before the public. The great thing is that if we can get the Danzig people to work with Poland under a scheme like this, the prosperity of the town will increase enormously, and it will come into its rightful position of being a great port with a very large hinterland, and should be one of the largest cities on the Continent. It ought also to be good for British trade which has, so far as I can understand, almost disappeared since Danzig was annexed by Prussia. I should say that it is a solution which is anti-Prussian, but goes a long way in recognizing non-political German feeling . . .

Letter to Mr Philip Kerr   *16 April 1919*

Have you seen anything more of Paderewski? I am going to lunch with him tomorrow but shall probably not have any opportunity of talking to him privately. I have seen Zaleski two or three times. Zaleski leaves for Switzerland I believe on Friday. It would have been very desirable to get some clear understanding with him before he goes if it were possible, but it is no good doing this unless we get the French in too. I suggested to Zaleski the importance of having good guidance given to the Poles from Polish correspondents here, and have seen the correspondent of the

Manchester Guardian. I see that there was a notice in *The Times* yesterday about Danzig for which I presume you were responsible.

What disturbs me most is that we have no responsible person at Warsaw at present who can keep in touch with Pilsudski. I know that Crowe has been urging the importance of this on the Foreign Office, but the omission to keep someone there is very unfortunate. It is no good putting up proposals for a solution of this and similar questions unless they are accompanied by a carefully thought-out connection, both diplomatic and, if necessary, military; I will confess I sometimes begin to despair of getting any good result when I see how this essential point is over-looked.

Extract from letter to the Rev. Canon Headlam   *16 April 1919*

I have been having a rather more interesting time lately as I was called in by the Prime Minister to advise both about the Saar Valley and Danzig, which are perhaps two of the most difficult points to be settled, and then was put on a Committee to do the Saar Valley with a Frenchman and an American, and have been working at Danzig also, though in rather an informal way. The whole situation is often difficult and delicate as the Prime Minister is apt to disregard all matters of official routine and pre-ferred to deal with me directly and not through the proper Foreign Office hierarchy; however, they are very good about it and the procedure has this advantage that we can get on much more quickly than if things were done correctly. We have got the Saar Valley settled, as you will see in the papers; I am not sure whether the settlement will work, but it is really a very honest attempt to solve an extremely difficult problem, and if it fails, it will really be because too much trouble has been taken to make it as nearly fair to all sides as we could. I believe the French are rather sore about it; they had a great fight, chiefly with the Americans, on many points, but Tardieu, with whom I had to deal, was extremely pleasant and carried the whole thing through very well.

I think, as far as I can make out, that the solution we have put forward about Danzig has also been accepted; here again it is a solution which will certainly not please the Poles, and will be equally disagreeable to the Ger-mans, but I think it is one which ought to make both sides feel that we have really tried to do the best. I had quite a long talk to President Wilson about it; he was very pleasant and on the whole left an agreeable impression though it is that of a man who holds very tight to certain principles and has not much knowledge or capacity for details. However, he was quite prepared to listen and discuss things like an ordinary man, and there was nothing of the Olympian about him.

I went to lunch with the Prime Minister to meet Paderewski, which was quite interesting. Paderewski gave me the impression of a man who was really sincere and trying to do all that he could for his country; he is a very good talker and made a great impression, both on the Prime Minister and on Bonar Law, who was there. I am going to lunch with Paderewski tomorrow . . .

I have been to three or four meetings of the Supreme Four; I think I had better not tell you more about them just yet. When I was there they were very jovial and happy with one another, but I imagine that the atmosphere is not always so peaceful . . .

I had hoped to get away for a short time, but there is, I think, no prospect of it now and I certainly should be rather disappointed if I was not here when the Germans come.

Memorandum of interview   *17 April 1919*[1]

Together with Mr Philip Kerr I had a long conversation today at luncheon with Monsieur Paderewski; Monsieur Zaleski was the only other person present. The conversation eventually, after turning on many other subjects, concentrated on the urgent Polish problems. Monsieur Paderewski said that the two cardinal points of Polish feeling were Danzig and Teschen. Teschen could be postponed, as it did not come into the treaty of peace with Germany; so also could Lithuania and the Ukraine. With regard to Lithuania and the White Ruthenians, he expressed himself strongly in favour of a federal solution; apparently there have been conversations here between the Poles and the Lithuanians;[2] the Poles are ready to recognize Lithuanian independence, but ultimately want a system by which Poland will be the centre of a large federal union, and he represented that this state of 42 millions would be strong enough to save eastern Europe from becoming Balkanized. He represented that Poland would perform the function which Austria had tried to perform in the Danubian territories, but would do it better, for the nucleus of Poles was larger than the nucleus of Germans in Austria. I objected that Poland would have to convince the world that she had the administrative capacity, and pointed

[1] Printed in P.C.M. Danzig.
[2] These talks were held between August Zaleski on the Polish side and Voldemaras on the Lithuanian. Captain Gielgud was appointed as British observer by Lloyd George; see K. M. Dziewanowski, *Joseph Pilsudski: A European Federalist*, pp. 119, 121.

out that she had not the historical background and experience; he demurred to this. All of this was, of course, the point of view which had repeatedly been put forward by the [Polish] National Committee.

The matter of immediate urgency is that of Danzig. The result of the discussion was very unsatisfactory. I explained to him as a kind of solution that might be suggested the scheme which has already been put forward, viz: Danzig an independent state under Polish suzerainty or protection. This had been tentatively accepted by Monsieur Zaleski. As I was not surprised to find, Monsieur Zaleski had gone rather beyond his brief. Monsieur Paderewski definitely refused to accept this. He said that he was not speaking so much for himself, but that if he were to accept it, it would be suicide for himself. He spoke of Polish sentiment. He said that he had received yesterday a letter from Monsieur Pilsudski, which apparently was to the effect that Polish feeling was getting more difficult to control. He implied that the situation was beyond what any leader could keep in hand. I said that I knew the difficulties; I was quite sure that in the long run the Poles would find out that they had got under this scheme all they really required; the point was whether he would be able to support it and whether his influence would be strong enough to get the Poles to accept it, so as to get over the critical period which is impending. He practically said that he could not do so. I therefore said that I could do no more, and that the only thing was for him to take the matter up again with the Prime Minister.[1] (Of course my instructions were that Polish sovereignty could not be given, and the Prime Minister objected even to the use of the word suzerainty; on this point I went beyond my instructions.)

I asked whether the Poles would accept a treaty of peace with Germany which consisted of the one clause, that Germany would transfer all her rights and titles over Danzig to the Allied and Associated Powers leaving the future destination of the city open; this also he would not agree to; he wanted transference to Poland.

The essential point is whether in taking this line he is really acting on information received from Warsaw or is not strong enough to meet the influence of the other Polish representatives here. Of course this topic was not mentioned. The conversation throughout was of an extremely friendly character.

[1] There is no evidence that Paderewski took up the question with Lloyd George. He faced, however, such strong criticism in Poland on the Danzig issue that he offered his resignation. After a brief crisis, he again took up his duties as Premier and strongly defended the treaty in the Polish parliament as giving Poland all that she needed for a secure existence. The Polish parliament approved the boundaries as set out in the draft treaty on 24 May.

The final moral I should draw from the whole situation is that it is impossible to carry on negotiations of this kind under the present conditions. It seems to me lamentable that at this moment we should be left without any British representative at all at Warsaw. Everything depends upon the situation there, but we are leaving Monsieur Pilsudski without advice or support, and we have no reliable means of knowing his views and the situation on the spot. Negotiations of this kind require, just as much as do military operations, a single authority at the head and concerted action, especially responsible British representatives on the spot who receive full instructions and are kept in constant touch with the situation here.

18 April 1919

Note. The draft articles for Danzig were considered by the Council of Four, and were returned for revision, by the Committee.[1]

Extract from letter to Mr J. W. Phillips
(Board of Education)   *18 April 1919*

I have been very busy here the last few weeks doing quite interesting work; I find it interesting doing diplomacy on my own. I found myself yesterday in a position which I never anticipated I should be in, viz: lunching with two other people with Paderewski, discussing the fate of Europe and trying to come to an agreement about Danzig. I have also had an arduous job in helping to settle the Saar Valley question; this is now done. I am not quite sure how the world will take it, but at any rate we can be quite sure of this, that the scheme has been drawn up with the best intentions on all sides. The real criticism is that in the attempt to be just to everyone all round, it may have produced something which is too complicated to work. Diplomacy seems to me very much like any other business; interesting because the personal element comes in so much, sometimes wearisome, when day after day one has to go on producing drafts which are rejected even more quickly than they are brought to life, and when everything has to be agreed between two or three different nations and translated into at least two languages. Always, however, one feels behind the extreme magnitude of the issues at stake and the serious consequences of failure. It does not help when one hears that the President has ordered his ship and is prepared to go back to America, and it is still worse when

[1] See P.P.C V, 86; Mantoux, I, 271–3.

one knows that Poland is at this moment perhaps the only protection in Europe against universal collapse, and that a false decision on a matter such as Danzig may bring about a revolution there, which would have incalculable consequences for the world. All this makes the delays, some of which are inevitable, some of which might I think have been avoided, very trying, and the whole thing might easily get on one's nerves, particularly when one remembers that all the time people are dying of starvation throughout a large part of Europe. It seems that the Germans are really going to arrive next week, but on our side it is still very doubtful whether the peace which they have to sign will be ready for them, and on their side, it is quite possible that things have been put off too long and that there will be no German Government left to come. However, I think it is probable that the fixing of the definite date will just enable them to carry things on for a little longer and, if so, we may get over the crisis, but nobody can tell.

Personally, it is interesting to get rather behind the scenes. I had a long conversation with President Wilson and several talks with Lloyd George, and I have been three or four times to the Council of Four meetings, which of course is the holiest of holies. It is amusing finding oneself sitting in a room with Lloyd George, Wilson and Clemenceau; at any rate one sees the raw material of which history is, or rather ought to be, made. Last night I went to a dinner given by the French press to the Belgian Delegation, and as I was the only Englishman present, found myself sitting in a post of honour, at the same table as Foch and several ambassadors, all of whom seemed to be very agreeable old gentlemen.

Memorandum   (undated – probably about 20 April)[1]

I have been having a collection made of such indications as we have either from public statements of prominent Germans, from the press, or from private information, as to the points with regard to which the Germans are likely to cause difficulties, when they are asked to accept the peace terms. Meanwhile it is clear that in the final revision the peace terms will have to be carefully scrutinized from this point of view.

The point to be kept in mind is that the fact that the German Government would probably reject some of the clauses is no reason for not insisting upon their acceptance, but great care will have to be taken that there shall be given to them no opportunity to justify the refusal in a man-

[1] The original of this memorandum is found in the Lothian Papers, GD 40/17/59, pp. 9–14, and dated 14 April.

ner which might cause political difficulty, either in England or in America. The whole question is extremely pressing, for from the discussion of a question such as that of Danzig, it is clear that already the possible attitude of the Germans is having considerable influence upon the decisions made here.

The matter of the contents of the peace terms cannot be separated from the procedure to be adopted in presenting them to the Germans, and it is to this point that I particularly wish to call attention. There seemed at one time to be a conception that the proper procedure would be to present the whole treaty *en bloc* to the Germans and demand unconditional acceptance. This is clearly impossible in this crude form. First of all, in such a very lengthy document, which goes into a large number of complicated details, there will certainly be a number of points on which the Germans will justly ask for interpretation. Secondly we cannot be sure that some essential points may not have been overlooked and that the Germans will not be able to show that some of the clauses as drafted will not work. To present the thing and refuse even interpretation and discussion on individual clauses would be acting precisely in the way in which the Austrians acted towards Serbia,[1] and by doing this we should put ourselves completely in the wrong. Moreover, if we acted, in this way we should be putting the Germans at an advantage, for they could refuse to sign the treaty, giving a number of general reasons and there would be no opportunity of fixing them to the particular points on which they really refused. They would be put in the position of being able to make a general appeal to the public opinion of the world, an appeal which the allied Governments would not then be in a good position to answer.

The procedure which I should venture to suggest would be something of the following:

(a) The treaty should at a public meeting be formally handed to the German Delegates and should be published (it is obviously impossible to publish it before it is communicated to them, but the demand for publicity is so great that we cannot refuse publication as from that time).

(b) The Germans should be informed that within a definite period they should hand in their observations in writing distinguishing between (1) clauses as to which they ask for explanations; (2) clauses as to which they propose emendations; (3) clauses or sections to which they object in principle.

(c) The Allies would then consider these observations and answer also in writing. Their answer would in some cases state categorically that the

[1] Reference to the Austrian ultimatum to Serbia of 25 July 1914.

clauses objected to must be accepted and were not open to discussion. As to the other points, they would either give the explanation asked for or agree that the points raised were such as might properly be discussed. Discussion on these points would then take place, either between the plenipotentiaries or between other members of the Delegations.

This method would, I think, simplify the procedure, keep the discussion within defined limits and, if there was a fundamental difference, would have the advantage that the Germans, supposing they refused to sign, would have to state quite clearly the clauses to which they objected and the reasons for their objection.[1]

Extract from letter to Mr G. Saunders (F.O.)   21 April 1919

. . . I think our settlement of Danzig will be as satisfactory as can be, but, like you, I am more anxious about the transference of German-speaking territories inland to Poland; the whole thing has been spoiled by a certain weakness in the Polish Committee; they gave too much territory to Poland – though not very much in excess – and they did not insist as they ought to have done, on its being handed to the Allied and Associated Powers, and then by them to Poland, so as to enable us to make what conditions we like as to the cession. I think something may be got into the treaty to try and remedy this defect. What is most difficult is the right bank of the Vistula; I have hesitated very much about it and have been persuaded by Kisch, rather against my better judgement, to urge that Marienburg and Marienwerder should be given to Poland. The difficulty is to assure to the Poles a free and direct access to the sea, and at the same time to keep account of just German claims.

I am getting hopeless about the whole business; there is no fully responsible control exercised from the political side. Many things have been left until the last moment; the work is very much in arrears and I do not see how it is possible to have the treaty ready by the end of this week. What I fear is that the Germans will be able to put their fingers on a great number of points which show bad workmanship. Throughout nothing has been thought of in advance, and points of the greatest importance have been postponed until the very last moment.

I do not know the precise truth of what has happened about the invitation of the Germans, but it looks as if some serious mistake in form has been made. People will not realize how important it is to observe external forms in dealing with people like the Germans. As I see it, we always have

[1] For the procedure adopted, see P.P.C. V, 118–22.

to meet the influence coming from French military opinion. Foch is an admirable soldier and probably a delightful man, but good soldiers are nearly always bad politicians.

Extract from letter to Mr Koppel (F.O.) *21 April 1919*

I spent a happy Easter Sunday yesterday working in the Astoria from 10.30 till lunch-time, then at 3 o'clock I had to go down to the Crillon with Kisch to talk about Danzig, and at 5.30 went to a very wearisome meeting at the Quai d'Orsay to discuss legal amendments to the report on the Saar Valley. I should not have minded if we had had plenty of time, but it makes one very impatient if at this late stage one has to spend time on minute and sometimes punctilious discussions of details of draughts-manship. But it has to be done, so I did not get to church, and consoled myself in the evening by playing bridge after another discussion about Danzig after dinner. Bridge in the evening I find necessary as a sedative. Good Friday we spent about the Jews, seeing how much of their claims ought to be secured to them. In the old days I believe the right method of spending Good Friday was to massacre the Jews; this custom still prevails in Eastern Europe; the Church of England prays for their conversion; we have advanced, inasmuch as we were trying to devise means to prevent them being converted; so the world progresses! . . .

22 April 1919

Note. On 22 April the Council of Four resolved that the draft articles in regard to Alsace-Lorraine, which had been put forward by the French at a very late stage, should be examined in the first instance by a Committee composed of Dr Haskins (USA), Mr Headlam-Morley (British Empire) and Monsieur Tardieu (France).[1] In his chapter on Alsace-Lorraine in the History of the Peace Conference,[2] Mr Headlam-Morley says:

The work of the Committee was delicate and not unattended by difficulties, and it was one on which I would gladly have been excused from serving; it was, therefore, gratifying that when I applied for instructions as to the attitude which I was to take, the answer I received from my very wise and experienced Chief, was that I should 'take a back seat'. Owing to the late stage at which the French put forward their proposals it was absolutely impossible, if the work was to be completed within the

[1] See P.P.C. V, 112.   [2] See P.C.M. (13818).

short time available, to consider the question with the care which was necessary. In particular, it was impossible, even if it had been advisable, to put forward any alternative draft to that suggested by the French. All that we could do was to get eliminated from the French draft those clauses which were clearly inapplicable or inadmissible.

22 April 1919

Note. On this day President Wilson handed in to the Council of Four a revised draft of articles concerning Danzig prepared by the Committee on Danzig, and it was agreed that they should be forwarded to the Drafting Committee.[1]

24 April 1919

Note. Mr Headlam-Morley and Dr Haskins attended a meeting of the Council of Four and handed in a memorandum on the Saar Valley, pointing out some difficulties which had arisen about the settlement of the frontiers. They, together with Monsieur Tardieu, proposed to pay a visit to the spot on the following Sunday (27th), and this was authorized by the Council.[2]

Extract from letter to Mr Namier (F.O.)   *25 April 1919*

As I was out this afternoon I asked Carnegie to telephone and warn you that you would probably be wanted here for a day or two. The official papers were sent off tonight and will probably be in the Foreign Office tomorrow; from them you will be able to see the reason of this request. I believe Paderewski is going away for a day or two; I am writing to enquire when he will be back and will telephone or telegraph to you as soon as I hear when he will be able to see you.[3]

26 April 1919

Note. Mr Headlam-Morley and Dr Haskins, in accordance with the authorization of the Council of Four of the 24th, visited the Saar Valley

[1] See P.P.C. V, 313–14; Mantoux, I, 287.
[2] See P.P.C. V, 206, 208–9; Mantoux, I, 353–4.
[3] At Paderewski's request, Hardinge agreed to order Namier to Paris. Paderewski mainly wanted to discuss Jewish affairs with Namier. The latter's visit is covered in Lady Namier's biography.

in regard to a proposed modification of the frontier in the north-western boundary; they started on Saturday evening, 26 April and returned to Paris early on Tuesday morning. On their return they reported that they were of the opinion that the economic and other interests of the southern portion of the canton of Mottlach required its incorporation in the territory of the Saar, and proposed that the boundary should be modified accordingly. It involved the addition of about 10 square miles and a population of about 5,000.[1]

Note of interview with Monsieur Paderewski   24 April 1919

In a conversation on Thursday the 24th with Monsieur Paderewski I explained to him the proposed arrangements for Danzig. He obviously was seriously disturbed, but recognized that the matter was in principle decided. He asked, however, that two points should be provided for, to which he attached the greatest importance:

(1) That there should be secured to Poland not only the 'use and service' of the docks, etc., but the actual ownership, especially of those situated at the mouth of the Vistula and outside the walls of the city.

(2) He asked why nothing was said about military things. I suggested that the Polish control over Danzig would be secured by the disarmament of Germany and that, in order to help the general principle of disarmament, it would not be desirable that Poland should make any display of military force in Danzig. While acquiescing in this idea, he still wanted the power of protection against unorganized attacks by German freebooters or 'Heimatschutz'. I said that I would try and get something put in giving to Poland the right, if required, for the 'protection of Danzig against external attack'.

I mentioned these points to Mr Hurst; he said he would get alternative drafts prepared to meet them, but must have authorization before putting them in definitely.

Note in regard to Danzig   26 April 1919

I personally received instructions in regard to this (see Note of interview with Monsieur Paderewski of 24th) at the Council of Three today. With regard to (1) it was determined that the ownership could not be given

[1] The report was approved by the Council of Four, 29 April, see P.P.C. V, 335–6. A full descriptive account of this visit is given by Mr Headlam-Morley in a letter to Mr J. Bailey of 10 May. See below, p. 100.

I

to Poland, but that the full right of development should be secured. (2) It was determined that if there was danger of external attack on Danzig the right procedure was that the League of Nations should undertake the protection; they would of course be able to instruct the Poles to send forces for this purpose.

Letter to Mr Philip Kerr   *30 April 1919*

I have just been speaking to Sir Percy Wyndham who is going out to Warsaw. It is, I think, absolutely essential that he should take a personal message from the Prime Minister to Pilsudski. Could you arrange that this should be done? There is not the slightest use in his going unless he is able, as soon as he arrives, to make clear that he comes with full authority to clear up the misunderstandings which have arisen and in view of the manner in which the Prime Minister's name has been put in the foreground, it is necessary that he should be able to say that he is expressly charged by the Prime Minister personally to give such message as might be determined on.

I have spoken to Lord Hardinge about this; he entirely agrees and authorized me to mention the matter.[1]

30 April 1919

Note. The Alsace-Lorraine Committee attended a meeting of the Council of Four, when the draft articles were considered and approved.[2]

Extract from diary   (*undated – probably end of April*)

When I came to Paris I proposed to keep a diary. Like many other intentions this has not been carried out. It seems, therefore, incumbent upon me at least to put down some reminiscences; this is all the more justifiable because, through more or less accidental circumstances, I have during the last period of the Conference seen rather more than I did at the earlier stages of the working of the machine, and have been brought into closer intercourse with some of the leading people and had a small amount of influence on some of the decisions.

[1] Headlam-Morley's suggestion was acted upon. Wyndham carried with him a personal letter to Pilsudski from Lloyd George in which the latter explained the Supreme Council's decision to make Danzig a free city as well as taking the opportunity 'to renew the expression of my goodwill towards Poland and towards the Government over which you preside'. See 'Lloyd George to Pilsudski', 2 May 1919. Lloyd George Papers, F/57/5/1.
[2] See P.P.C. V, 373–86; Mantoux, I, 431–4.

On my arrival here (11 January 1919) I found that, as had been agreed in London, I was put down in the list of the staff as Head of the Political Branch of the Intelligence Clearing House under Sir Henry Penson, with Mr Leeper, Mr Toynbee, Lord Hartington[1] and Mr Powicke. I found, however, that Allen Leeper, who had arrived before me, was already doing full political work in connection with the Balkan Section, and Toynbee, who came over the same day as I did, was at once taken over by Sir Louis Mallet. I found that a room for me had been reserved on the Foreign Office floor in the Political Section, adjoining Sir William Tyrrell's. As to my duties and functions, I received then and throughout the whole of the time I have been in Paris no single word of instruction. So far as official duties went, I had none. I had, therefore, to determine my own duties for myself. As the result of conversation with Sir Henry Penson, it seemed to me that the whole functions of the Intelligence Clearing House were very ill-defined; the general idea was that it should be a centre of information to which each of the sections into which the Astoria was divided should send material, and that it should then distribute this material as requested to other sections. This was the scheme which had been elaborated by Penson and Parker before leaving England, and it obviously was, if properly carried out, an essential part of a complicated organization such as that of the Astoria. As regards my own particular position in it, it seemed clear from the beginning that if the Intelligence Clearing House was to work in connection with the Foreign Office Section, it required somebody in the Foreign Office Section who should act as the channel of communication to the Intelligence Clearing House. As my own room was on the Foreign Office floor, and as I was very anxious not to sever my connection with the Foreign Office work, I appointed myself liaison officer in the Foreign Office Section. There was a certain amount of justification for this, for officially my only position was that of Assistant-Director of the Political Intelligence Department. During the period succeeding the Armistice, this Department had been the centre of all the work done for the preparation of material bearing upon the Peace, and I was the only person who knew the details of the organization. There was still a considerable amount of material to come from London. We had charge of the stock of all the papers and memoranda which had been prepared in London, and it was obvious that one of our (by 'our' I mean Miss Hughes and myself) duties would be to distribute these papers to whoever wished to see them. In consequence I established myself in the Foreign Office Section, making myself in a sort of undefined way a general

[1] Captain the Marquess of Hartington, the military adviser to the Intelligence Clearing House.

depository of material and information of a political nature, bearing upon the Peace.

During the first weeks, which for many reasons were rather a trying time, a considerable amount of work of this kind had to be done, and it was, I think, of some use. The difficulty then and throughout was the entire absence of any general and active control, either of the Astoria as a whole, or of the Political Section in particular. The position was an interesting one, capable of great development. For the first time in the history of England a selected staff from a large number of Government Departments was working together as a single body in the same building. It was to be anticipated, therefore, that all the chronic difficulties which had existed in London, arising from inter-departmental friction and jealousy, would disappear, but to get the full advantage out of this, it was desirable that there should be some general supervision. As the particular object in view was a diplomatic one, viz: the drawing up of a treaty of peace, it was obvious that this general supervision could only come from the Foreign Office, or, as it was called, the Political Section, and it appeared that no one was more suitable for this task than Lord Hardinge; his high position, his experience and many of his personal qualities seemed to indicate that he was a man under whom all would be willing to serve. This, I believe, was in fact the case. But for some reason, which I have never been able entirely to understand, there was a curious reluctance on his part to take up this responsibility. To a certain extent I believe this was caused by the conditions under which he came out. In the scheme drawn up by Parker, he was assigned the position of Superintending Ambassador, but I understand that the Cabinet had never given any formal approval to this scheme, and he came out without any instructions, holding the position merely as Permanent Secretary of the Foreign Office. He had therefore no authority – I will not say to issue instructions to the other sections, for instance to the Naval and Military – but there seemed to be no positive recognition that the Political Section must be the bond of union between all the other Departments. The result was that week after week went by, each of the sections continued working by itself, and no official arrangement was made for communication and consultation. Practically, owing to the fact that we were working in the same building and living in the same hotel, a great deal of informal and personal consultation took place, but this was at the beginning only very partial and, as far as I could make out, some of the sections – especially the Economic and the Financial, which were of very great importance – continued to work on their own without any consultation or communication with others.

1 May 1919

Note. At a meeting of the Council of Four President Wilson said his attention had been drawn to the position of the Jews in Poland and Romania, etc. He put forward draft clauses prepared by himself and by Dr Miller which he proposed should be included in the treaty. Mr Lloyd George said he had received a note on the subject from Sir Hubert Llewellyn Smith which opened up some wider aspects of the conditions which should be accepted by the new nations. After some discussion it was agreed that a Committee composed of Dr Miller (USA) Mr Headlam-Morley (British Empire), and a French representative to be nominated by Monsieur Clemenceau (Monsieur Berthelot was appointed), should meet immediately to consider the international obligations to be accepted by Poland and other new states created by the treaties of peace, including the protection of racial and religious minorities and other matters raised in the following documents: the two drafts produced by President Wilson; the clauses forwarded by Dr Miller; memorandum by Sir Hubert Llewellyn Smith; all of which should be regarded as an indication to the Committee of the subjects they were to consider.[1]

Extract from letter to Mr A. E. Zimmern (F.O.)   *1 May 1919*

... There is a frightful rush of work here just now which really makes it impossible to write letters; in some way or another the text of the treaty is to be ready by Monday, and all kinds of problems are constantly coming up which have been overlooked or neglected. I have been busy with the Saar Valley, which I think is now settled, with Danzig and Alsace-Lorraine, and have just this afternoon been put on a new job about minority rights and a lot of miscellaneous problems. I went for a short visit to the Saar Valley for a couple of days, which was very interesting; tell Bailey that I will try and send him an account of it as soon as I possibly get time, but as I keep Miss Hughes working on fully official work up to midnight every night, I do not think it would be fair to occupy more of her time with semi-official communications. ...

Extract from letter to Sir Maurice Hankey   *2 May 1919*

With regard to the Committee on New States, apparently at the time of writing, 6.15 p.m., the French have not yet appointed a representative. I assume that anything to be inserted in the text of the treaty with Germany

[1] See P.P.C. V, 393–5; Mantoux, I, 440–2; also Headlam-Morley P.C.M. Minorities Treaties (13507).

must be ready by tomorrow at the latest. You will see, therefore, that the situation is a very difficult one. I have already had a meeting with my American colleague and after discussion with him I have drawn up the following draft report which I hope to persuade him to accept at a meeting we are holding at 9 o'clock this evening; I think he will accept; if not, I propose to stick to this and send it in.[1]

The suggestion that we could insert in the treaty with Germany, without very thorough discussion, the suggestions made by President Wilson, is one quite impossible to accept. What Mr Miller, who is advising the President on the matter, has done is simply to take in their crude form certain Jewish suggestions, which we have had before us here for several days, and have been trying to persuade the Jews to withdraw. I will not at this moment enter into details, but it would be quite out of the question to accept them without a thorough revision, and it is essential that before accepting anything, we must hear the Polish point of view. I saw Paderewski today and he promised to send an authorized Polish representative who might discuss the matter with us tomorrow. The only thing that is possible, therefore, is to adopt the procedure I suggest in my draft report and to confine ourselves at this stage to merely a clause binding the Poles to accept certain guarantees which will be inserted in the separate treaty.

I am writing to you in advance about the matter because it must come up before the Council of Three tomorrow and I should like the Prime Minister to know as soon as possible the line which I should venture to advise him to take on the subject. If he asks why the President's proposals are impossible, I need only point out that No. 6 proposes to impose upon Poland a particular form of electoral procedure; No. 4 constitutes the Jewish population a national minority, an expression which would be bitterly opposed by the Poles, and Article 5, though I think it may stand in principle, will want very careful revision in detail. The clauses are also insufficient from the Jewish point of view because what is really essential to the Jews is that there should be secured to them in some precise manner the direct right of appeal to the League of Nations if the Poles violate their engagements.

P.S. Lord Hardinge at my request has appointed Mr E. H. Carr to be British Secretary to the Committee; there is so much work in these special Committees that I cannot get on without formal help officially supplied, and he will be responsible for the communication of drafts, etc.[2]

[1] See Annex A of the 'Report to the Council of Three by the Committee on New States', P.P.C. V, 442–3.
[2] The records of the Committee on New States are found in FO 608, Vol. 61.

3 May 1919

Note. A preliminary report was presented for consideration by the Committee on New States, including articles to be inserted in the chapter of the treaty with Germany relating to Poland. These were accepted with slight modifications. (On 6 May an extension of the terms of the Committee to include Romania and Greece was made.)[1]

Extract from letter to Sir Maurice Hankey   *5 May 1919*

I am writing to you in reference to your letter of 3 May to Monsieur Dutasta, regarding the decisions taken at the Council of Three that morning.[2] I do not quite know what the precise official arrangements are for recording action taken as a result of instructions from the Council of Three, but as I went down myself to the Drafting Committee that afternoon to explain the instructions and to give what help I could in getting them embodied, it may be useful that I should write to you in order to place on record precisely what has happened.

With regard to the Report of the New States Committee, Annex A has, in accordance with the instructions, been inserted in the section dealing both with Poland and with Czechoslovakia. Nothing of the kind had hitherto been inserted in the section dealing with Czechoslovakia; in the section dealing with Poland, there already was a clause dealing with part of it. But the clause was one which was much weaker. The result is that the matter is now satisfactorily dealt with uniformly for both states.

As regards Articles 1 and 2, this had already been partly provided for in the Czechoslovak section, but there was nothing in the Polish section. The whole of the substance of the two articles is now inserted in both sections. It was not possible at such a late stage to get precisely identical wording and arrangement, but here again there has no doubt been considerable improvement made.

With regard to the other matters, the draft article on railway facilities was inserted. Owing to the late stage at which this was done, there is, as was pointed out at the Drafting Committee, a certain amount of overlapping which, had there been more time, it would have been better to avoid, but the essential point is now secured.

Serious difficulties arose about the other two points. With regard to

[1] See P.P.C. V, 439–44, 483.
[2] Since Orlando had withdrawn over the Fiume and Dalmatia question, the Council was now sometimes called the Council of Three. See Note on 3 May above.

the navigation of the Vistula and building fortifications, etc., which might threaten the free navigation of the Vistula, it was pointed out that to a certain extent this was in direct and open contradiction to a clause in the military terms which had, I understand, been inserted by the desire of President Wilson, to the effect that nothing should be imposed upon Germany requiring any kind of alteration in the military defences of her eastern frontier. At this late stage it was therefore clearly impossible for the Drafting Committee to deal satisfactorily with the matter without a further reference to the Council of Three which could not be made. They have, however, inserted a clause preventing Germany 'erecting fortifications' in the defined area. This is not all which was desirable, but it is perhaps better than nothing.

With regard to the clause preventing Germany from requisitioning or injuring the territory to be ceded, it was pointed out that this could not be done in the treaty of peace, for the acts which it was proposed to prevent are acts which, if they take place at all, would take place before the coming into force of the treaty; an engagement in the treaty therefore not to commit these acts would have been of no effect. If it is desired to take steps to prevent, for instance, the Germans destroying or injuring the Silesian coal mines during the period which would elapse before they are in fact ceded to Poland,[1] this will have to be done by some other machinery than by the actual treaty of peace. Whether or not there is a real danger of such a nature as to make it necessary to take precautions, I am not in a position to say, but I think the matter is one on which those who are in a position to know, both political and military, should be consulted. If they are of the opinion that it is necessary to take precautions, then the method of so doing should be discussed.

The whole matter, however, raised a question which will, so far as I can make out, cause very serious difficulty. I write in some uncertainty, but so far as I can understand, none of the clauses of the treaty will in fact become effective until after the ratification. If this is the case, there will be an interval, which will at least be of some weeks, after the signing of the treaty, before it becomes effective. The result of this will be that all action will be suspended, and it will be impossible to get on with such matters as the organization of plebiscites in those areas in which they are enjoined, as for instance, Slesvig, East Prussia, or the evacuation by the Germans of the territory to be ceded. The political results of this may be at the least extremely inconvenient and I venture to suggest that if the matter has not been discussed, it should be at once taken into consideration.

[1] The draft treaty stipulated the cession of Upper Silesia to Poland.

Letter to Sir Eric Drummond[1]   7 May 1919

I enclose some notes on Danzig and the Saar which are so written that they can be shown to anyone, and just for that reason ignore the most difficult and important problems. With regard to the Saar, everything depends upon the personality of the Chairman of the Governing Commission. Nothing was said during the discussions at the Committee about his nationality, but I think we may take it that the French assume that he will be a Frenchman. It is quite clear that the French could, if they wished, make the whole scheme unworkable, for with their complete ownership and control over all the mines which are the chief industry of the district, with the inclusion of the Saar Basin in the French Customs Union and the very close connection with France, the whole thing would obviously break down unless there were a thoroughly good understanding on general matters between the French and the Commission, which means in effect the Chairman. On the other hand, if the Chairman were a characteristic representative of the more advanced French nationalism, he would undoubtedly set to work to use his position to further French interests and so to influence and forestall decisions which will come after fifteen years.

Of course the best thing would be that the Chairman should be a Frenchman whom one could trust to behave with absolute impartiality and, if necessary, hold his own even against the French Government. We in England have plenty of people who are accustomed to this sort of thing; my impression is that the very conception of such an attitude is very rare among the French. I have no personal knowledge of important French people; the only Frenchman with whom I have had any close connection is Tardieu. There is no doubt that he has seen the importance of putting a check on the immoderate demands of French Government Departments and technical experts, and as he is closely identified with the whole scheme, it might be worth while consulting him confidentially about the matter. It might be possible to get a suitable man from Alsace-Lorraine; if so, this would create a good impression.

I do not think there ought to be much difficulty in getting a representative of the Saar Valley itself. He should of course be a man of high position, preferably someone who has himself large industrial interests in the Basin, so that he would look at things from the practical point of

---

[1] This was written in reply to a letter from Balfour's private secretary, Sir Eric Drummond, asking for Mr Headlam-Morley's views as to the best method by which the League of Nations could undertake the duties specifically assigned to them in the treaty with regard to the Saar Valley and Danzig.

view rather than the political. Some of the big businesses, other than the mines, are owned by trusts and syndicates connected with similar institutes in Westphalia and elsewhere; the owners or managers of these would probably be the most dangerous type of the big German industrialists, who are of course more responsible for the offensive side of modern Germany than even the soldiers, but I expect that one could find some other firms which have remained in the hands of local people and would therefore be German, and not Prussian. I spent a couple of days in the Saar Valley a little while ago and stayed a night with General Andauer, who is at present the Military Governor of the district. He appeared to be a sensible, level-headed, honest man; he is I think an Alsatian. It is possible that the French may put him forward as their candidate; if so, I should think that he would do well, though I doubt whether he has great ability. If he is not put forward as their candidate, he is certainly a man who ought to be consulted.

As to Danzig, I think it is most desirable that the High Commissioner should be an Englishman. The ultimate guarantee for the settlement undertaken by the League of Nations must of course depend upon the possibility, if necessary, of applying armed force. Armed force here must be primarily naval, and naval should certainly mean British. Before Danzig was annexed by Prussia, there was good British trade, and it is in our interests, as also it is our duty, to use the opportunity very definitely and deliberately to develop British influence and trade in the eastern Baltic. We have had suggestions that Danzig should even be made a British naval base; this I think is going too far, but I should like quite definitely to see an Englishman at Danzig and that the people should get accustomed to having one or more British ships of war, if not stationed there, at least constantly visiting the coast. Whoever is chosen should certainly know Germany and the German language.[1]

Memorandum on the Saar Valley[2]

The first thing to be done is to select the people to form the Governing Commission, and particularly the Chairman. The object with which the

[1] The first Allied Administrator, then High Commissioner of the League in Danzig, was in fact an Englishman, Sir Reginald Tower. The Danzigers asked for an Englishman. Balfour supported this on the grounds that Great Britain could more easily supply Danzig and the adjoining plebiscite area with troops by sea, while France could more easily transport troops to the plebiscite area in Upper Silesia. See P.P.C. VII, 625-8. The French agreed on 18 August that the Allied Administrator in Danzig should be an Englishman. See FO 371/3925.
[2] See Headlam-Morley P.C.M. Saar Valley (12150); also Nelson, *Land and Power*, ch. X.

scheme was devised is to try and get a form of administration which will avoid the complete helplessness which has characterized international administrations in the past. In order to do this, the Chairman of the Governing Commission has been made the executive officer of the Commission. It is obvious that if a good man is found for the work he will be able to have the whole power in his own hands, and it will work out, and is intended to work out (that was in fact my own feeling, and this particular part of the scheme is my device), to a large extent a one-man control. The other members of the Commission would, I hope, not take much part in the details of the government, but they would have to be consulted and give their consent on all questions of general principle, and would be the court of reference if difficulties arose either with the French or with the Germans.

It follows from this that the Chairman ought to have a very much larger salary than the others and he ought to have an official residence. I do not think it is necessary that the others should reside permanently on the spot; they would have to be there at the beginning for some time to start the whole thing, but when that was done, I should hope that they would be content with, say, monthly meetings, and I should not therefore be inclined to give them a very high salary. The Saar Valley is easily accessible and they might combine the position of members of this commission with other work in their own countries. What they ought to bring in is valuable administrative experience, particularly in matters connected with industry, railways and labour problems. We must always remember – and this was clearly brought to the minds of the Committee during their discussions – that one of the chief dangers may arise from the management of labour. It would be preferable that the three other members, in addition to the Frenchman and the local man, should be an Englishman, a Swiss and perhaps a Belgian.

You will note that the Governing Commission have been given full powers to determine all matters arising out of the interpretation of this chapter of the treaty. I was a little doubtful myself as to what view the League of Nations might take about this; they might conceivably regard it as trespassing upon the powers of the Council. This makes it all the more important that the members of the Commission should be people who are to be thoroughly depended upon. In this case the Commission will naturally enter upon its duties the moment that the treaty is ratified; I suppose that then the district will be at once evacuated by the French troops who now occupy it. Nothing has been said about this in the treaty. There is also nothing said about the provision of the troops which would be necessary in case of disturbance or difficulty in enforcing the settlement. All that the Commission have power to do is to make a levy on local gendarmerie. One hopes that the question will not arise, and I do not think that it is likely to do so because the whole period for the new system is limited to fifteen years, and during that time the French will in fact be in occupation, as I understand, of the neighbouring German districts. Of course if there was difficulty, troops would have to be sent in and this would have to be done under the authority of the League of Nations. Obviously they would have to be French troops, but the question to be decided would be whether they should be a French contingent acting purely under French command, or whether in some form or other, they should be given the form of an allied occupation, for instance, by the presence of a small number of troops of other nations. If there was any necessity for occupation immediately, a small British and American contingent should be added; there would be no difficulty about this so long as the British and Americans are occupying part of the left bank of the Rhine. The less said about this publicly the better, but it ought to be considered privately.

My opinion is that there is at present very little Bolshevism or Spartacism in the district; if there were trouble it would, as I have already said, probably be labour trouble rather than German nationalism, but we know that in some parts of Germany the Spartacists are working with the Nationalists, and we must be on our guard against this.

As to the membership of the Commission, if it was desired to put on, for instance, an American representative, it could be one who has other duties, either diplomatic or in connection with the League of Nations, in Europe, so that it should be clearly indicated that his work in the Saar Valley was not expected to occupy the whole of his time.

Extract from letter to Mr Koppel (F.O.)   *8 May 1919*

... Of course we have all been very rushed for the last fortnight. It has affected me particularly because, for some reason or another, they seemed to put me on to a new Committee about once every three days. First of all I had, though not on a Committee, the whole of the Danzig business, which was amusing and interesting; then the Saar Valley, which meant working through very complicated articles, about sixty in number; then when that was not quite finished, they set me on to the Alsace-Lorraine business, which was much more complicated, far more contentious and had to be done under great pressure of time. Now they have invented quite a new kind of thing, viz: a Committee to consider what guarantees have to be found for the protection of Jews and other minorities in the New States, especially Poland. This ought to have been provided for in the treaty with Germany, but they only woke up to the fact that something had to be done last Thursday, and the orders had already gone out that the treaty was to be closed by Saturday night. However, our Committee did a record; we had our first meeting on Friday afternoon at 3 o'clock, and had our first report ready and presented to the Three at 12 o'clock on Saturday. It was passed by them and I went down to the Drafting Committee in the afternoon and got it put in myself. This of course was only the beginning. Now we are sitting day by day drafting clauses to put into a special treaty with Poland. This means considering the whole question of the Jews in Poland. It is very fortunate that Namier is here and I have kept him two or three days longer as he could give me lots of information about the matter, and I think he is really doing useful work buzzing about between Poles and Jews. I like this new Committee. There are only three of us on it, an American, a Frenchman and myself. We are all quite nice and intelligent; each of us brings an assistant (Carr is mine) and we are getting on quite well. . . .

In addition to all these other things I went down to help the Drafting Committee at the end of their labours. They had a most appalling job and it was an extraordinary sight. They had to go through the whole text of the treaty again and again to be sure that it was all right. One morning Malkin was there at quarter to seven and did not get back till 10 o'clock in the evening. The next night they had to sit up all night with the printers, and when I came down to breakfast at 8 o'clock, I found Malkin and Payne,[1] of the Commercial Section, who has just returned. Malkin has been quite ill and is going home today for a short holiday. Hurst really carried the thing through entirely on his own shoulders, and it is owing to him more than to anyone else that there is a treaty of any kind to present to the Germans. The thing was done at the end in extraordinary time and, except the Drafting Committee people, I do not think that anyone read through the whole of the treaty; the result is that there are, I believe, many inconsistencies in it and lots of points of detail on which the Germans can put their fingers.[2]

[1] Sir Henry A. Payne, the Comptroller of Companies Department of the Board of Trade. A member of the Economic Section of the British Delegation.
[2] The task of printing the draft treaty was so rushed that only three hours separated its completion and presentation. No time was allotted to a review of the treaty once printed in its entirety. Foreseeing the need for a careful review, Headlam-Morley in mid-April had written to Kerr urging that the necessary arrangements be made. In addition to pointing out

I am sorry the Germans seem to have made an extremely bad impression yesterday.[1] I saw the Prime Minister after the concert last night and he was full of indignation. He said they were insolent beyond description, not so much in what they said, but the manner in which they said it; he said that he had never been so angry with the Germans throughout the war, and that the Colonials were in such a state of indignation that they would like to have gone for the Germans at once. This is no doubt partly the result of bad manners, but whatever the cause may be, the effect will be very lamentable.

Now I must go off to my meeting. I have, I am glad to say, now got a private sitting room which makes life much pleasanter, and I can do a certain amount of work there in the morning before going to the office, and it makes it possible to work in the evening under pleasanter conditions than one could before.

Extract from letter to Mr John Bailey (F.O.)   10 May 1919

It is a very long time since I have written to you and there is much which I should like to have talked to you about. Among other things, a fortnight ago I went down for a couple of days to the Saar Valley. A difference of opinion arose as to the boundaries and so Haskins, my American colleague, and I went down to view the place on the spot. I was very glad of the opportunity of getting away from Paris and I have always felt that it was perfectly absurd to sit here tracing in detail the boundaries of a place which one knew nothing about.

We had a very pleasant tour. We started late Saturday night and went by train to Metz, where we arrived about 7 o'clock in the morning and had breakfast. I had never been there before and was astounded by the heavy and elaborate teutonism of the railway station; a very ambitious piece of architecture in early Romanesque style, but forbidding and

---

the obvious need to make certain that the different chapters, when put together, formed 'a coherent, consistent and workable scheme', he stressed as well the importance of eliminating all opportunities for the Germans to justify a refusal to sign 'in a manner which might cause political difficulties'. See 'Headlam-Morley to Kerr', 16 April 1919, Lothian Papers, GD 40/17/59, pp. 9–12.

[1] A reference to the Plenary Session of 7 May at which the German Delegation received a draft copy of the peace treaty. There was an outburst of indignation because Brockdorff-Rantzau, head of the German Delegation, read his speech sitting down. Harold Nicolson noted that a colleague who was standing near by thought he was on the verge of collapse and could not have stood up even if he had wanted to. Balfour, when he was asked about it, said he had no idea: 'I make it a rule never to stare at people when they are in obvious distress.' Harold Nicolson, *Peacemaking*, p. 330.

depressing to a degree. Then we motored straight away through Lorraine to Saarbrücken, where we arrived at about 11 o'clock and went at once to see General Andauer, who is Military Governor. He was billeted in the luxurious and comfortable house of one of the chief industrial proprietors; he was extremely cordial and asked us to stay the night, so that we got all the benefit of the German comfort, and I slept in a real German bed with a large feather bed over me. It was curious seeing a French officer and his staff in a house full of all the family treasures of a typical German family. There was one curious relic in it; on the cellar door, an inscription written in French, addressed 'Messieurs les Prussiens', to the effect that the writers had not wished to break open the cellar, but as they wanted the wine it was necessary to do so. This had been written by the French when they went over the frontier into Saarbrücken in 1870 at the beginning of the war, and had been religiously preserved ever since with a glass over it. The Germans had little imagined that some day it would be read by a French General occupying the house. After luncheon we started on our tour through the district. It was Sunday, and everything very quiet; of course we could not see much of the people, but I do not think that anyone who had not known would have noticed anything different from an ordinary Sunday; the people were on the whole well dressed with good boots and shoes; many of the children looked quite plump, a few of them a little pale, but they were playing about in the streets just as usual. The French said that they had been very underfed at first, but that things were improving. No doubt the French do everything in their power to make them comfortable. We stopped at Saarlouis and found the French officer in command in the old town hall. This had been built in Louis XIV's time, a beautifully proportioned building looking out on a typical seventeenth-century French town. On the strength of this the French are quite convinced that Saarlouis ought to belong to them. The real truth is I believe that they destroyed the old town, built a new one in French style on the old site and have ever since considered that this is sufficient title to the possession of the district. They were on stronger grounds when here and elsewhere they pointed out the contrast between French art and decoration and the appallingly oppressive and laboured modern art which the Prussians have introduced. Then we went on right to the outskirts of the district; an extraordinarily beautiful valley entirely surrounded by hills, with a pottery factory in an old abbey, which we decided should belong to the Saar Valley. Here we went to call on a German proprietor who was obviously very pro-French; that was clearly the reason why we were taken to see him.

We had a very pleasant evening playing bridge with the General and his staff and started early the next morning, going this time north and east. It was Monday and there was a certain amount of work going on in the factories and mines, though not, I should say, very much. They told me that there were no serious labour troubles; they had been warned of some Spartacist agitators, but an enquiry had shown that there was really little being done. On our way back we went through Zweibrücken, which is not to be in the Saar, much to the disappointment of the French. They are very keen on getting it for themselves. It was curious seeing them there. It is a picturesque old town with a great deal of good building of the French late seventeenth and early eighteenth centuries. The French Commandant carried us off at once to see an exhibition which he had started, the chief objects in which were contemporary pictures of the Prince of Nassau-Zweibrücken[1] in French uniform, and testimonials from the Grand Monarch as to the admirable conduct of the Saarbrücken regiment. There were many really fine specimens of French art and workmanship and a special room with the latest millinery and hats from Paris. Here again the moral of the whole thing was meant to be that French culture was so superior to German that Zweibrücken must obviously belong to France. One could not help feeling that in a moment all that has happened in the last fifty years was wiped away; the French soldiers were back again in the place where they used to be under the Monarchy and the Revolution: confident, debonair, quick, feeling themselves completely at home in their historical task of bringing a higher civilization to the Germans. One felt as one saw them that there was no essential difference between them and their predecessors of a hundred and twenty or two hundred years ago. I have always said that, perhaps unconsciously, the French of today are just the same as the French of Richelieu and Louis XIV, and here on the spot I felt more than ever how true it was. We had a long motor drive back through Lorraine in blinding snow storms, got to Metz just in time for dinner and a short look at the cathedral, then took the train and arrived back in Paris about 7 o'clock the next morning, after a sleepless night without a sleeping berth, to find any amount of work waiting.

I find that the Saar Valley scheme is generally looked upon very critically; it is the special and peculiar child of the Great Four, who themselves invented the plan of putting it under the League of Nations. After visiting the place, I feel convinced that under favourable circumstances it might be made an extremely interesting experiment in the form of a rather

[1] The Prince of Nassau-Zweibrücken commanded a regiment in the army of Louis XIV.

autocratic government of a fortunately placed and prosperous community. The whole district outside the actual mining towns is hilly, with large forests, and might be made a model of government for a small and self-contained industrial area. Whether it will succeed will of course depend largely upon whom they chose to govern it. I am inclined to think that probably the inhabitants will accept without much difficulty.

You will now have seen also the Alsace-Lorraine provisions; I had a good deal to do with them and do not like them, but I like them better than the original French proposals. Again and again one finds the same thing; the French Departments of State and the inferior people seem completely defective in all sense of justice, fair play or generosity; the people at the top have for political reasons to defend the proposals sent up to them, but are, I think, often glad when they are refused. The difficulty is to distinguish the points on which the best French really attach importance, and those which they are only defending because they are told to do so.

I wonder what you think of the treaty of peace as a whole. Personally I think that the territorial clauses are not bad, but everyone I have talked to agrees that the treaty as a whole is quite impossible and indefensible. The cumulative effect is such that the provisions will be impossible to be carried out by the Germans.

Extract from letter to the Rev. Canon Headlam   *11 May 1919*

... We have been very busy the last fortnight getting the treaty finished. Everything was in arrears; the whole French organization for printing proof-reading, drafting, etc., was extremely unsatisfactory and so it was very difficult to get the thing through. I spent last Sunday from nine in the morning until 8 o'clock at night down in the Quai d'Orsay doing what I could to help. After all our work, the treaty as printed still contains a large number of blunders and some really serious ones.

I do not think it is a good treaty at all; the territorial clauses, apart from certain details in the Polish settlement, are on the whole justifiable, but there will I think be serious trouble about Upper Silesia, where things have been stretched too far against the Germans, and they will have a very plausible ground of complaint that we are assigning a population which has been German for over five hundred years to Poland without giving them an opportunity of expressing their wishes.[1] This of course will be all

[1] Headlam-Morley was one of the first Allied representatives who realized the likelihood of a strong German protest over the cession of Upper Silesia to Poland.

K

the more serious because this transference of territory means the transference of some very valuable coal mines. The economic and reparation clauses are, as far as I can understand, in their cumulative effect really impossible. I do not understand them all myself, but those who do assure me that this is the case. Obligations have been put upon Germany which, owing to other clauses in the treaty, it will be practically impossible for her to carry out. However these things can be rectified later and I do not myself expect that this will prevent the Germans from signing. It is a pity that we have stretched things too far; if the clauses had been rather less severe, we should have got just as much and been in a much stronger position. With regard to the disarmament clauses, severe as they are, they could be defended if there were some real guarantee that the Allies would themselves begin disarming. No doubt France wants to reduce her forces, but we have to remember that new countries such as Poland and Czechoslovakia are only anxious to build up a large army as soon as they can. Here, however, much depends, not so much on the treaty itself, but on what is done during the next few months, and I am frightened that everyone will be so tired that nothing will be done. . . .

Extract from letter to Mr G. Saunders (F.O.) 12 May 1919

. . . I think I agree with you about the treaty of peace. The cumulative effect of it is to put on Germany disabilities of such a nature that no nation could be expected to acquiesce in them. On the other hand, I do not take the situation so tragically. By far the most onerous are the economic and the reparation clauses; these are obviously, even if they are accepted without fundamental change, of such a nature that revision will be almost inevitable. In particular Germany could not possibly come into the League of Nations without the whole scheme being thoroughly revised, and I hope it will be found necessary and possible to admit Germany at a comparatively early date. The territorial clauses are on a different basis; it must be assumed that the cessions of territory made now are to be permanent. Abhorrent as they may be to the Germans, I think that the territorial clauses are on the whole just, with the exception of some of the details of the Polish-German frontier. This has been stretched too much against Germany. My own expectation is that the question of Upper Silesia will turn out to be the real crux of signing. In this case we have assigned to Poland a considerable district with a very mixed population, a district which has not been Polish for over five hundred years, and are fixing the boundaries absolutely without even attempting to consult the population. As a large part of the population is, I believe, a shifting mining population, a vote under the best of circumstances would be very unsatisfactory. The position therefore is at best a difficult one, but it will be represented by Germany, and I think not without justice, that we have stretched the case against them here and avoided consulting the population, just because this district contains very valuable coal mines. I anticipate therefore that the Germans will make great opposition to accepting this part of the treaty and that even if they do so, there will be great difficulty in practically enforcing it; we may, I think, be sure that there will be violent opposition to Polish occupation and that the German Government will say they have no power to control it. Curiously enough this point seems always to have been neglected; the recommendations of the Polish Committee were accepted in regard to it without demur; I do not think the Prime Minister understood the situation. Again, an assignment of the district round Glatz to Czechoslovakia is very difficult to justify.

The fundamental fault of a good deal of the treaty, especially the Ports and Waterways, many of the economic clauses, and to a certain extent also the disarmament clauses, is that what ought to be a general agreement under the League of Nations is imposed by force upon Germany, without reciprocity. This is a great blunder; the only way of avoiding this would have been to separate the preliminaries of peace with Germany from those portions of the treaty which are in the nature of reconstruction for the future. Most of the imperfections arise from this not having been done. To take a particular case, it is very invidious that Germany should be compelled to accept international control for the Elbe and Oder, while the Allied and Associated Powers are not under any obligation to accept international control for any rivers within their territories. I do not think that the clauses imposed upon Germany are in themselves necessarily bad, but it is a bad start of the new system to do things in this way.

Letter to Sir Maurice Hankey   13 May 1919

The New States Committee today completed the first part of their work, viz: the consideration of minority rights in Poland. A report, accompanied by draft articles for the proposed treaty will, I hope reach you in good time tomorrow.[1] The report is unanimous, with the exception of an article safeguarding the use of the Sabbath by the Jews, which I proposed,

[1] The report as well as minutes of the New States Committee can be found in David Hunter Miller's *My Diary at the Peace Conference*, 21 vols. (New York: privately printed, 1924), Vol. X.

but none of the other members accepts. This will therefore have to come up for decision by the Four. I hope very much that the Prime Minister will support me in this. As he will see, we have been extremely moderate in the demands we have made from the Poles for the protection of the Jews. I have myself been fighting the battle of the Jews throughout and got very little support from my American colleague. On every other point we have managed to come to an agreement, but not on the Sabbath. Everyone who knows Poland, even including those who tend to be anti-Semitic, assures me that the matter is of real pressing importance, and I could not therefore give way on this point.

I hope that the Four will be able to deal with the matter as quickly as possible, for until they do, we cannot get on to the other States; their approval of our proposals will be a precedent.

There is one other point on which there is some difference of opinion, the proposal for the guarantee of the League of Nations. The matter is a very difficult one and I have got a paragraph into the report simply saying that we should ask for more time to consider it. I will send you a copy of the memorandum I am writing on the subject.

P.S. With regard to Danzig, I think that there is in this case no deliberate interference by anyone. It is simply a case of that kind of misunderstanding which almost inevitably arose in consequence of the haste with which at the end the drafting was done, and also owing to the fact that there was no one officially charged with the Danzig business to whom the Drafting Committee could send their draft when completed. I did, as a matter of fact, see the final draft when I was down at the Drafting Committee and ought to have noticed the change then. I will talk to Hurst about getting out of the difficulty and send up any proposal which I can make.[1]

Memorandum of interview with
Monsieur Sokolnicki   *15 May 1919*

Monsieur Sokolnicki, Secretary of the Polish Delegation, came to see me today; he said he had heard that there was a Committee appointed to deal

---

[1] Following receipt of the approved scheme for Danzig prepared by Headlam-Morley and Mezes, the Drafting Committee on its own initiative made several important alterations. For one thing, it stipulated that Danzig should become a free city, not after a special treaty with Poland had been negotiated as Headlam-Morley and Mezes had proposed, but immediately upon the conclusion of the peace. Headlam-Morley's efforts to restore the original clause are described in his résumé of his Peace Conference activities. As a result of his intervention, the articles were redrafted in the form in which they appeared in the final version of the Versailles treaty, p. 181.

with certain Polish questions and that he had heard that I was a member of it, and he wished to ask if I could give him any information or guidance. I said that it was a matter that it was quite impossible for me to say anything about at this moment. I refused to answer any questions or even to receive any semi-official suggestions on his part.

He then said that he was rather anxious about the general relations of the British Government to Poland. He said that he recognized that it was perhaps unfortunate that no official representative of Poland had been appointed in London. He suggested that there might be some want of understanding as to the general direction of Polish policy. He mentioned in particular Polish policy in regard to Lithuania, Galicia, and generally the eastern frontiers. I said that I had myself nothing whatever to do with these matters and that Sir Esme Howard was the proper person to approach with regard to them. He asked, however, none the less if he might at some later date have a quite private and unofficial conversation with me with regard to them. In conversation I said that it was quite probable that there might be some difference as to details between Great Britain and Poland, but that between friends such differences would always occur and would not affect the amicable relations between the two countries. He said that it was not only on matters of detail that differences might arise, but from a misunderstanding as to the wider and more general principles involved in the whole future of Eastern Europe. I agreed that this was a point of great interest and said that quite privately and unofficially I should be very glad to talk over these matters with him.

I think it might be useful that I should do so. If I did, I should take the opportunity of pressing merely as my own personal view the idea that the security of Poland in the future will be safer if Poland depends on the new system which we hope to be able to build up in which states will not base their existence on the rivalry of armaments. The moral I should draw from this would be that Poland should take the opportunity of the temporary disarmament of Germany to encourage the general principle of disarmament and not use the opportunity to start to build up a strong military force which would undoubtedly be regarded by Germany as a menace. I should press strongly that if Poland does this, she would inevitably bring about in a short period an attempt by Germany to re-establish strong military forces, and that if this rivalry ever begins, Poland will be placed in the most dangerous position. I should also take the opportunity of suggesting that in the long run Great Britain cannot, as a single Power, make herself responsible for any kind of military intervention in Eastern Europe, and that however friendly and well disposed we are to

Poland, there are necessary limits to the military help which we could give.

I should suggest also that it would be a very unwise proposal to claim territories on her eastern frontier, possession of which would inevitably involve future dissensions with Russia and that therefore if the British Government was inclined to discourage some Polish claims, it was no evidence of ill-will, but the true act of a friend. The safety of Poland would depend not merely upon the extent of territory which she governs, but on the fact that she governs a contented population and that she can live in the most amicable and peaceful relations with her neighbours on the eastern side.

Memorandum on the right of appeal of minorities to the League of Nations   16 May 1919

Past experience shows that it is of little use to insert in the clauses of a treaty obligations undertaken on the part of any Power as regards certain classes of its subjects unless there is also provided some definite means by which the violation of these provisions can be dealt with. In the past there has been no authority capable or qualified to enforce any such obligations except the Great Powers, and the experience, for instance, of Romania, has clearly demonstrated that under the older condition of affairs it was practically impossible to get that unanimity between the Great Powers which was essential.

In the future this difficulty will to a certain extent be overcome by the establishment of the League of Nations. There will be an authority which has the right to intervene, and it is hoped that it will be able to do so without creating the risk of a European war. As soon, however, as we approach the matter more in detail we come across very serious difficulties. In order that the League may act in a matter of this kind, it is necessary that provision should be made by which it may be formally seized of the case; that is, if for instance there are pogroms of Jews in Poland, there must be someone whose right and duty it is to bring the matter to the official cognizance of the League.

We therefore come to the problem of to whom this right and duty should be assigned. There are two answers not mutually exclusive: (1) any Power, member of the League of Nations, necessarily has the right of bringing any matter before the Council of the League; (2) a right might be given to the injured persons themselves to approach the League directly. The question at issue is whether it is desirable to give this right to the minorities, whose rights as guaranteed under a treaty, are being violated.

As a general principle it is, I believe, now accepted that it is most un-desirable and would be most dangerous to allow the inhabitants or citizens of any state direct approach to the League except through their own Government. If we once allow this principle to be neglected, we should get into a position in which, for instance, the French in Canada, the Jews in America, the Roman Catholics in England or in France, the Welsh, the Irish, the Scottish Highlanders, the Basques, Bretons or Catalonians, might approach the League and complain of injustice to which they were sub-jected. If we once begin on these lines, the League would, if it became an effective and active body, acquire a practically unlimited right of criticizing and supervising the internal constitution of every state. It is needless to point out the danger of this, for it would enable the League, under circumstances not at all impossible, to be used as a weapon for imposing particular forms of Government on all states.

It follows from this that if the right is to be given to individual inhabi-tants, citizens or communities to approach the League, this can only be recognized as a quite exceptional and, it is to be hoped, a temporary measure, allowable only in the case of specific bodies in definite states. There are only two justifications for allowing any deviation from the main principle: (1) as a matter of fact there have been established as a result of the late war new states which, just because they are new, in-experienced, and have no established traditions, may justly be treated in a different category from the older established states; (2) in certain cases the Allies have transferred large territories, which have a considerable population of aliens, against their will to hostile states. In these cases there is a direct obligation lying upon the Allies to protect these people against flagrant injustice or persecution.

In these two cases it is, I submit, justifiable as a special and exceptional measure to give the direct right of appeal to the League of Nations. If, however, this right of appeal is given, it should I think in all cases be given specifically to a named definite body, and it should not be given under the general heading of 'Minorities', and it should be strictly limited to those definite cases in which there is real reason for anticipating that injustice will be done. If this principle is accepted, then it would be necessary to determine which are the minorities to which in the case of each new state, this specific right should be given.

It will be generally agreed that at least in the case of Poland and Romania, it must be assigned to the Jews. I feel very doubtful whether it is necessary or desirable to give the same right to the Jews in all the other states with which our Committee deals. Our information is that in Yugoslavia certainly the number of Jews is so small that it is not necessary; Czecho-slovakia is a doubtful case; if it is necessary to do anything of the kind in Greece, it should be limited specifically to the Jews of Salonika. My reason for desiring not to give the right generally to the Jews in all these states is that this might be taken as a precedent for giving similar rights to the Jews in other old-established states, and this would, I think, be most dangerous and undesirable.

The case of other minorities is very different from that of the Jews; this exceptional right should, I think, only be assigned to those of the minorities who are transferred as a result of the Peace. To take a specific case, there might be strong justification for giving such a right to the Germans in the transferred territory; it would, I venture to suggest, be most undesirable and most unfair to the Poles to give this right to all Germans who live in what was formerly Russian Poland. In regard to Poland, therefore, I should suggest that the right of appeal should be given (a) to the Jews through-out the whole of Poland; (b) possibly to the Germans in the transferred territory, to the Ruthenians or Little Russians, to the White Russians and to the Lithuanians in any territories which might eventually be assigned to Poland, in which they form a considerable proportion of the population.

There is a positive reason why the right of appeal should be given to these minorities. If it is not, in case of necessity they will have to turn to other Powers for protection and persuade one or more of these to bring their grievances before the League of Nations. The result would be that, for instance, the Polish Germans would turn for help to the Government of Germany, the White Russians to the Government of Russia. It is submitted that it is extremely desirable to avoid this situation arising. It seems, there-fore, that in reality the dignity and independence of the Polish state would be better safeguarded by allowing the direct right of appeal in these ex-ceptional cases to the League of Nations than it would be if in the absence of such an appeal the Great Powers and their representatives at Warsaw, were put into the position of being individually the protectors of certain classes of Polish citizens. We want to get rid of this old system, which has always worked badly, and to substitute a better.

17 May 1919

Note. The Report No. 2 of the Committee on New States was considered by the Council of Four.[1] There was a discussion mainly about the Jewish

[1] For the minutes of the Supreme Council's meeting, see P.P.C. V, 678–81.

Sabbath and Mr Headlam-Morley was asked to state his views. He said that he was supported by Mr Lucien Wolf, Mr Namier, as well as by Sir Esme Howard, but he thought it desirable to consult the Poles. It was agreed to approve the report in principle, that the Committee should communicate it officially to the Polish Delegation in Paris and confer with them on the subject, and that the gist of the report should be telegraphed to the Polish Government and its views invited. A telegram was accordingly sent to the French Minister at Warsaw for presentation, in conjunction with his allied colleagues, to the Polish Government.

Extract from letter to Mr Namier (F.O.)   *17 May 1919*

... I am enclosing very confidentially a copy of the Report of our Committee on the Jews, etc; this is only a first copy and, as you will see, there are a great number of misprints, but I do not want to delay until I get the revise. I am adding to it a typed copy of one paragraph which is being altered, dealing with the nature of the appeal to the League of Nations. You will, I expect, be disappointed in some ways with the result; on some matters I should like to have had it a little stronger, but I could get no support; Miller, the American, was on essential points even more difficult than the French. As you will see, I have stuck out about the Sabbath, though in a modified form, but on the whole I thought it better not to divide the Committee on what after all would have been apparently small modifications of language. The one point on which I felt that I had not sufficient information was about hospitals. I pressed very much that the Jews should be given the administration of public funds assigned to hospitals, as well as schools; curiously enough I met with very strong opposition on this point and as I had no proper information, could not carry my point. There may be an opportunity of revision in detail after it has been to the Four, so I should be much obliged if you will tell me whether this is a matter of importance. *A priori* I should have expected that it would be.

We decided that as soon as the report was prepared it must be kept absolutely confidential, and therefore I have not been able to consult Mack, Marshall or Wolf about it. Very unfortunately, however, Miller, the American representative, gave a copy to Marshall, who has already, I believe, shown it to other people. I am very anxious about this because it will have a disastrous effect if the Poles learn that a copy has been given to the Jews before the Polish official representatives have seen it. Wolf, hearing that Marshall had a copy, asked me for one, but I refused to give it to him. It is most important that even in London it should be kept strictly confidential.

What I suppose will happen is that if the Four approve, they will communicate it officially to the Polish Delegation and authorize us to consider any minor alterations which the Poles may wish to have inserted; if they do this, I think that perhaps we may be able to get any minor alterations strengthening the report inserted on our side; for this reason any detailed criticisms from you would be valuable.

Extract from letter to Mr Namier (F.O.)   *17 May 1919*

Since writing the enclosed, I have been called to the Council of Four and the whole thing is through. No one else was there except myself, as they only wanted to discuss the Sabbath article. They accepted the first paragraph of it without difficulty, but were rather troubled about the second paragraph and asked me why I put that in; I said that I had done so at the request of Sir Esme Howard, and at once all opposition disappeared and the Prime Minister said that if he asked for it, it must be all right. I am quite sure from my conversation that I was right in not making too many points of difference. The treaty is to be sent out direct to Poland for the observation of the Polish Government, in addition to consultation here with the Polish Delegation. It was clearly, they felt, that this was a matter on which the Polish Government should be consulted directly and not allowed to speak merely through the mouth of the first Polish Delegate in Paris.[1]

Extract from diary   (*undated – probably about 18 May*)

Protection of minority rights in the new states

From the time when we first occupied ourselves with the problems of the Peace, it became apparent that serious problems would arise from the fact that the new states created in Eastern Europe would in all cases have considerable minorities, either Jews or other races, which were often bitterly hostile to the governing nationality. The matter was therefore, from November onwards, the subject of desultory conversations and minutes. At first there was, so far as I recollect, a proposal that there should

---

[1] The Council's decision for the most part reflected Lloyd George's view that the head of the Polish Delegation, Monsieur Dmowski, 'did not represent the democratic opinion in Poland'. See P.P.C. V, 680.

be inserted in the League of Nations some general clause giving the League of Nations the right to protect minorities in all countries which were members of the League. This I always most strongly opposed and I believe did so on paper, for it would have involved the right to interfere in the internal constitution of every country in the world. As I pointed out, it would give the League of Nations the right to protect the Chinese in Liverpool, the Roman Catholics in France, the French in Canada, quite apart from more serious problems, such as the Irish. This point of view was, I think, not seriously opposed by any except the unofficial bodies who wished the League of Nations to be a sort of super-state with a general right of guarding democracy and freedom throughout the world. I think that in one of the original schemes something of the kind was included, but it was soon dropped out.

My own view always was that any right given to the League of Nations must be quite definite and specific and based on special treaties entered into because of definite exceptional cases, and that such a right could only be recognized in the case of a new or immature state of Eastern Europe or Western Asia. Even if the denial of such right elsewhere might lead to injustice and oppression, that was better than to allow anything which would mean the negation of the sovereignty of every state in the world.

It was from the point of view of the Jews that the matter really attracted the most attention, and numerous memoranda and petitions were sent both by the Zionists and other bodies asking for special protection to the Jews. The influence of the Zionist movement led them to lay stress on the 'national' aspect of Judaism. They wanted the Jews in each country to be recognized as a national entity and to be given the same rights as other national minorities.

After we came to Paris, as soon as the work of the boundary Commissions began, the matter naturally came up from time to time. Again and again minutes were written, but nothing was done. I discussed the matter with Malkin, and eventually, through him, got a minute issued instructing those responsible for each state or group of states to say what particular clauses would be applicable to the cases with which they had to deal. This was done, but nothing at all followed. No notice was taken of the minutes; they were never sent up to the Heads of the Office, and week after week went by without the matter progressing further. So far as the higher authorities went, the question remained absolutely undecided until less than a week before the time when the Germans were to receive the copy of the treaty.

On Thursday, 1 May, the matter came up before the Council of Four,[1] being brought before it by President Wilson, who put forward a scheme suggested to him by Mr Miller, for providing guarantees to the Jews in Poland and elsewhere. At the same time a minute was sent up by Llewellyn Smith, pointing out the necessity of binding the new states to provide fair treatment in commercial and other matters. As a result the Council of Four (or Three, for the Italians were absent at that time) appointed a Committee for dealing with the problem, with instructions to propose clauses for insertion in the treaty with Germany. There were at once appointed Mr Miller and myself; there was some difficulty about the choice of the French representative. Mr Miller and I received the notice of our appointment on Thursday, 1 May. The Treaty of Peace was to be ready on Saturday. Our French colleague had not yet been appointed. The situation was really rather absurd. I saw Mr Miller while at the Crillon in connection with the Alsace-Lorraine scheme, and arranged that he should come and meet me at the Astoria at 3 o'clock on Friday afternoon. He put forward the scheme which the President had already produced and suggested that that might be incorporated in the treaty with Germany. It was a scheme which, while couched in general language, contained clauses which obviously required very careful scrutiny. We had another meeting on Friday evening at 9 o'clock, at which each of us produced alternative reports. I disliked many of the details of his scheme, which were much too much in the style of the American Constitution, but I took the line that anyhow we could not get through anything in the time available, and drafted a short clause for insertion in the treaty with Germany, simply binding Poland to accept such principles as might be determined upon. The next morning we went to the Council of Three. We had a meeting in the President's house first, at which Monsieur Berthelot (our French colleague) was also present, and he accepted the report in which the difference in the point of view was put forward. We then went in to the Three.[2] Mr Miller propounded his scheme. I suggested to the Prime Minister the reasons why it could not well be accepted. He saw them at once. He said that he did not know how long it took to draw up the American Constitution, but he imagined that it took up some months, and the scheme before us evidently aimed at drawing up a Constitution for Poland within two hours. On this it was turned down with very little discussion, and the proposed clause approved for insertion in the treaty with Germany, with two modifications by President Wilson.

[1] See P.P.C. V, 383–95; Mantoux, I, 440–1.
[2] See P.P.C. V, 439–40; Mantoux, I, 474–5.

(During the course of this meeting I took the opportunity of giving the Prime Minister my picture postcard of the Saar Valley. He passed it on to Clemenceau, who at once said: 'This is not the Saar; there is a river; it must be Fiume. And there is a statue; President Wilson, here is a picture of Fiume with a statue of you.' When the Prime Minister admired the picture and said it looked nice, President Wilson said: 'It is too beautiful for Germany.' Finally the picture was presented to Monsieur Clemenceau.)

We were very lucky in getting the new states matter taken, as there was an immense crowd waiting, consisting of financial and reparation people. However, Hankey got us a quarter of an hour. That afternoon, having got the decision from the Four, I went down to the Drafting Committee, explained the point to their great indignation, and got the clause inserted. It was possible to do this without any alteration in the numbering of the clauses.

I may add that before leaving the Council of Three I got an opportunity of mentioning the clause for giving mutual railway facilities to the Poles and the Germans, which I found, as explained elsewhere, had been omitted by the Drafting Committee from the treaty. The Prime Minister was very indignant and they all gave Hankey instructions to write a letter immediately to the Drafting Committee to get it inserted. Even then I had considerable difficulty in getting it done, but succeeded by pointing out that this also could be put in without altering the actual numbering of the clauses.

The rest of Saturday and the whole of Sunday I spent with the Drafting Committee. Akers Douglas, Carnegie and Strachey[1] were all there reading through proofs and trying to get the work on. It was an extraordinary sight; in the large room upstairs, the whole floor littered with papers, Fromageot[2] at the head of the table, Hurst and Brown Scott[3] opposite one another, Malkin hovering about, and the rest of us in the background. All the work was done by Fromageot and Hurst. Brown Scott seemed to do nothing except at times to interrupt with irrelevant petty jokes and futile anecdotes, until Hurst stopped him, saying 'don't chatter, Scott' – an admirable illustration of the friendly relations of the two great nations. Fromageot and Hurst are most admirable people, with

[1] Charles Strachey, a member of the Colonial Office.
[2] Henri Fromageot, chief legal adviser to the Quai d'Orsay, one of the technical advisers on the French Delegation and French representative on the Drafting Committee.
[3] James Brown Scott, technical adviser on legal questions in the American Delegation. A member of the Commission on Responsibility of the Authors of the War and of the Drafting Committee.

a great power of work, and fortunately most equitable tempers; they have, however, one great fault, that they insisted on doing everything themselves and have spent their whole time reading through the treaty word by word, and doing all the spade work. The result was that there was no one who had any leisure to decide important matters of principle when they were brought up to them, and it was most difficult to get attention. Hurst was really annoyed, as I had to bring two or three important changes about the Danzig clauses and Poland, which I had to insist on being put in. The whole arrangement was in reality the acme of mismanagement and want of organization; Hurst, Fromageot and Malkin were worked to death. My first duty was to set to work and go through the treaty, cutting out the Italians wherever they were referred to. Of course two days afterwards somebody else had to go through and put them all in again. The work was extraordinarily difficult because of the change of decision made by the Council of Four. On Sunday they asked us to go down again early; I asked what they meant by early, and was told that Malkin was going at quarter to seven; I went down with Akers Douglas at nine and got back at eight o'clock in the evening. We read through all the first part dealing with Europe, correcting misprints and drawing attention to obvious errors and blunders; in particular, the Saar Valley and Alsace-Lorraine had to be read with great care, as the English and French did not always agree. With great difficulty we got it all done, the corrections made on one copy, which we handed to Strachey, who was to give them to the messenger for the printers. Everything seemed satisfactory, but when the treaty appeared in print, we found that a considerable number of passages had been printed from the uncorrected copies, so that a good deal of our labour was in vain. The work went on on Monday and Tuesday; it was not until Monday that the final text of the reparation clauses was ready.

On Monday I had to go and see Mr Balfour because the French had suddenly asked to put in a new clause about the Swiss rights in Savoy. They treated the English with very great discourtesy in the matter, as they arranged the whole thing with the Swiss, and the first official intimation which came from the French was an urgent request to Mr Balfour, which he received about half past twelve, to go down to the Quai d'Orsay and agree to a clause being put into the treaty. I objected to it strongly and if he had had any power of will he would simply have refused to discuss the question at all at that late stage; however, what he did say was that he would not come down until after lunch. When he went he agreed, and this new clause had to be put in.

During the rest of the week I was chiefly occupied with the Committee on New States. It was quite pleasant except that Miller, the American, was a dull fellow. I was a good deal pestered by Jews who, however, turned out to be quite reasonable and we succeeded in turning down the most American of the American proposals. There was some difficulty in persuading Mr Miller that the Christians of Warsaw would not have their religious feelings offended by seeing Jews working on a Sunday; he seemed to think that the Continental Sunday was that to which he is accustomed in Boston or in New York.

I really had to fight the battle of the Jews almost alone; luckily I had been well coached by Judge Mack, Mr Marshall, Mr Namier and Lucien Wolf. I explained to them that I could not support any claim to 'national' rights, and we agreed that it would be quite sufficient to get educational privileges if this were coupled with really stringent clauses assuring them of citizenship and the ordinary protection of the law. We therefore easily agreed on the Committee that the first thing was to get in the essential clauses about citizenship, and we also agreed that the other clauses should be drafted as far as possible in general language; as Berthelot pointed out, if one attempted to be precise, one almost inevitably ruled out special cases of which one had not thought. On these lines we agreed pretty well, the only ultimate point of difference being the protection of the Jewish Sabbath about which I held out as against the other two. During the latter part of the week an Italian turned up. The Committee has been kept singularly quiet; nothing about it has appeared in the press; even the Poles have apparently not found out who are the members of it, and the Foreign Secretaries have never heard of its existence at all. We got finished on Thursday (15 May) and sent in our report to the Council of Four. On Saturday I was telephoned for and found that I was sent for alone; the reason for this is that they wanted only to discuss the one clause which I had proposed. I had very little difficulty in persuading them to agree to it. When I was asked about the elections not taking place on Saturday, I said that this had been suggested to me by Sir Esme Howard; the Prime Minister at once said that he was a Roman Catholic, and this carried the matter. In the end I myself raised the question of the method of appeal to the League of Nations. Were the minorities themselves to be allowed direct access? A short conversation took place in which the President seemed rather definitely opposed. However, I asked, as the report also asked, that the matter should be allowed to be brought up again if necessary, and so the whole thing finished quite satisfactorily.

Letter to General Smuts   *19 May 1919*

I have just been reading with very great interest your memorandum on the negotiations for the Peace Treaty.[1] I hope you will allow me to say how glad I am that someone has said what many are thinking. I feel myself, and I know that there are many who agree with me, that the treaty in its present form is indefensible and cannot in fact be carried out.

So far as my observation has gone, the main reasons which have got us into this unfortunate position are two. First of all, throughout all the discussions here, it seems to me that we have been too much influenced in our attitude towards Germany by the point of view of the French military. In saying this, I do not wish to attach any blame to the French, the difficulties and dangers of whose position every one must realize, but it is just because of these difficulties and dangers that their interpretation of the German situation cannot be depended upon. Secondly, as you yourself know, there was no opportunity to read the treaty through as a whole after the separate sections had been determined, and before it was submitted to the Germans. To this I attach great importance. With a few exceptions, it seems to me that a defence can be made of each one of the individual clauses, but I feel convinced that if any responsible person had read through the whole at leisure, he would have felt that the cumulative effect would be such that a thorough revision must be made.

The reason that I am venturing to write to you is not so much to inquire into the question of how we have got ourselves into this very awkward situation, but to investigate the practical measures to be taken to remedy this position. It is no good dwelling too much on the past, but we must look to the future.

Now, it seems to me that in regard to the treaty, we ought to make a distinction between the cessions of territory and the other clauses. The cessions of territory, at any rate on the Continent of Europe, when made, must be considered as final. These clauses, subject to certain minor modifications, should I think stand. The essential thing is that Germany must give up Alsace-Lorraine and the indisputably Polish provinces. I only wish that this had been determined and embodied in a preliminary treaty immediately after the Armistice. Had this been done, many misfortunes would have been avoided. But if these clauses, if and when accepted, necessarily become permanent, the same is not true of many other parts of the treaty; in their nature, the financial, the reparation, the commercial and the military clauses are easily capable of revision at a later stage. A

[1] See W. K. Hancock, *Smuts: The Sanguine Years, 1870–1919*, pp. 522–4. See also p. 150.

revision would certainly be necessary at the time when Germany is admitted to the League of Nations. I hope that this admission will take place soon.

If this point of view is accepted, and if it can be brought about that the Germans would understand it, then, subject always to minor modifications, to which I shall refer directly, it would make it easier for them to sign it and easier for those who think, like you, to accept it. How an understanding with regard to this matter is to be brought about is a question for very careful consideration and suitable action. Even if this view is accepted, I agree that it is desirable that, as you suggest, reasonable and fair modifications proposed by the Germans should be frankly and openly accepted. There are in fact a certain number of modifications which I think that we ourselves ought to put forward.

The particular case which you mention is that of the Saar Basin, and it is one which, as I was a member of the Committee which drew up this section, specially interests me. I enclose a copy of a memorandum which I have just written on the matter. From this you will see that I entirely agree that Article 38[1] is untenable, that it should be withdrawn and some other article substituted for it. I should like, however, to say that I do not think that the provision for repurchase was really 'a cunning device for the perpetual confiscation of the Saar Basin'. I always disliked and opposed the clause; the justification put forward for it was that in negotiations with the Germans it was necessary to have a very strong weapon; it was put forward, however, as a means of coercion which it would not in fact be necessary to use. While I regretted the procedure, I felt that these provisions, which are not to become effective until after fifteen years, would certainly be revised under what one hopes may be much better conditions.

I have to go this afternoon to a meeting to discuss the reply to the last German note, and I will do what I can to get it drafted in accordance with your wishes.

Letter to Sir Maurice Hankey   19 May 1919

So far as I recollect, at the meeting of the Four on Saturday, nothing was said about referring the draft treaty with Poland to the Drafting Committee. Perhaps it was intended to defer doing this until it had been submitted to the Poles. I venture, however, to suggest that it is very desirable that it should be sent to them at once; our experience in the treaty with Germany as to the inconveniences which arose from the material going to the

[1] This refers to the repurchase of the Saar Valley mines. See pp. 122, 167.

L

Drafting Committee at the last moment makes it clearly desirable to avoid the same rush of work at the end. In drawing up the clauses of this treaty, there were obviously some very complicated points – as for instance in regard to double nationality – which make it especially important that it should have the careful criticism of skilled jurists. At the meetings of the Committee I took the view that it was much better that we should not spend our time on matters which certainly some of us did not really understand, but should deliberately leave the final revision to the lawyers.

I think therefore that it ought to go to the Drafting Committee with instructions that they should carefully review and revise the articles and suggest any alterations that may seem to them advisable in order to carry out more effectively the principles and objects with which the treaty has been drawn up; and that they should be asked, if there are any material alterations that they would wish to suggest, to report them to and confer with the Committee. I am very anxious to avoid the misunderstanding which arose with regard to some of the clauses in the treaty of peace with Germany, and I think some such form as this ought always to be adopted in referring the different chapters of the treaties to the Drafting Committee.

Letter to Mr P. N. Baker   20 May 1919

I have been reading your memorandum on the right of appeal. You make out a very strong case and I expect you are right, but feel that the matter wants very careful consideration. As far as our treaties are concerned, the whole thing is extremely urgent. The draft treaty with Poland has been approved by the Council of Four; we still can propose a modification of the article dealing with the appeal to the League of Nations, and if we are to do so, must act very rapidly. For practical purposes, therefore, the immediate question is what, if anything, must be put in to the treaty with Poland and the other new states, in order to bind them to recognize the special rights of the League of Nations and to permit such right of appeal as may be considered necessary. If Article 13 is left without any addition, then difficulty might arise from the fact that there is no definition of the expression 'protection of the League of Nations', and I do not know that the words 'of which the League of Nations has jurisdiction' in Chapter I have, as they now stand, any binding force. Hurst, whom I spoke to, seemed to think they have no meaning. It seems to me, therefore, that it will be necessary to have some kind of discussion on the point.

Would I be allowed to communicate your memorandum, or the gist of it, to the other members of our Committee, or at any rate to Miller?

There is one point on which I think that your scheme would not be satisfactory. It regards the whole matter purely from the point of view of law and would no doubt work in the case of normal conditions; it would give a remedy against legislation or decisions of the court inconsistent with the principles of the treaty and also against denial of justice. I doubt, however, whether it would be a satisfactory means of dealing with popular persecution on a large scale, extensive riots and pogroms. What is in my mind is that if acts of the kind which now are going on continue, for instance, if the Polish army enters a town and subjects the Jewish population *en masse* to insults and violence, it would be rather absurd to attempt to deal with this simply by means of a complicated system of legal procedure, which at the best would certainly take some months before it came up to the League of Nations. We must, I think, keep open the possibility of a direct appeal, to take place immediately and to produce immediate action when we have to do with flagrant facts.

Minute addressed to Lord Hardinge   *20 May 1919*

May I ask if some arrangements could be made by which copies of the sections of the Austrian treaty as they are drafted might be made accessible. In connection with the treaties which are being drafted with the new states, it is absolutely essential that we should have before us the clauses of the Austrian treaty. At present the only copy in the Astoria appears to be one which belongs to Mr Malkin personally as member of the Drafting Committee.

Great difficulty arose in the later stages of the German treaty from the similar difficulty which we experienced in getting copies, and in more than one matter this had the result that clauses were left which will have eventually to be modified. It is, I think, very desirable that we should profit by our experience and avoid the same difficulties in connection with the Austrian treaty. The cause of the trouble is that the printing is done by the French; we can only get copies from them, and I cannot find out whose duty it is to apply for them.

22 May 1919

Note. The Council of Four had before them two letters from the German Delegation, together with two draft replies drawn up by the Saar Valley Committee. At this meeting the Prime Minister drew attention to the clause concerning the conditions for the repurchase of the mines by the

German Government at the end of fifteen years. After some discussion the meeting adjourned in order that the Committee might revise the two draft letters; these were considered later in the day and approved subject to a few small modifications.[1]

Extract from diary   24 May 1919

The writing of a letter: I have been much occupied during the last week in composing the answer to Rantzau's[2] two letters about the Saar Valley. About ten days ago the first letter (dated 13 May) came in.[3] I got a copy of it at 12.30 with the greatest difficulty, the meeting to draft the answer having been summoned for 3 o'clock. I met Crowe, who was in charge, in the lounge and mentioned it to him; he said that he had not yet got a copy of the letter. I therefore sent him up to Norman's[4] room to look at it. This meant that when the meeting began, none of the members had had time even to read through the letter which they were to answer with care; none the less, at the meeting they drafted a reply which they proposed to send off.[5] It was in many ways unsatisfactory, in particular because it laid too much stress on the political side. This was sent up to the Council of Four, but before it had been passed a second letter came in from Rantzau, dated 16 May,[6] about the Saar Valley. In the same way a meeting was called at Tardieu's office in great haste to answer this, and this time I was present. Another letter was then agreed upon, based on a French draft.[7] A short meeting was called for final approval of the two letters. I disliked them very much and began drafting a different version in one letter; I found that if two letters were made, it would be impossible to avoid repetition or to bring out the essential points.

The most important point of the German letters was the stress they laid on the proposal that if the mines were not repurchased by Germany, the permanent possession of part of the territory should go to France. I had always strongly opposed this clause which seemed to me quite unjustifiable but my objection had been overruled on the ground that this had been definitely accepted by the Council of Four. We agreed that this must be withdrawn, and that in consequence some alteration must be made in the text of the treaty. On this we went to the Council of Four, put in the two

[1] See P.P.C. V, 813-15, 826-9; Mantoux, II, 165-7.
[2] Count Brockdorff-Rantzau.
[3] See P.P.C. V, 817-20.
[4] H. Norman, British Counsellor of Embassy as well as British representative on the Peace Conference Secretariat.
[5] See P.P.C. V, 823-4.   [6] See P.P.C. V, 820-2.   [7] See P.P.C. V, 824-5.

letters, and raised the point of the alteration in the treaty. They were all horrified at the words as they stood; the Prime Minister said that it was quite impossible that such a proposal should be made; I took the opportunity of pointing out that they had themselves definitely approved of it. They instructed us to propose an alteration. Tardieu, Crowe, Haskins and myself, with Loucheur,[1] went into the ante-room and there succeeded in drafting what I think was a satisfactory alternative. We then went back; they agreed to this and instructed us to put in a sentence saying that the result of the clause which the Germans anticipated in their letter was one which emphatically had never been intended. The situation was rather difficult as we had to say that we did not intend the result which was clearly and specifically put down in the text of the treaty.

We had another meeting to make the necessary changes in the two letters. On further reading they seemed to me, however, so unsatisfactory in the general drafting and arrangement that I put in the beginning of a draft of a single letter. They read this and they all said, 'une belle lettre', but preferred to stick to their old plan. We went back again to the Four and explained what we had done. We did not get a proper hearing as there was a great crowd in the room and Wilson and Lloyd George were walking about. However, they accepted. I at once went back to my room and got out a copy as finally approved and sent it to Hankey. I was, however, so dissatisfied that I went to him personally and said the thing could not stand. He said the only thing to do was to go to the Prime Minister, I might just catch him before he went out to dinner. I therefore went to his flat, arriving there about ten minutes to eight and waited for half an hour, although I had Carnegie and other people waiting to dine with me at 8 o'clock, as Carnegie was going home the next day. The Prime Minister came in about 8.15. I explained the situation to him and showed him a new draft I had prepared. He read it quickly, said it was much better and that he had been disappointed with our procedure, as he had expected that we should subject the draft to a much more general revision. He had in fact explained this personally to Crowe and Haskins as we were leaving the previous meeting. I got Miss Hughes to come down early after breakfast the next morning (Friday the 23rd), went to Crowe and explained the situation, then went to see Mezes (Haskins being away) and examined my draft with him carefully. He approved. At 6 o'clock that evening I got a letter from Aubert approving my draft with certain modifications. We got an English version typed out that night before dinner, sent a copy to Hankey and after dinner we went down in a car, with Malkin, to the

[1] See p. 167.

Crillon, leaving a copy at Tardieu's office on the way. On Saturday morning I went through the papers between 7 and 8 o'clock, telephoned Miss Hughes at 8 o'clock to come down as soon as possible after breakfast when I dictated a new draft incorporating most of Tardieu's alterations, but making further changes in the arrangement. At 10 o'clock Aubert and Mezes came to the Astoria; we went through this final draft carefully and agreed on it. At quarter to eleven I went to the Council of Four, met Tardieu on the staircase, who read it through and approved; then we went upstairs. I handed the final revision to Hankey, who exclaimed in despair that I was 'dreadful'; he had got out my last draft for signature and now we wanted another change! However, he was very nice about it. I handed a copy to the Prime Minister; Tardieu explained to Clemenceau that we were all agreed. I told President Wilson that Dr Mezes had just agreed in my room, so they accepted it without any further inquiry and I handed the final draft again to Hankey.[1]

With this I hope, at the moment when I am dictating this (11.30 Saturday morning), that the matter is really at an end. I think it was worth while taking the trouble, though it caused a good deal of inconvenience and delay, but, to specify one point, I verified at the very last moment this morning that the original draft quoted the German letter as saying that the Saar Valley would be put under 'French control'; as a matter of fact it said nothing of the sort; the words used were not 'French control' but 'foreign control'.

The draft as finally approved lays down specifically that no change can be made in the general scheme, but introduces an important modification in the one point on which the Germans were clearly right. I could wish that this readiness to accept changes, when clearly an improvement, could be shown in all the answers to the German notes. While we do not want to give way on fundamental matters, it is for every reason most desirable that we should show that we are reasonable in points of detail, and we want to make it easy for the Germans to sign by pointing out to their own people that their expostulations have not been without effect, when there was a real justification behind them.

Extract from letter to
Mr A. E. Zimmern (F.O.)   26 May 1919

... I have not changed my mind in the least since the time when we were writing minutes together about the reparation points. I think that all we

[1] See P.P.C. V, pp. 912–13, 915–17; Mantoux, II, 195.

said then is completely justified and the truth of it is shown by what has happened since. This of course has made the whole position here very difficult. Personally I had nothing whatever to do with the reparation clauses; I said my say after we came here; I have reason to believe that what I said was considered and I received indirectly a delicate hint that I had said it sufficiently often. That being the case, all I could do was to do what little I could to help in getting the other parts of the treaty, with which I was more immediately concerned, as well done as was possible. Frankly, I think that the territorial clauses in their general outline are necessary and right; they are open to criticism on details; my own work was chiefly connected with Danzig – in which I think we have gone as far as was possible to anticipate just German criticism – the Saar Valley and Alsace-Lorraine. The real difficulty about the whole thing is that owing to certain faults of organization, the delay at the beginning, and the haste at the end, there has never been time to get the whole treaty reviewed from the point of view of the general situation.

My own view is very strongly that even those who dislike many portions of the treaty should do all that can be done to make it easier for the Germans to sign. There can, I think, be little doubt that many of the clauses, particularly the reparation clauses, will have to be thoroughly revised, but it would be much easier to get the revision after the treaty is signed than it would be to get the revision now. There is all the difference between these clauses, which do not begin to work for two years, and the territorial clauses which ought to be definitive. It is, I think, most important that just at this juncture the Germans should not be led to believe that there will be fundamental difference among the Allies, or serious opposition in England, for if they did so, they might speculate on this and refuse to sign. Whatever one thinks of the treaty, this I am convinced would be a great disaster. We have to look at the thing from the practical point of view and at the moment I am sure the best attitude to take is that we must get the peace as quickly as possible, but that there shall be a general understanding that an opportunity will be made for modification of those points which seem either to be unworkable or to be really too severe . . .

. . . I do not know if I told you I was working on the protection of minorities in Poland and other small states; this has brought me up against the whole Zionist problem of which hitherto I have known little. It is interesting and rather attractive work, as one feels that one is occupied in construction and not merely in destruction, I have consistently refused to give any support to the Jewish claims to what they call 'national' rights, and I think we have got a series of clauses which may do a certain amount of good and will not encourage what I have always regarded as the very dangerous aims of the more extreme Zionist party.

Extract from letter to Mr Hurst   *26 May 1919*

You will either have received or very soon be receiving an official notification sent to the Drafting Committee that the Prime Minister today at the meeting of the Council of Four brought up the point whether in the treaty of peace Austria should be regarded as a new state or as the inheritor of old Austria.[1] I feel rather guilty at having raised so fundamental a point at so late a stage, but I am sure it is one of real importance and I am very anxious that the treaty should be a document which treats in a suitable manner the complicated situation which has arisen from the dissolution of the Austro-Hungarian Empire. The reference is worded in such a way as practically to give full control to the Drafting Committee and to enable them to reject the point if they wish to do so. Frankly, I hope they will not.

I have been going through the political clauses of the treaty and I think that if the modification is accepted, the changes will not be so great as might at first sight appear, and as soon as I can get it finished, I will send you proposals for carrying them through. I may say that what more than anything else induced me to press this point, which indeed has been very long in my mind, was a perusal of the clauses dealing with such subjects as the revision of the Balkan treaty. It seemed to me absolutely impossible that we should recognize that the new Austria has any kind of claim which she could renounce, arising our of these old treaties made with Austria-Hungary.

With regard to the name by which the new state is to be called, it was mentioned at the Council of Four this afternoon that the credentials of the Austrian plenipotentiaries had been handed in and accepted in the name of 'German Austria'. If so, we are, I presume, bound to accept the name 'German Austria'.

With regard to the financial, economic and reparation clauses, I might point out that the financial clauses have been drafted on the assumption that Austria is a new state, and in them, therefore, comparatively little, if any, alteration would be necessary. The commercial clauses apparently have been drafted on the assumption that it is an old state. There would in any case have to be a thorough modification of one of these sections. If the commercial section is the one to be altered, then all that would be

[1] See P.P.C. VI, 26–30; Mantoux, II, 205–10.

necessary would be to apply to Austria the clauses which are being drafted by the commercial section for insertion in the treaties with the other new states, with no doubt small changes. If this procedure were adopted, there would not be much waste of labour. I understand that the reparation clauses are at present in a completely inchoate condition. I do not think that Ports and Waterways will require much alteration.

Note on the draft Austrian treaty   *26 May 1919*

I have been looking through the draft of the Austrian treaty so far as it is in print,[1] with the object of considering the problems which come up with regard to the new states. It seems to me that the whole basis on which the treaty is drafted is open to very serious criticism. So far as I can understand, the theory underlying it is that what we may call the new Austria, is juridically identical with the old Austria. This seems to me to be wrong in fact and dangerous in principle. Surely new Austria is as much a new state as Czechoslovakia. What happened during the course of the Revolution was that the old Austro-Hungarian Monarchy completely broke up; certain portions, Bohemia, Moravia, etc., formed themselves into one state; other portions, Croatia, Dalmatia, etc., united themselves with Serbia; other portions, Upper and Lower Austria, Tyrol, Carinthia, Styria, etc., also formed themselves into a new state.

It is, I think, of real importance politically that this should be clearly expressed. By adopting the principle on which the draft treaty is drawn up, we are driven to recognize that the new Austria, being identical with the old Austria, inherits from the old Austria all the rights of sovereignty and jurisdiction which the Habsburgs exercised over the seventeen territories comprised within the Austrian half of the Dual Monarchy. It is no doubt the case that the treaty provides for the renunciation of these rights, but the very fact that we ask Austria to renounce these rights means that we recognize that she has them. Suppose now – an improbable but not impossible contingency – that owing to some unforeseen accident the treaty was never signed, we should be left in the situation that the Allied and Associated Powers had definitely recognized the continued existence of these rights. To take a particular instance, German Austria has during the last months been repeatedly claiming to be heard as the advocate of the rights of the Germans in Bohemia. It is clearly essential for political reasons that no right of this kind should be recognized. If German Austria is regarded as a new state within certain limited frontiers, then no such

[1] See P.P.C. V, 836–58.

right can in fact be claimed; if she is the inheritor of the old Austria, then it is difficult to deny that she has now a legal right to be heard on the matter, and even if the legal right were renounced, it would be very difficult to get rid of a vague moral right. Moreover, it is certainly not outside the range of possibility that in some form or other the Monarchy will be restored in Austria. The present era of revolution will probably be succeeded by one of reaction; the Emperor is not a party to the treaty; might he not find in it some justification for reasserting the rights, the existence of which is recognized in the treaty?

If the new Austria does not join Germany, it is quite probable, and I think desirable, that some economic union should in the future be established between the Danubian states. Any such union will be easier to establish, and much less dangerous, if it is clearly understood that the new Austria is not in any sense the heir of the old Austria, but a new state just like the others.

I notice that the financial chapter has been drawn up on the theory that Austria is a new state; in this way it differs from, for instance, the commercial section. They will have to be brought into harmony with one another. I should suggest that the principle of the financial chapter is the right one to adopt.

The whole treaty as drafted is simply an attempt to transfer to Austria the terms of the treaty with Germany with such verbal alterations as are necessary. The circumstances are, however, completely different. In the case of Austria we have not only to put an end to the state of war, but to deal with one of the greatest events which have ever taken place in European history, the dissolution of one of the oldest, the greatest and the most extensive states on the Continent of Europe. I should venture to suggest that it is encumbent on us to recognize this and to find appropriate and dignified language in which we place on record what has happened. What we have to do is not merely to end the war, but to arrange the liquidation of the Austro-Hungarian Monarchy. I will not now spend time by going through the articles in detail, but I put forward a preamble and certain general clauses which might be used as a basis.

If this view were adopted, then I should suggest that to a large extent the commercial chapter should be based, not on the commercial chapter of the treaty with Germany, but on the commercial section of the treaties with the new states. In dealing, for instance, with the international conventions we should adopt the views, not that Austria renounced rights under certain conventions made with the old Austria-Hungary but, like other new states, she undertook to join those international conventions which it was desirable that she should join. All those clauses in which, for instance, Austria renounces rights in Morocco, which the Austro-Hungarian Monarchy held, seem to me to be essentially unsound.

Might I also raise the question of the name of the new state. As Mr Leeper points out to me, the name by which they have always called themselves is Deutsch-Österreich. There ought to be careful consideration whether it would not be desirable to adopt this name; if we did so, then the confusion between the old and the new Austria would naturally disappear. With regard to nomenclature, there is I think some difficulty about the use of the word 'Austria'. In its Constituent Law of 1867, by which the arrangements with Hungary were made, the word 'Austria' is never used, and those parts of the Monarchy outside Hungary are spoken of as 'the territories represented in the Reichsrat'. I believe that technically the word was avoided until the accession of the Emperor Charles when (I have no books of reference by me) there was a decree that the word 'Austria' should be used for the government of this part of the Monarchy. It has, however, sometimes been used, as for instance, in the Treaty with Lichtenstein in 1878. It would therefore be desirable that there should be inserted a definition stating that when 'Austria' is used in this treaty, it means the territories represented in the Reichsrat.[1]

26 May 1919

Note. On 26 May the New States Committee presented draft articles for inclusion in the treaties with Austria and with Hungary, which were approved. It was at this meeting that Mr Headlam-Morley caused some consternation by asking whether Austria was regarded as a new state or as an old state, the inheritor of the Austro-Hungarian Empire. Some parts of the treaty appeared to have been drafted on the former hypothesis, some on the latter. It was dangerous to treat Austria as possessing the rights formerly belonging to the Austro-Hungarian Empire. He produced a memorandum[2] and some draft articles on the subject. It was decided to refer the question to the Drafting Committee.

[1] The lands represented in the Reichsrat were: Austria, Galicia, Bohemia-Moravia-Silesia, Croatia and Slovenia. If the definition suggested by Headlam-Morley were adopted, the new Austria would have no rights in territories assigned to Poland, Czechoslovakia and the South Slav Kingdom (renamed Yugoslavia in 1929). Ultimately, these states were burdened with a share of Austrian reparations and Poland also had to pay a part of German reparations and of the Russian debt. Poland was also refused the right to claim reparations from Germany. See T. Komarnicki, *The Rebirth of the Polish Republic* (London: Heinemann, 1957), pp. 304–7.
[2] See P.P.C. VI, 45–6, 54–6.

Letter to Mr Hurst   *28 May 1919*

The point which was in the minds of the New States Committee was that if Austria alone renounced rights over the territories included in the new Czechoslovak state, this would imply that the new Austria inherited the rights which the Habsburg Monarchy held or claimed. It was felt that this was an incorrect and a dangerous view and that there should not be anything inserted in the treaty which implied that any of these common rights adhered to new Austria rather than to any of the other states into which the Monarchy is being dissolved. The draft before you was drawn up on the idea that there would be no harm in the renunciation by the new Austria, if there was also renunciation by Czechoslovakia; this would put the two states on a complete equality in regard to the heritage of the old Austrian Empire.

Of course the point whether or not something of this sort should be inserted depends on the view which the Drafting Committee has taken as to the legal position of the new Austria. The point to which you draw attention in your letter, that there is no similar renunciation in the treaty with Germany does not, I think, really apply, for there is nothing similar in the relations between Poland and Czechoslovakia on the one hand, and Germany on the other, and those between Czechoslovakia on the one hand, and the old Austria – and possibly also the New Austria – on the other. I think your proposed new clause would meet the point, though I confess I rather prefer my own version which I put forward, that new Austria renounces all rights and titles which might arise from the former connection of her territories included in the former Austro-Hungarian Monarchy, though if this form has been adopted it should, I think, also have been reciprocal, and Czechoslovakia should have made a similar renunciation.

To take a particular illustration of the problems which will arise, I presume on the principle on which the treaty was drafted, foreign embassies will belong to the new Austria and to the new Hungary together; in my view Czechoslovakia would have an equal legal right with either of these other two new states. This is perhaps not a very important point, but it puts the difference of view clearly.

Extract from letter to Mr Koppel (F.O.)   *30 May 1919*

The latest amusement was that yesterday we got the German answer, a really voluminous document.[1] The Prime Minister ordered that it should

[1] The detailed German reply is printed in P.P.C. VI, 795–924.

be translated the same day, so that everyone was turned on to that; luckily I was away at a meeting, so they did not get hold of me, but I helped Akers Douglas for about ten minutes after dinner with two pages, which I translated, although I entirely failed to understand it. Now that the work has been completed, we are told that the Germans themselves are sending in a supplementary document of the same length as their original, and also a complete English version. . . .

The Austrian treaty is in a most awful mess. A Plenary Session was summoned yesterday to receive it, though as a matter of fact, by the time it was summoned, essential decisions had not yet been made on some of the frontier questions and some of the chapters are not in the least agreed upon. Romania and the small states, however, made a protest and said that they must read the text of the treaty before they agreed to it, a demand which I suppose will be considered extraordinarily impertinent. However, they got their way; the Plenary Session was adjourned till Saturday and the Austrians will not get the treaty until Monday; by that time perhaps some of it will be ready.

I am much tied up at present with the New States Committee; everyone who had got a good idea which has been ignored in the main treaty dumps it upon us. . . .

When the Austrians presented their credentials, they were in the name of German Austria and were accepted in that style; two days later it was discovered that this was a thing which could not be permitted for a moment, so an ultimatum has been sent to them telling them to change their name during the next two days.[1]

Extract from letter to Mr Rex Leeper　　　　　　　*30 May 1919*

There has been so much to do here lately – often under great pressure of time – that it has been quite impossible to think about anything else. I read your letter about Russia with great interest, but am afraid it is quite impossible for me to form any opinion as to the merits of the alternative policies. For a long time I have given up attempting to follow the events there, and Kolchak and Dennikin[2] are little more than names to me. Of course I hear a certain amount of conversation on the matter, but I have not even time to read the telegrams. It does not do to attempt to take part in problems for which one has no responsibility and for that reason

[1] See P.P.C. III, 424–30.
[2] See Appendix pp. 207–8.

I have never been able, as I should have liked to do, to press home in any way a request for you to come out. I wish very much that it could have been arranged.

On the general question of principle in the Baltic states I quite agree with you that any arrangements now made ought to be, frankly, provisional. It is clearly quite unjustifiable on strict legal grounds that we should attempt finally to dispose of any old Russian territory without the assent of Russia, and on political grounds it would be most undesirable to do so. I should extend this principle also to the eastern frontiers of Poland and should say that any frontier assigned now ought to be made provisional, pending the consent of Russia. Whether ultimately it is desirable that the Baltic states should be reunited to Russia, either under a federal system or as autonomous states under Russian sovereignty, or whether they should ultimately gain full sovereignty in some kind of federal union, is quite a different matter, and on this it would be presumptuous of me to attempt to form an opinion. If we look at the matter from the frankly utilitarian point of view, the essential thing is to prevent, if it is possible, a political understanding between Germany and Russia against the new settlement in Eastern Europe. All that we have done hitherto is of such a nature as to make such an understanding almost inevitable. Much will depend upon the events of the next few days which will probably determine our attitude towards Germany after the Peace.

Extract from diary   31 May 1919

On Friday night (30 May) there was a dinner got up by Curtis to consider his proposal for the establishment of an institute for the study of foreign affairs, and a year-book; the whole thing is to be a co-operation between England and America. His idea was that Beer should be editor, but that the thing should be printed in England. General Bliss was in the chair, with Lord Robert Cecil. There were about ten Americans and some twenty Englishmen present. Curtis introduced a discussion after dinner which lasted about an hour; Crowe made a rather critical speech on the ground that he feared Government influence; it was pointed out that there was really little fear of that in England and America. The difficulty of co-operation of officials was raised and the question of official secrets. I suggested that the importance of official secrets was very much overestimated; that Government officials did not really differ from others so much in the amount of their knowledge as in their sense of responsibility. It was eventually agreed that a small Committee should be appointed to draft definite proposals. The British members consist of Eustace Percy, Latham,[1] an Australian and myself, with Curtis as Secretary.

The difficulty is the establishment of an institute. Curtis and I agreed this morning that we must look rather to the Royal Society as a model, for if the thing is to be effective, admission must be difficult so as to avoid a great mass of incompetent members who are admitted to many other learned societies in order to get funds. We should start as a nucleus with members of the Delegation here, and this should give the personal element which would help to get the thing going. There is to be a meeting of the Committee on Thursday after dinner.

Extract from diary   *1 June 1919*

I went yesterday to a meeting of the Plenary Session;[2] Abraham succeeded in getting me in. I was glad to go as I had never been to any of these before, and it was particularly interesting as almost the whole of the discussion turned on the minority clauses which are being imposed upon the new and other states. The whole matter is worth recording.

Our Committee, after dealing with Poland and Czechoslovakia, got on to Romania. We decided to write a fishing letter to Bratianu, asking him what measures the Romanian Government proposed to take to safeguard the rights of minorities. He answered stating in a vague and general way that they had the best possible intentions, but concluded his letter with a categorical statement that they would not admit the interference of any external powers in any internal Romanian matters and would accept no obligations except such general obligations as might be accepted by all members of the League of Nations.

This raised the general question in a very acute form. Our view has always been that the League of Nations should have no general obligations for insuring a regime of justice or interfering at all in the internal affairs of the constituent states. On the other hand, it is generally agreed that these new states in Eastern Europe must be treated in an exceptional way; it is absolutely necessary to secure adequate guarantees for the protection of the minorities, especially the Jews. These guarantees must be secured by treaty as a condition of the recognition of the state or the transference of new territories, and the guarantee of the League of Nations will come in in the ordinary form of the guarantee.

The position of Romania is particularly important, for of course it is

[1] Lt.-Col. J. G. Latham, British technical expert on commercial and industrial matters.
[2] See P.P.C. III, 424–30.

not a new state and there are difficulties in imposing obligations on the old territories. On the other hand, the Romanian record is so bad that we cannot merely accept their assurances. Moreover, Romania is still bound by clauses in the Treaty of Berlin,[1] and we cannot therefore adopt the position that we are not creating new obligations, but substituting a new form of guarantee for old obligations.

On receiving this answer, the Committee determined to send it at once to the Council of Four and ask them to insert in the Treaty with Austria a clause binding Romania, similar to that inserted in the treaty with Germany binding Poland and Czechoslovakia. They did so and immediately sent instructions to the Drafting Committee.[2]

There was a secret Plenary Session summoned for Thursday. Monsieur Bratianu was present and he objected that they had not had time to see the text of the treaty and they must do so before they gave their assent to it.[3] On this the meeting was postponed till Saturday and the presentation of the terms to Austria postponed from Friday to Monday. On hearing this, I anticipated that Romania would not only raise questions of frontier, but also of the minority clauses, and would very probably be supported by the other smaller states. I therefore drew up a memorandum on the point in great haste and sent it in at luncheon time Friday morning. I sent a copy to Lord Robert Cecil and warned him that there might be difficulty. He promised to take the matter up and to support us.

At a meeting of the New States Committee on Saturday morning, Berthelot said that on Friday Bratianu had called on Pichon and officially informed him that Romania would refuse to sign the treaty if the clause was inserted. He had also had a long conversation with Monsieur Berthelot about it. By this my anticipations were completely justified. I was called away from the meeting at 12 o'clock by Lord Eustace Percy, who came down to fetch me to a Conference at the rue Nitot. I went there with him and found the Prime Minister, Mr Balfour, Crowe, Esme Howard, Paton and the private secretaries. They were discussing the German answer.[4]

---

[1] The Treaty of Berlin, 1878, recognized Romanian independence but, according to Article XLIV, the Government was obliged to promise protection to the Jews. Little was done to implement this article.

[2] See P.P.C. VI, 131.

[3] This refers to the Austrian treaty.

[4] See P.P.C. III, 391–3; Spector, *Rumania at the Paris Peace Conference*, p. 140.

In their reply of 31 May, the German Delegation accused the Allied and Associated Powers of not having based the Polish-German frontier on ethnographic factors. Moreover, they condemned the ceding of Upper Silesia as a violation of Wilsonian principles and protested not only against the holding of plebiscites in Allenstein and Marienwerder, but against what they described as 'the rape of Danzig'. P.P.C. VI, 795–924.

The Prime Minister was much disturbed about the Polish frontier and Paton was explaining the details, pointing out that in some cases they had perhaps been pressed against Germany too far. The Prime Minister said that he was very disturbed by the situation supposing the Germans refused to sign, and wanted to deprive them of any just reason for this. Paton explained several detailed points in which concessions might be made, especially those in which the frontier had been advanced too far west either for strategical reasons or because of railways. The conversation then turned on Upper Silesia and as a general result it seemed to be agreed that a plebiscite ought to be offered here. Of course the report of the Polish Committee on this is quite indefensible; we have assumed that because there is an ethnographical majority of Poles, the country ought to go to Poland without consulting the wishes of the population; as I pointed out, we ought not to assume that political attachment will always go with the language and race. It is particularly unfortunate that this decision should have been made in a district which is of such great economic importance, for the Germans will be able to make it appear that our real object has been to deprive Germany of coal mines, which are essential to her existence.

There was to be a meeting of the British Empire Delegation and the Cabinet on Sunday, and the Prime Minister asked for memoranda on this point, and from me on the Saar Valley, in preparation. At the end of the meeting I mentioned the Romanian point to Mr Balfour and the Prime Minister and just got Lord Robert Cecil as he was going to lunch, and told him also what I knew as to the afternoon meeting.[1]

The meeting of the Plenary Session was very interesting and amusing. It was held in the *salle à manger*;[2] Clemenceau in the chair, with Wilson on one side and Lloyd George on the other, all the delegations seated in order round the table, the secretaries at the back tables. The meeting began by Clemenceau calling on Bratianu, who at once made a protest complaining of the delay in delivering them the copies of the treaty. Clemenceau at once lost his temper, spoke with great rapidity so that it was difficult to hear what he said, was very rude to Bratianu, and then turned all his indignation against Dutasta. Bratianu's protest was, as far as I can make out, completely justified. The text had not reached him at the time agreed upon. Bratianu then made another speech in which he

[1] For the minutes of the meeting, see FO 374/22, pp. 230–5. A summary can be found in Nelson, op. cit., pp. 333–8.
[2] For the minutes of the Plenary Session, see P.P.C. III, 395–410.

M

objected to the financial clauses, some of the frontier arrangements, but most of his speech was devoted to the Minority clauses. As to the financial clauses, Tardieu made a short speech and it was agreed that they should be withdrawn and not presented to the Austrians on Monday. Bratianu spoke very strongly on the main principle that the Allies were pledged that small states should be treated on a complete equality with the large states; the proposed procedure, as he pointed out, was an infringement of their sovereignty. He was followed by Krammarsch, Paderewski, Trumbitch and Venizelos. Krammarsch proposed in the clause to omit the words 'the Allied and Associated Powers', so that it would read 'Romania agrees to accept such provisions as are necessary' instead of 'such provisions as the Allied and Associated Powers consider necessary'. This of course would deprive the Allies of the power to impose terms and would clearly not meet the situation. Paderewski was very moderate and I think his speech meant that he would make no difficulty. Trumbitch objected to the different treatment of, for instance, Yugoslavia and Italy, and laid stress on the point that any guarantees must apply merely to the new territory and not to old Serbian territory. This meant that they would be allowed to do what they liked, for instance, in Macedonia. I pointed this out afterwards to Mr Balfour, who had not taken the point. Venizelos said that the proper means of dealing with the matter was to have discussion between the principal Powers and the states interested. Wilson made a speech of some length which was impressive. He took the line that it was owing to the exertions of the great Powers that Romania and the other states had got their independence or their increase of territory, and very strongly emphasized the point that the new order was to be guaranteed by the Great Powers. It was their strength on which the smaller states depended and on them, therefore, was the responsibility. If they were to guarantee the settlement they must see to it that it was a just one and that causes of disorder and conflict were not left. There were historical reasons why this matter could not be neglected. He avoided everything which could appear invidious; no mention was made of the Jews, but he said enough to indicate what was in his mind. He laid stress on the point that the American nation, which had the highest ideals, could not be asked to support a peace unless they were assured that it was just. Lloyd George and Balfour nodded approval during his speech. Bratianu answered again; while he was speaking, Lloyd George turned round, and in a very loud aside said: 'This damned fellow; he cannot even get coats for his soldiers without us!', an observation which, though it presents a substantial truth, might perhaps have been expressed more discreetly. The result of the whole thing was that the Four were to reconsider the point. I do not know what decision they have come to.[1]

After the meeting I went back and hastily composed a memorandum on the Saar Valley for the meeting of the Cabinet and British Empire Delegation today, which I took in for Clement Jones at about 8 o'clock. I have received a notice that I am to hold myself in readiness today (Sunday) from 11 o'clock onwards in case I am needed.

Extract from letter to Mr Namier (F.O.)   *2 June 1919*

One point I should like to have your opinion on. In our draft treaty with Poland, which you have, we had conferred Polish nationality on all residents on 1 August 1914. We chose that date because we understood that there had been considerable forced migrations of the population during the war; we wanted to include all those who were living in Poland before the war, but had been driven out, but to exclude those whom the Germans had introduced. The Drafting Committee proposed to change the date to 'the date of the coming into force of the treaties with Germany, etc.', which means about the end of this month. I am not disposed at present to accept this. I should like any advice that you can give me on the matter as quickly as possible. It may be too late as the thing will have to be settled within a day or two, but probably I can get it postponed until Wednesday.

[There follows a résumé of the previous document.]

We are also having interesting discussion on the guarantee of the League of Nations for our minority rights. I got in Lord Robert Cecil to help me; he is taking up the matter strongly and I hope we shall get something satisfactory inserted in the treaty, but the French do not like it and the Americans are curiously unsatisfactory. Miller has gone and we have only Hudson,[2] who is very young and inexperienced and frightened of coming to any decision on his own responsibility. The situation is not easy; without Cecil I do not think I could have done anything.

Extract from letter to Mr Randall[3] (F.O.)   *4 June 1919*

... I hope that eventually they may make a business-like job of the Austrian treaty; they cannot do it, especially on the financial and reparation

[1] The Council of Four approved draft letters answering the reservations of the Romanian and Serbian Delegations on 4 June. See P.P.C. VI, 181.

[2] Manley O. Hudson, an adviser to the American Delegation on legal affairs and the alternate representative for David Hunter Miller on several commissions and on the New States Committee.   [3] A. W. G. Randall, a member of the Foreign Office News Department.

side, without consulting the Austrians themselves. I do not know whether they will condescend to give up their principles as far as this. Of course the Italians are a great difficulty; they are just as obstructive and tiresome in dealing with Austria as the French are in dealing with Germany. I feel sure that we ought to work for a good understanding between the states which have grown up out of the old Austria, so as to bring about, if possible, an orientation of Vienna in that direction rather than a union of German Austria with Germany. I am very much disturbed about the Tyrol; to give it to Italy seems to be the most unjustifiable action of the Conference and I cannot understand how Wilson ever came to consent to it,[1] but we have found here that it is impossible to place any real reliance upon Americans if we attempt to carry through Wilsonian principles....

As to Austria and the Germans in Bohemia, I look on it definitely as a question of frontier. Most of the Germans in Bohemia are in districts which could not possibly be united to Austria; as they therefore do not fall within the frontiers of new Austria, new Austria ceases to have any official interest in them. I believe there are certain small districts in the south of Moravia and Bohemia which might conceivably have been transferred to Austria; this is a question which might be argued, but my point is that German Austria had not in virtue of the old position of Vienna any claim to interfere in any way in any part of the Austrian Empire, whatever the inhabitants of it may be, which is outside its own frontiers. In the same way, Czechoslovakia has no voice or no claim to represent or protect those Slovaks, and they are a considerable number, who are left in Hungary.

4 June 1919

Note. At a meeting of the Council of Four it was determined that a Committee should be appointed 'to work out the basis of articles for amending the portions of the draft treaty of peace with Germany concerning the eastern frontiers'. The following were appointed to be members of the Committee: Dr Lord (USA), Mr Headlam-Morley (GB), General le Rond (France) and Marquis della Torretta (Italy). Their terms of reference were clearly defined. On 6 June the question was raised by President Wilson as to the position of the original Polish Committee, and it was agreed that 'the Polish Commission should for the present reserve taking action with regard to the German treaty, leaving the matter in the hands of the special committee'.[2]

[1] President Wilson in this case accepted a 'natural' geographical frontier for Italy and one assuring her economic unity. See P.P.C. V, 185, and VI, 213.
[2] See P.P.C. VI, 186-7, 221.

Memorandum   *5 June 1919*

At an earlier stage I was in favour of trying to get some system by which the representatives of the minorities could appeal directly to the Council of the League. Further discussion and investigation has convinced me that it would be difficult under any circumstances to do so, and in particular, I should feel very reluctant under present conditions, particularly in view of the discussion which took place at the Plenary Session last Saturday, to impose upon Poland, Romania and the other states the necessity of allowing individual citizens or groups of citizens of these states to appeal directly to the Court of the League of Nations, over the head of and as against their own Government. This would be represented as a serious infraction of sovereignty, which would inevitably draw forth most energetic protests. These protests would be dangerous because they could point out that the Great Powers themselves did not allow such an appeal to their own nationals.

It seems to me, therefore, that the soundest view to take is that the League of Nations can only deal with disputes between states; infringement of the clauses can only be brought to the cognizance of the League of Nations in so far as they are a breach of a treaty obligation; it follows from this that only the states themselves can be principals in any dispute of which the Court can take cognizance.

After studying carefully Article 14 of the Covenant,[1] it seems to me that this is the only possible interpretation. I think that if the American version were adopted, the Court would necessarily have to decide that they could not hear private individuals or groups of individuals, and that in fact the minorities themselves would not get the privilege which it is attempted to secure for them. If this view is correct, it is all the more undesirable that the Great Powers should, under the circumstances, incur the very grave unpopularity which would attach to them if they tried to no purpose to impose such a possibility upon the small states. But my chief reason is that if we once let it be supposed that anyone but states can appear before the Court, we should be opening the way to a very dangerous agitation for allowing minorities in other countries the same privilege.

---

[1] Article 14 reads as follows: 'The Council shall formulate and submit to the Members of the League for adoption plans for the establishment of a permanent Court of International Justice. The Court shall be competent to hear and determine any dispute of an international character which the parties thereto submit to it. The Court may also give an advisory opinion upon any dispute or question referred to it by the Council or by the Assembly.'

Note addressed to Sir Hubert Llewellyn Smith   5 June 1919

A Committee has been appointed by the Council of Four, of which I am the British member, to carry out certain revisions in the treaty with Germany, which have in principle been agreed upon. Among these are the two provisions, a copy of which is attached.[1] The matter is urgent, and it would greatly facilitate the work if members of the British Delegation who are responsible for these matters could draft articles for insertion in the treaty to carry out the instructions of the Council of Four.

I should be very much obliged if you could let me have a draft of this kind as soon as possible.

Extract from letter to Mr Edwyn Bevan (F.O.)   11 June 1919

... In a way I was glad to be put on the Commission for the Eastern Frontiers of Germany, but I very much wish that nothing had been said in the papers about it;[2] it makes it very much more difficult if these things are published. The position was an extraordinarily difficult one, both for public and personal reasons; at the present moment I think I had better say nothing at all about the result; it is to be discussed at the Council of Four this afternoon and I am to be there, to which I look forward with some trepidation, as the whole atmosphere is extremely electric and the prolonged controversy, combined with the heat, is putting everyone's nerves on edge, and I am myself beginning to find it very difficult to keep my balance and my temper; I never mind losing my temper with an Englishman, and not much with an American, but when Frenchmen and Italians come in, then of course it would be fatal.

I think that probably we differ about the justice of the territorial settlement in Eastern Europe. I have always maintained that to give Danzig to Poland without guarantees was quite unjustifiable. I am prepared to defend the present solution by which Danzig is taken away from Germany, but not annexed to Poland. The question of West Prussia is in my mind more difficult than that of Danzig. I have never been quite able to make up my mind about it, but on the whole I am not prepared to say that the solution in the treaty is an unjust one. Anyhow no one is proposing to alter it and that will stay, at any rate so far as I am at present informed. The chief concession proposed, as you will see from the papers, is with regard to

[1] These concerned the plebiscite in Upper Silesia and the supplies of coal, etc.
[2] The members of the Committee were given in *The Times* of 7 June. The work of the Committee is discussed in detail in Nelson, op. cit., pp. 349–56.

Upper Silesia; from the general political point of view it is clear that this is the danger spot of Europe and any solution which will prevent the outbreak of open war here ought to be welcomed.

Letter to Sir Maurice Hankey   11 June 1919

I wonder whether the Four are likely soon to come to a decision on the point which our Committee on New States referred to them as to the method of the guarantee of the League of Nations for the minority rights. The whole of the rest of the treaty is now ready and if we could get a decision on this we could set it up in its final form for approval, and the matter could then be submitted for signature to the Poles and the Czechoslovaks, and the whole affair concluded. It would be a great relief if we could get this finished off.

Extract from letter to Mr Namier (F.O.)   11 June 1919

Many thanks for your letter; you will excuse my answering it in detail at this moment, all the more so that I rather think we differ fundamentally. I cannot reconcile myself to the position that it is the right thing to satisfy the Poles by giving them more than they can justly demand on their western frontiers, so as to relieve the tension on the eastern. Of course this arises from the fact that I really know nothing about the problems on the eastern frontier of Poland, but I feel that it would be a fatal thing to give to the Poles more than they can justly demand at the expense of Germany; in my mind Germany is more important than the White Russians.

I hope that our minorities clauses will soon be finished; I have had so much to do with other things the last week that the work has had to take rather a second place and we are being held up because the particular nature of the guarantee by the League of Nations had to be referred to the Four, and they have not yet given their decision. As soon as that is done, I hope the whole thing will be finished. What I have been trying to get is a real and effective guarantee, but after long consideration I did not feel that it was wise to ask that the minorities themselves should be given the right of appeal to the League of Nations. I went round to the rather strict legal view, that the League of Nations was a compact between states and that only states should have immediate access, either to the Council or to the Court. I got Cecil to come and talk to the Committee about the point; he differs from me completely, but frankly I do not think that his view is reconcilable with the text of the Covenant of the League of Nations, and politically it would be very difficult to press it at this moment. However, the problem has been put up to the Council of Four and they must decide; they have so much to do that it will, I expect, be some days before we get their verdict.

The whole situation here seems to me to be getting very dangerous and critical, especially owing to the advance in the east of Europe.[1] The real source of the difficulty seems to me to be this, that the same people have to determine all the problems of the peace and also to determine the action to be taken from day to day, and this is more than anyone can manage. The result is that matters which require urgent action, dealing with the military situation, the Baltic provinces and Hungary, etc., are postponed and it is obvious that a condition of affairs is arising which may wreck the Peace before it is signed. Keynes has thrown up the sponge and gone away, and Falk[2] (I do not know if you know him) also; this is a very serious loss, as it leaves our staff weakened at the most critical period on one of the most important points. A lot of the Americans have gone, some because of private business and some as a protest against the Peace, others in order to try and influence opinion in America. I have seen a little of Lord for the first time during the last three or four days; we differ of course on many points, but I find him less difficult than I had been led to expect.

11 June 1919

Note. The Report of the Committee on the Eastern Frontiers of Germany was considered by the Council of Four; the members of the Committee were present and General le Rond made a statement as to the points on which the Committee were in agreement and as to those on which they disagreed. The report was approved with certain modifications and was sent to the Drafting Committee the following day in order that the necessary revision in the German treaty should be made.[3]

Extract from letter to Mr G. Saunders (F.O.)   *12 June 1919*

I am very much interested in your observations on France, and especially on Tardieu; I know he had the reputation of being an unscrupulous enemy

[1] This apparently refers to the Soviet regime of Bela Kun in Hungary and to the capture of Riga on 22 May by General von der Goltz from the Bolsheviks. In April the Poles had forced the Bolsheviks to abandon Vilna and in June began an advance eastward.
[2] Oswald T. Falk, a member of the Financial Section of the British Delegation.
[3] See P.P.C. VI, 316–17; Mantoux, II, 382–7.

of England; very likely he is that still, but if so, he is sufficiently clever not to show his hand. I have had a good deal to do with him and find him very easy and agreeable to work with; I have been quite frank with him and told him when necessary that the whole French policy, as for instance, about Alsace-Lorraine, was radically and completely wrong and unjustifiable. I made it clear at the same time that we did not intend to oppose it because we recognized that this was a matter on which France was to judge for herself. I did not want him to think that when we supported him it was because we approved of what he was doing, or thought it wise. He has always taken observations of that kind very well, but once he looked as if he was rather taken aback. Once or twice we had a fundamental difference of opinion about some of the Alsace-Lorraine clauses and the matter had to be taken up to the Council of Four. He defended his view, which was eventually almost contemptuously rejected by the Council of Four; Lloyd George said, 'I think Monsieur Tardieu has been ill advised in putting forward these claims; they are a bit too thick.' Clemenceau acquiesced at once and the matter was finished. On going out of the room Tardieu said that he never wanted to defend them, but he was forced to do so by representatives of other ministries; that he had not a free hand and that often put him in a very difficult situation. The truth about him anyhow is this, that he is so clever, has had so much experience and is so quick, that he can distinguish better than many Frenchmen what is defensible and attainable and what is not. The chief point I have noticed that he is not playing the game is the use of the French press; there is no doubt that there was a good deal of leakage and that matters which we were keeping strictly secret were the subject of articles, anti-English, in the *Temps* and other papers. This I attributed to him. I do not think it has made the slightest difference. On one or two points on which I think he was possibly playing a double game, he has certainly been defeated. He, like all other Frenchmen, was obviously at bottom very sore at not getting the 1814 frontiers; I think that they were trying to manipulate the Saar scheme in such a way as to insure the territory falling to France at the end of the fifteen years. I had a long struggle about this; the Americans did not play up, but eventually the obnoxious clauses were cut out, as I knew they would have to be, in consequence of the German remonstrances. . . .

It has now been decided to have a plebiscite in Upper Silesia. As you know, I have always been very anxious about the situation there, and I am sure that it would not have been possible to hand over this district direct to the Poles. The disadvantage of a plebiscite is that it will leave the question undecided for some considerable period – I think it is to be one or two years. This means Allied occupation with a Commission and Allied troops, which the military will not like, but anything is better than having an acute state of civil war, which would have been the alternative. We have also got important concessions to Germany, giving them a right to purchase coal from Upper Silesia even if the mines are eventually transferred to Poland, and freeing them from the danger of confiscation of German property in the territories transferred to Poland. This, combined with some minor modifications of the frontier, is I think a real improvement, which ought to make it possible for the Germans to sign so far as this part of the settlement goes.

We are putting up a stiff defence of the Saar Valley scheme; I am enclosing a copy of a minute which I wrote in case you have not seen it. What distresses me is that after all we are going to let down Belgium about Luxemburg. This is, as far as I can understand, merely the result of the curious want of energy and initiative which all through has characterized the conduct of the more purely diplomatic side of the business. We do not seem to have taken any trouble to do what we could to help Belgium; we have not taken her into our confidence, not discussed things frankly, or explained, as we surely should have done, the reasons why in some cases we could not support her claims.[1]

13 June 1919

Note. The Report of the Committee on the Eastern Frontiers of Germany as to the answer to be given to the German note was considered and approved, subject to certain amendments.[2]

Extract from letter to Mr Philip Baker   *13 June 1919*

I have just been looking at some of the papers about the pressure to be brought on Switzerland to force her to become a member of the League of Nations. I understand that the difficulty is that Switzerland does not wish to lose the privileges of neutrality which at present she enjoys, while of course if a sovereign state joins the League of Nations, it must necessarily undertake obligations which every sovereign state, a member of the League, has to hold in carrying out the decisions of the League.

I will confess that there seems to be a good deal to be said, if not for the

---

[1] A reference to Belgian hopes for an economic union with Luxemburg.
[2] See P.P.C. VI, 398. The Committee's discussions and report are in FO/608/126. For the organization of the Committee, see 4 June, p. 138 above.

Swiss point of view at present put forward, at least for a point of view which is not very far removed from it. I should have thought that the territory in which the seat of the League is placed should be in a different position from that of any other state: it should, that is, not be a sovereign state, a member of the League, with the responsibility of joining with other members of the League; it should rather be a territory in international relations, passive, without responsibility, dependent entirely upon the protection of the League.

That the whole of Switzerland should be put into such a position might appear rather exaggerated; I should have suggested that the best thing of all would be that Geneva should be established in this special condition. But even as regards Switzerland as a whole, I should venture to suggest that there was something to be said for the whole territory being given a special position if the Swiss Government and the Swiss people would be willing to accept all the implications of this. I am very anxious about the future of Switzerland with the French on one side, the Italians on another, and the Germans on another, if at any time the rather artificial equilibrium should collapse. The preservation of Switzerland seems to be a European necessity, and if we can preserve it more easily by leaving it under a form of neutrality different from that enjoyed by any other state, there would be much to be said for this.

Letter to Sir Maurice Hankey   15 June 1919

You will, I hope, receive tomorrow the full text of the treaty with Poland drawn up by the Committee on New States. May I once more draw attention to the extreme urgency of the matter. It is essential that this treaty should be ready to be signed by Poland on the same day as that on which the treaty with Germany is signed. This may be, I assume, possibly within a week. It is the more important that there should be no delay as I have learned confidentially through a reliable source that it has been intimated to the Poles that they need not really trouble about the matter as the Quai d'Orsay do not intend the treaties to be signed, and the suggestion is that dilatory methods will be used. I do not know whether as regards the French this is true, but the very fact that this is being said makes it all the more essential that we should press on the thing with the greatest urgency. Although the treaty has been officially communicated both to the Polish Government at Warsaw and to the Polish Legation here,[1]

[1] A copy of Clemenceau's covering letter and the treaty can be found in P.P.C. XIII, 791–808.

we have had no response from either. The only thing to do therefore, is to get the final matter reserved by the Four decided, and then at once to communicate the treaty to Poland with an official intimation that they will be expected to sign it on the same day on which the Treaty with Germany is signed. The same procedure will have to be followed in regard to the Czechs.

I do not know whether at the last moment the Poles will make serious difficulties; if they do, they will probably adopt the course of asking for further delay. As against this, our answer would be that they have not taken advantage of the opportunity given to them to communicate their criticisms with regard to the minority clauses. I must note, however, that the commercial clauses have not yet been communicated to them. If they made serious difficulty, the question would arise as to the means to be adopted to overcome their reluctance or refusal. I must point out that we are absolutely bound in honour to insist at any rate on the minority clauses, and a reference to them will be included, I believe, in the answer to the German note.

You asked me to communicate with the Poles about the answer which is being expected from Monsieur Paderewski. I spoke to Monsieur Zaleski, who is one of his confidential advisers about the matter and he said that he would see to it. He was not himself informed as to the matter.

Letter to Sir Maurice Hankey   *16 June 1919*

The Reports of our Committee on Poland and Czechoslovakia ought to reach you tonight, but it is very difficult to be sure that they will, so I am sending you unofficially the enclosed copies. As so often happens, these copies are full of misprints, but they show, I think, sufficient for the purposes of the Four, what the reports contain. If by any chance you do not receive the official copies before the meeting of the Four tomorrow, the fact that you have these advance copies privately in your possession might enable you none the less to get the matter considered. Berthelot today at the meeting of the Committee read a long letter from the French Minister at Warsaw to the effect that the Poles had not the slightest intention of signing; this I expect is bluff, but speed and decision are necessary if the whole thing is not to be lost.

Extract from letter to Mr Namier (F.O.)   *17 June 1919*

I have just been reading the long telegram to Sir Percy Wyndham, in which I seem to recognize your handiwork; I must congratulate you on it.[1] We have been having rather a busy time lately and I have found it difficult to keep up with all the active steps necessary in regard to the minorities question. We have been delayed by the difficulty of getting a decision from the Four; I have been pressing as hard as I can and hope that they are going to take the matter this afternoon and then the whole thing will be finished. They have been so occupied with the answer to the German note and the alterations to the Treaty of Peace that they have had little time for anything else; I believe they are going to have a holiday tomorrow, so the situation is getting serious as unless one can get an immediate decision, I do not see how we can get the Polish signature on the same day as the German treaty is signed, supposing it is signed. I imagine that there will probably be secret forces working for delay, and delay is so easy that unless one does a great deal of fussing about, things of great importance may easily be neglected.

I have just had a visit from Young[2] on his way home from Prague; as usual he has a good deal of sound information; I hope he will see Sir George Clerk. Seton-Watson has also come back and is going to London today; you ought to make a point of seeing him too. He sent us very useful letters from Prague.

Owing to the trouble about the Germans, Austrian affairs have been rather in the background; have you seen Renner's protest?[3] Much of it seems to be quite justified, but it is almost hopeless to attempt here to get any serious interest taken in Austria; there is practically no one on the spot who has really sound knowledge and experience, and of course the Italians are very difficult. They are always trying to get some advantages for themselves. However, if the Germans do sign, then things will be immensely eased all round, and I expect that they will, after making a great protest. Our present difficulty is that we have not available a single copy of the revised treaty so that we do not really know what modifications have been introduced into it. These small things mean an immense waste of time and energy and add to the difficulty of getting the important things done.

[1] This may refer to the F.O. answer to Sir Percy Wyndham's Warsaw telegram of 13 June. In it he reported that the British officers sent to inquire into the situation in East Galicia had corroborated reports of Ukrainian atrocities against the Poles and had also reported that the Ukrainian peasants welcomed Polish rule since it meant peace. FO 688/1/Misc. no. 47. Namier was of the opinion that the British officers sent to East Galicia had been shown only what the Poles wanted them to see, e.g. his remarks of 5 June on the report of Major A. L. Paris, FO 371/3907/f.20811/pc. 8284.

[2] R. F. Young, of the Board of Education.

[3] The Austrian observations on the draft treaty (Treaty of Saint-Germain) were presented to the Conference on 10 June. See Temperley, *History of the Peace Conference*, vol. IV, p. 394.

Perhaps I look on things in rather a critical light as I was kept up the whole of Sunday night working almost without stopping from 9 o'clock on Sunday morning till 1 o'clock on Monday afternoon on work much of which could quite well have been avoided if there had been any reasonable foresight.

Zimmern has just arrived here; I believe he has come out for the Supreme Economic Council; the last time I wrote to him I said that he would not remain long at Aberystwyth.

17 June 1919

Note. The Council of Four dealt with a draft treaty with Poland submitted by the New States Committee. A long letter from Monsieur Paderewski was read to the meeting by Mr Lloyd George, who said that it was a fundamental challenge to the whole policy of the Powers concerning New States. It was agreed to refer the letter to the Committee on New States to consider the objections raised to their treaty and to see whether some of these objections could not be met. It was further agreed that states only, not individuals, should have the right of appeal to the permanent Court of International Justice.[1]

Extract from letter to Mr Randall (F.O.)   *17 June 1919*

... I am afraid I have been too busy to reply before as we have had to get off the answer to the German note, and this, like everything else, had to be done under immense pressure. Difficulty is added by the fact that everything is printed by the French; they of course make innumerable printer's errors in any English stuff, and these have to be corrected; of course nobody thought to get a skilled proof-reader to do this very mechanical work. I wonder what you think of it; I have read most of it so often that I am tired to death of it and can hardly judge it. The introductory letter, which is by Philip Kerr, is a very able piece of writing, but seems to me too much like an article in a review;[2] it ought to have been much more like a serious State paper. This, I am told, is Clemenceau's criticism. The rest is very unequal and much of it unsatisfactory. I am much annoyed by the whole thing because if it had been properly edited and revised, a really good piece of work might have been made of it.

---

[1] Paderewski's letter can be found in Lloyd George Papers, F/57/5/2. See also P.P.C. VI, 529, 530, 535–40.
[2] For Kerr's letter see P.P.C. VI, 926–35.

However, the Committee of Reivision was only appointed on Friday; the whole thing had to be ready and printed by midday on Monday, and it was quite out of the question to get any thorough revision. Philip Kerr was the British member of the Revising Committee but he ran me in to help him, and that meant practically continuous work from Saturday till yesterday afternoon. . . .[1]

The Austrian treaty has been rather neglected lately but I imagine we shall have to turn to it now. So far as I understand it, much of it seems to me the sort of thing which might have been published in *Alice in Wonderland*; it has almost the same relation to actual facts. Renner's protest, which you have doubtless seen, is much of it just, but of course his claim to represent the Germans of Bohemia must be steadily rejected. The cession of mid-Tyrol to Italy seems to me to be absolutely unjustifiable. I do not know whether there will be any opportunity of getting a revision of this; I shall do all I can to get it reconsidered, but it is rather wearing to go on trying to get an alteration in things that have already been settled. . . .

With regard to the Rhine and the lateral canal. I quite agree with you. I tried hard to get this altered; the only thing to be said for it is that it is not nearly as bad as the clauses which the French originally wanted to put in. The thing was done by the Ports and Waterways people, and as so often happens here, they kept it in their own hands and it was extremely difficult to get any kind of political criticism listened to. As they were working under the Economic Section, they ought at least to have looked after British interests, but the whole discussion was warped by the fact that they accepted the first French draft as a basis of discussion. The result was that all the prolonged and at times acrimonious negotiations were devoted to cutting down the worst French demands, but it would have been much wiser if our people had put in an alternative and insisted on that being taken as a basis. Had they done this and got the support of the Americans, something respectable might have come out of it. I had rather a sharp argument about the matter some weeks ago, but could get no effective support.

Extract from diary   *19 June 1919*

I propose to put down a very brief record of the events of the last fortnight so far as I have been personally concerned, and, let me add, so far as I

---

[1] Headlam-Morley wrote that section of the Allied reply which dealt with German criticism of the Polish settlement. See P.P.C. VI, 945-9.

can recollect. But the pressure of work has been so extreme, the number of topics to be dealt with so various, the importance of the matters at issue so great, and the difficulty of getting any decisions or knowing what the decisions are when they have been given so constant, that even after this short space of time, it is almost impossible to get a clear recollection of what has happened.

A new stage in the negotiations began when the German reply was received on 29 May. The first task was to get it translated. Apparently only one copy was available and the Prime Minister required that the translation should be completed in twenty-four hours. This threw an immense amount of work on to the staff and it was done on the whole with great success. From this I was exempted as I was supposed to be too much occupied with other things. The note, having been translated and made available, raised the whole question as to the character of the Peace. On I think it was Saturday morning, I was summoned to the rue Nitot, where I found the Prime Minister, Mr Balfour, the Private Secretaries, Paton and Esme Howard discussing the nature of any concessions which might be made in the Polish clauses. The Prime Minister said that the one thing he was anxious about was that the Germans should sign and he wanted to know what modifications they might justly require. Paton had his maps and there was a good deal of talk about the details of the frontier. Paton explained how in certain cases the frontier had been unjustly biased against the Germans and this led to the conclusion that the criticisms they had made in their note on certain details of the frontier were justified. There was also a good deal of discussion about Upper Silesia, and I strongly supported the proposal for having a plebiscite there. There was an interesting discussion between the Prime Minister and Mr Balfour (the details of which I cannot recall at this moment), but it ended with a general agreement that there should be a plebiscite in Upper Silesia. Before this General Smuts had circulated a memorandum expressing his serious dissent from the general terms of the treaty. I wrote a letter, a copy of which will be found in my correspondence,[1] to him. Mr Barnes did the same thing. I had some conversation with Mr Barnes on the matter and suggested to him the point of view that unsatisfactory though the treaty was in many points, the important thing was to use every effort to get the Germans to sign, because it was quite obvious to see that the treaty could not be carried out in the form in which it stood, and it would be easy to get alterations afterwards. He said that this was all very well for me, but I did not have to sign the treaty, and he would find it very difficult to

[1] See p. 118 above.

put his name to a document of this kind. This is the view which General Smuts also took. On the Sunday there was a meeting of the British Empire Delegation, at which members of the Cabinet were also present. I was instructed to hold myself in readiness in case I was wanted, so I sat in the Majestic most of the day waiting for a telephone message which never came and thereby lost the opportunity of going out for a 'joy ride' with Abraham. In preparation for this meeting I had written a defence of the Saar Valley scheme.

As a result of these discussions it was eventually agreed by the Council of Four that there should be certain modifications of the treaty and a fresh Committee was appointed to consider the modifications in the Polish clauses, on which I was the British representative. The other members were General le Rond, who was Chairman, Lord, the American, and Marquis della Torretta for Italy. The Committee was appointed on 4 June. The situation was for me an extremely difficult one, for all the other members of the Committee had been either members of, or closely associated with the original Polish Commission, whose decisions were to be reversed. Our instructions made the situation even more difficult. We first of all received definite instructions to draft modifications of the Polish clauses in order (1) to leave with Germany three districts which were to be assigned to Poland, in which there was a German majority; (2) to arrange for a plebiscite in Upper Silesia; (3) to introduce economic concessions to the Germans in regard to Upper Silesia supposing it were eventually given to Poland, viz: (a) to give the Germans the right to purchase coal on the same terms as the Poles, (b) to exempt property held by the Germans from confiscation without just payment.[1]

In addition to this it was determined that the general reference to the Committees for considering modifications in the treaty and drafting a reply to the German note should, so far as regards Poland, be sent to our Committee and not to the original Polish Commission. I was responsible for this, as I pointed out to Hankey that a very awkward situation would arise if our Committee were to sit and deal with these matters from one point of view, while the Polish Commission at the same time considered them from another point of view. There had been a very awkward scene the day before. Monsieur Cambon had summoned the Polish Commission without authorization; Kisch, therefore, after receiving instructions, went down to the meeting of the Commission and simply stated that there was no authority for summoning the meeting and that he could not take any part in the proceedings. He thereupon left the room.

[1] See P.P.C. VI, 186–7, 190.

N

I asked Kisch to come with me to the first meeting of our Committee. The Chairman[1] began by suggesting that our first duty was to review the modifications which we might suggest, and obviously he intended to draft our report on the lines, not of carrying out our instructions, but of criticizing our instructions. I strongly objected to this and nearly all the meetings of the Committee were prejudiced by this difference of opinion as to our procedure. I had, however, the support of Lord, who, though he expressed in the strongest terms his dissent from the instructions we had received, acted in a very straightforward way in recognizing that it was our first duty to carry them out. He went so far as to say, and it was put down in the records, that the idea of a plebiscite in Upper Silesia was monstrous. I found myself from the beginning thrown into complete opposition to all the other members. However, ultimately I succeeded in getting the report in a general way based on the lines which seemed to me the only ones legitimate, that is, there were to be two reports, one carrying out our instructions and the other drafting the reply to the German note and suggesting any further alterations which might be desired. The French, supported by the Americans, were very anxious that the modifications in favour of the Germans should be balanced by other modifications of the frontier in favour of the Poles; we had received a third set of instructions from the Council of Four authorizing one such modification which Paderewski had asked for, i.e. the district of Namslau in Silesia. This therefore was easily agreed to. They wanted further modifications in the district of Schlochau, Bomst, Filehne. Filehne is the district from which two Polish peasants had found their way to Paris and le Rond said that they had come to his office and with tears besought him that they might be given to Poland. I said that I could easily get hundreds of Germans who could come with tears in their eyes and beg not to be ceded to Poland. This did not seem to make much impression. The proposed modifications were referred to a sub-Committee on boundaries in order to procure the necessary statistics. I said I was quite prepared to consider these proposals, but fought very hard against the principle of compensation. The French were always wanting to argue the thing on the ground of compensation; they seemed to assume that it was our duty to see that if an injustice was done to some Poles by leaving them in Germany, we should do an equal injustice to some Germans by transferring them to Poland. The view I took was that each case should be considered on its merits and I consistently refused to allow the word or idea of compensation to appear in the report. In this I was successful. It seemed to me that

[1] For minutes of the Committee's meetings, see FO 608/126/17493.

it was owing to the use of this principle of compensation that some of the worst features in the original Polish report were due. On the report of the sub-Committee, it appeared that there was no justification for giving Bomst to Poland; this therefore was rejected. After a long and difficult argument, which spread over two or three meetings, I agreed to the other districts, but got in exchange for that the separation of the two reports and an agreement on the main principle on which the reports should be drafted. During the course of the discussion I went to the Prime Minister in order to ask him whether it would be inconvenient to him that I should be in a minority of one on the report presented. He said that he was in a very difficult position; he wanted to get the Germans to sign; he insisted on the definite point of a plebiscite in Upper Silesia; he was prepared to give way on smaller points and it turned out that it might be convenient to him that I should hold out on some of these points so that he might then throw me over; that would strengthen his position.

There was another serious difference of opinion as to the length of the plebiscite period in Upper Silesia. I wanted a short period of about six months; they began by asking for a period of two to three years. On this we asked for further instructions and were summoned to the Council of Four. We were not invited in, but the President came out and told us that what they would like would be that the arguments on the two sides should be presented so that they could decide. He obviously wanted to see Lord and myself alone, but General le Rond was there, took the conversation into his own hands and rather pressed his point of view that the Committee had not merely to carry out modifications, but to criticize them. The President said nothing else to this but looked rather annoyed. In accordance with our instructions we then drew up two alternative schemes for the plebiscite and went down again to the Four with our report, which was in rather an unsatisfactory condition. Le Rond was asked to make his statement; he began in French; he was asked to speak in English so as to save time; he demurred and said he could not do so; however, he then made a very vigorous statement in English, explaining the point of view for the long plebiscite. The President then suggested that I should make my statement for the shorter plebiscite. The Prime Minister said it was quite unnecessary; he had been very much struck by what General le Rond had said and did not wish to press the point. That is, he threw me over completely. He whispered to me that his reason for doing this was that he understood that the Germans wished for the longer plebiscite period; I do not know what his authority for this was. At the end he said that he had been much impressed by what General le Rond had said; there was only one point on which he completely differed from him and he thought he was quite wrong. Everyone sprang to attention and expected some serious issue to be raised. The Prime Minister then went on: 'The one matter on which General le Rond is perfectly wrong is when he said he could not speak English; I must congratulate him in the most hearty manner on the ability with which he has presented his case.' It was admirably done: General le Rond was as pleased as Punch, his vanity was entirely satisfied and it was most cleverly devised for removing the effects of the friction which might otherwise have arisen. Crowe told me afterwards that he was delighted and I gather that the gossip was that I had been completely overthrown. The further history of this is curious; Paderewski was heard by the Council of Four, said that he was in favour of the shorter period, and eventually they changed their minds and adopted my solution! Hankey told me that the Prime Minister was very pleased and said that I was right after all.[1]

Extract from diary   *19 June 1919*

On Friday (13 June) Seton-Watson, who had just come back from Prague, was lunching with me. He had sent an urgent telegram to me personally dealing with the dangerous situation created by the state of war which had arisen between Hungary and Czechoslovakia[2] and arrived himself the next day. I went to Philip Kerr and tried to get an interview between them, but I do not think one was ever arranged. Kerr then asked me to help him as he had been appointed British representative on the Committee for revising the answer to the German note. He tried to get Percy too, but they agreed that Private Secretaries could not give sufficient time. The first meeting was Friday afternoon and the work went on almost continuously till 2 o'clock on Monday afternoon. We were busy all Saturday, started on Sunday soon after nine, worked all the morning and most of the afternoon; I came back to dinner early, returned to the Quai d'Orsay at 8 o'clock, remained there till 6.30 a.m., then came back for a short rest, a bath and breakfast and went back again at 9 o'clock; about 10 o'clock Hutchinson[3] and I went down to the Imprimerie Nationale where we continued revising and passing proofs until 1 o'clock. At 1 o'clock I left him as I had an important meeting of the New States Committee at

[1] See P.P.C. VI, 449–51.
[2] On 28 March Bela Kun's Soviet Hungary had declared war on Czechoslovakia and the Hungarian army tried to regain Slovakia.
[3] H. J. Hutchinson, Private Secretary to Sir Hubert Llewellyn Smith.

3.30. He stayed on till 2.30. I asked him to help me, and also got Turner[1] of the Economic Section, who was extremely useful at the more mechanical work of proof-reading, which was very important owing to the number of misprints which always arise when the French print the English text. The work was arduous. The procedure was that the drafts went up to the Council of Four from the different Commissions who had prepared them. They passed the drafts and sent them down to us for final revision; of course we never knew whether any particular phrase was part of the original draft of the Commission who prepared the material or whether it had been inserted by the Council of Four, unless it happened that Kerr or somebody else knew precisely what had happened. It was very difficult therefore to know what authority we had for altering the drafts. This arose, for instance, in regard to the expression that the Germans might be admitted to the League of Nations 'in the early future', which occurred in the League of Nations draft; in the covering letter the phrase used was 'within a reasonable period'. The French objected that these two expressions were inconsistent with one another and wanted to get them made uniform. What I particularly wished to do was at any rate to preserve the expression 'in the early future'. The French said it was impossible to translate this into French; however we succeeded in preserving it and this, I think, is the most important thing in the whole of the answer.

21 June 1919

Note. The Council of Four considered the remarks of the New States Committee on Monsieur Paderewski's letter of 15 June. After President Wilson had read a summary of the letter it was approved, and the Committee was authorized, in consultation with the Drafting Committee, to embody the changes proposed in a final text of the treaty with Poland. They were also instructed to prepare for consideration of the Council a draft of a letter forwarding the text of the treaty to the Polish Delegation. At the request of Mr Headlam-Morley the Committee were also authorized to consider the nature of alterations in the draft treaty with Poland in order to provide that, in all except the primary schools, Jewish children should be instructed in Polish and not in the Yiddish language, thereby avoiding the risk of encouraging the use of Yiddish as one of the national languages for a part of the population of Poland.[2]

[1] W. T. Turner of the Board of Trade and technical adviser to the British Delegation on commercial and industrial questions.
[2] See P.P.C. VI, 569–73.

23 June 1919

Note. There was a long discussion at a meeting of the Council of Four, at which Mr Headlam-Morley, Mr Hudson, etc., were present, concerning the Polish treaty and the covering letter thereto. It was agreed (1) with regard to the use of languages other than Polish, that the Polish Government should be given a free hand in all schools except primary schools. But in those cases where there was a considerable minority, as provided in certain articles of the draft treaty, the children of Polish citizens speaking a language other than Polish should be given facilities for receiving instruction in the primary schools through the medium of their own language (2) the draft letter to the Polish Delegation was approved subject to a redraft of the passage dealing with schools, in accordance with the above decision.[1]

Extract from letter to Mr Carnegie (F.O.)   *23 June 1919*

Slesvig

... On Saturday week, at the last moment, without telling or consulting anyone, the Council of Four made up their minds to restrict the plebiscite to the first two zones.[2] I really know nothing more about it than this. I do not know who was present when they did it and I only heard when we were revising the reply to the Germans that a sentence referring to the plebiscite must be altered because they had come to this decision. The only comment one has to make is that if they had intended to do it, it would have been much better to have done it sooner. I have only just got a copy of the treaty as finally printed, and I have not yet been able to see how the plebiscite clauses stand.

I had a visit from Holstein[3] last week; he of course wanted to come and be condoled with about it, but on the whole he took it very well. The Danes asked also for an alteration in the article about payment. It gave us a great deal of trouble and I tried to get something which would more or less meet their wishes, but in the hurry and turmoil which attended everything at the beginning of last week, it slipped out altogether. We had also got an alteration of the plebiscite clauses with regard to Eupen and Malmédy, which improved them greatly, but that also had to be sacrificed; the Council of Four rejected it last Monday at the very last moment

[1] See P.P.C. VI, 624–8, 629, 634.
[2] See P.P.C. VI, 454.
[3] Count Holstein, a Dane residing in mid-Slesvig, who sought to secure through Headlam-Morley its inclusion within the zone of the proposed plebiscite.

after the answer to the Germans containing a reference to this alteration had been drafted and printed.[1] I was at the Imprimerie Nationale
up to 1 o'clock on Monday and had passed everything for press, when
a telephone message came in and the whole page had to be reprinted
in consequence. This is the sort of thing which of course constantly
happens.

I have been much occupied the last few days with our Polish treaty;
we have had every kind of obstacle in our way. We must, if possible, get
the treaty ready to be signed at the same time as the German treaty which,
according to latest information, will be on Wednesday. I am doubtful
whether we shall succeed as it has to get through the Drafting Committee,
who have an enormous number of other things to do; at this moment they
are occupied in discussing whether the sinking of the German fleet was
a breach of the armistice.[2] I am inclined to think they will not get the
treaty signed until Thursday, in which case I hope we shall get things ready.
It has not facilitated matters that the Council of Four came to a decision
on an important matter on Saturday and reversed it again today. All these
things are rather wearisome. It would be easy enough if we had time,
but the Poles are, I believe, deliberately adopting dilatory methods and I
expect that they get support in Paris. As printing and all other technical
details depend upon the French, one never knows whether some unexpected obstacle or delay may not be interposed.

Letter to Sir Maurice Hankey   23 June 1919

I am sorry to have to trouble you again about our Polish treaty, but a
serious deadlock has arisen since Saturday which, so far as I can see, can
only be dealt with by the Four. The matter is one which ought properly
to be brought up before the attention of the Four by Monsieur Berthelot,
the Chairman of the New States Committee. Unfortunately he is ill. I
attempted to get a meeting of the Committee yesterday to consider the
matter, but was unable to do so; I think therefore it is my duty to bring up
the matter myself at once, in view of the extreme urgency.

On Saturday the Council of Four passed a resolution that 'The

[1] The proposed change in the Eupen and Malmédy plebiscite clauses involved the substituting of a secret in place of an open ballot. Neither Mantoux nor P.P.C. include the minutes
of that Supreme Council session of 16 June at which the decision was taken not to alter the
original clauses.
[2] Rather than allow their former adversaries to assume possession of their much-prized
battle fleet, then interned at Scapa Flow, the German officers on board ordered it to be
scuttled on 21 June, to the outrage of the Allies. Seventy-three ships actually sank.

Commission was also authorized to consider the nature of the alterations required in the draft treaty with Poland in order to provide that in all except the primary schools, Jewish children should be instructed in the Polish and not in the Yiddish language, thereby avoiding the risk of encouraging the use of Yiddish as one of the national languages for part of the population of Poland.' A meeting was held that afternoon at which four delegations agreed to add the following provision to the article dealing with Jewish schools:

> Nothing in this article shall preclude the Polish Government from making the teaching of the Polish language obligatory in these schools or from making the use of the Polish language as a medium of instruction obligatory in higher classes and higher schools.

The American Delegation however refuses to assent to the insertion of this article. I understand that the objections are not to the phraseology or wording, but are based on a dissent in principle.

The majority of the Committee are of opinion that in inserting this article they are carrying out the instructions they have received; the American delegation does not interpret the resolution passed at Saturday's meeting in this sense. It is necessary, therefore, to ask for precise instructions whether or not an article to this effect is to be included. It would obviously be improper for me to attempt to put forward the arguments advanced by the American Delegation in support of their contention. I think, however, I shall be expressing the views of the rest of my colleagues if I again state the reasons why we are desirous of inserting this provision.

We were instructed to do all we could to meet the specific points raised in the note of Monsieur Paderewski. As regards the German schools we have gone far to do so, by expressly limiting the particular privileges given to the Germans to those parts of Poland which are territories transferred from Germany to Poland. In other parts of Poland the Germans will have no special educational privileges.

It was necessary to consider what could be done to meet the very strong apprehensions which were felt by the Poles as to the Jewish schools. We remain of the opinion that it is right and desirable that the Polish Jews should have the right as a religious community to their own schools. There is, however, a real danger that if these schools are placed under Jewish management, the more extreme national elements among the Jews may use these schools in order artificially to foster the use of the Yiddish language in such a way as to increase the separation which the use of this language produces between the Jews and other citizens of Poland. We do not consider that the Allied and Associated Powers would be justified in compelling the Polish State to permit public funds to be used for this purpose. On the other hand, we are informed that for the younger children, it is necessary, at any rate at present, that the instruction should be given in Yiddish, for the children come from their homes knowing no other language. We think, therefore, that the right system to be pursued is that Yiddish may be used as the language of instruction for young children, but not for older children. In particular, we should be very reluctant to see those Jews who are receiving higher education in Secondary Schools having their training in Yiddish; if they are to take their place as Polish citizens, they ought in our opinion to acquire the habit of using Polish as their natural language.

We consider that the position of Yiddish is quite different from the position of German in the transferred territories; in a town such as Bromberg, eighty per cent of the population of which is German, we hold that the Germans should be allowed to have secondary schools in which German is the medium of instruction. These schools, however, will not be under the management of the Germans, but under the direct management of the Polish State. Yiddish, moreover, is not a language such as German, which is of high value for educational and cultural purposes and we do not wish that its use for those purposes should be deliberately encouraged. Personally I should add that after the most careful consideration, and after discussing the matter with Jewish advisers, I should be very reluctant to take the responsibility of imposing such an obligation upon the Poles.

If this clause receives the approval of the Four, a small consequential amendment would have to be made in the draft letter to Monsieur Paderewski, copies of which were sent to you last night. I must urge very strongly that this matter may be settled at the earliest possible moment, for we wish to get both the letter and the text of the treaty communicated to the Poles today, in order that the treaty may be ready to be signed at the same time as the German treaty.

Letter to Sir Maurice Hankey   *24 June 1919*

I enclose herewith a corrected copy of the English version of the letter from Monsieur Clemenceau to Monsieur Paderewski, enclosing the copy of the Polish treaty.[1]

[1] See P.P.C. XIII, 791–808.

The matter and responsibility is now out of the hands of the New States Committee. I must, however, call your attention to the fact that unless precise instructions are given, we cannot be sure that the necessary preparations are being made to have the copy ready for signature; I do not know whether it has been decided, for instance, by whom it is to be signed on behalf of each of the Powers concerned; I presume that we may take it that the credentials which they have received for signing the treaty with Germany will be sufficient for this purpose also. It is quite probable that difficulties on this point will be raised by the Poles. If the Supreme Council desire to have the treaty signed on Thursday, as was intended, it is absolutely essential that they should take the necessary steps to see that their wishes are complied with. The final arrangements must necessarily be in the hands either of the French Foreign Office or of the Secretariat General, and we cannot depend upon their doing all that is necessary unless specific and precise instructions are given to them.

Copy of letter to Sir Eric Drummond 24 June 1919

One of the Military Section here came to see me again yesterday and asked me about the appointment of a representative of the Saar Valley on the Saar Valley Commission, and I have since been talking to Baker about it. It is very important to get a thoroughly sound person, who will have the confidence of the population; he must be for these purposes a good German, though not a Prussian or pan-German, a Chauvinist or a Bolshevik. I understand that the suggestion has been made that the best thing would be to have the Mayor of Saarbrücken if on inquiry he turned out to be suitable. I quite agree that it ought to be someone who has already held some important position of this kind. The difficulty is that it is practically impossible to get into touch with the people here except through the French, and probably the French will try and put up some leading man who is definitely Francophil. If it could be managed, I think the best thing would be that the League of Nations should send down someone to the spot, who should meet a small number of the leading inhabitants of the district, that is, the people who hold high official positions, the most important native employers of labour and perhaps some representatives of labour itself and talk over the matter with them quite frankly. This would have to be done during the interval between the signing and the ratification of the treaty, so that there is not much time. The arrangements would, I suppose, necessarily have to be in the hands of the French Military Commander, but if General Andauer, whom I saw when I was there, is still in charge, I think that we could trust him to do the thing honestly. Of course the proposal ought to come from the League of Nations as a whole, and not merely from the British Section, and probably two or three people would have to go in order to explore the ground. I hope you will have a British representative, and if so, that he will be someone who really knows and has experience of administration of mines and industries. The difficulties which will arise will probably come from the French management of the mines and we shall be able to meet these much better by having as British representative somebody who has technical knowledge and will have the experience which will enable him to use his position to help in administering and governing the territory for the practical welfare of the population. The great danger to avoid is having the thing run on political grounds.

Extract from letter to the
Rev. A. C. Headlam, D.D.   25 June 1919

... I am not surprised that you differ from me about the treaty, but I can only say that I have not found one single person here who approves of it as a whole. While in most cases particular clauses can be defended, the total effect is, I am sure, quite indefensible and in fact is, I think, quite unworkable.

As I see it the origin of the whole difficulty is the behaviour of the Allies since the Armistice, and in particular the long delay in beginning negotiations. For this unfortunately the British are to a great extent responsible. Everything was put aside because of the General Election, and by this we missed the opportunity of having immediately after the Armistice preliminaries of peace, in which all the main points could be settled. This could have been done perfectly well and then the very complicated matters of the financial settlement, etc., could have been arranged in a more leisurely manner. To a large extent also, the Americans are responsible, because we had to wait until Wilson came over. This delay spoiled the whole thing. You speak of the German behaviour under the Armistice; I think that our own action under the Armistice is equally or more reprehensible. One of the conditions of the Armistice was that we should let Germany have sufficient food. Four months elapsed before any food of any kind got into Germany, and the blockade, instead of being to some extent relaxed, was made even more strict than it was during the war. The newspapers kept talking about the conditions in Germany as if the Germans were pretending not to have enough food. I know that the

Northcliffe press refused to publish the telegrams from their representative in Berlin, who told the real truth. No one would believe the truth until a large number of British officers were sent to Germany, some of them passionate haters of Germany, and they were horrified at the state of things which they found. Cannot you imagine the feelings of the Germans when month after month went by after the Armistice and no step was taken towards bringing about peace or allowing food into the country, and they saw children and other people slowly dying from want of proper food? I am not in the least surprised that this has left a feeling of intense bitterness. It is I think an action, or rather an inaction, as indefensible as anything I have ever heard of. In other matters too, which I cannot explain in detail, we have repeatedly violated both the spirit and I think also the letter of the Armistice. Had we got at any rate the preliminaries of peace earlier, all the growth of bitterness which has taken place recently would have been avoided.

In another matter we are greatly to blame. The terms of the Armistice specifically determined the nature and extent of the reparation to be paid by Germany; this is categorically violated in the reparation clauses. I believe that the Cabinet never took the trouble to inquire carefully into the precise wording of the Armistice. But if we do this sort of thing, we have no right to accuse the Germans of want of good faith and no right to expect that they will trust either what we say or our intentions.

With regard to the French, I do not think that anyone in the least underestimates the difficulties of their position and I am sure there is no want of sympathy for them. The complaint that I make is that they are so extraordinarily short-sighted in their policy. They insist on small matters which will tend permanently to maintain the estrangement between the countries, but will not really weaken Germany. Many of the best Frenchmen themselves recognize this, but they are hampered, just as we are, by the press and people who allow themselves to be guided by their passions and not their reason. The best Frenchmen are very easy to deal with, but they have a great number of technical experts who put forward demands which are quite unjustifiable.

Whether or not it is better for Austria to join Germany I do not know; one thing I am clear about is that if they want to join Germany and we permanently prevent it by force, we should be just recreating in Germany the national race spirit which we want to see diminished. What I should like on the whole to see would be that German Austria should throw herself into an economic union with the other Danubian states, but here again, the policy which has been pursued towards German Austria is of such a nature as to drive them straight into the arms of Germany. This is what Tardieu, who is the cleverest Frenchman here, himself acknowledges. No one wishes to deny France everything that she can have in order to get started again, but the folly of many of the proposals, some of which have been accepted, is this: Germany cannot pay an indemnity unless her industries start again; if, therefore, you impose terms on Germany of such a kind as really to ruin her, you are depriving yourself of any hope of getting any kind of reparation. This applies especially to the coal clauses as originally proposed. I think there is no doubt that if they had been insisted upon, Germany would have been entirely without the coal necessary for starting production. You also have to remember this, that if you do not give Germany some hope to look forward to, she will be thrown permanently into opposition with the whole new system. She will inevitably be driven to an alliance with Russia and an alliance with Russia will sooner or later bring about a new conflict similar to the one which is just over. The French and others here wish to avoid this by making what they call a strong Poland, that is a Poland which will have in addition to all genuinely Polish territories large districts which were annexed by force contrary to the will of the inhabitants, simply in order to make the population of Poland and the territory of Poland greater. This seems to me a disastrous policy. It would weaken and not strengthen Poland and would inevitably bring about a coalition between Russia and Germany for a fresh partition.

The modifications introduced into the treaty have, I think, considerably improved it. Some of the clauses in the original treaty were clearly unjust. As regards Upper Silesia there is no reasonable doubt that if it had been handed straight over to Poland without a plebiscite, there would have been a violent explosion in a part of Europe where it is very difficult for us to exercise military authority, and whatever the final result would have been, it would, as people who come straight back from Warsaw tell me, have been the final blow which would have made it almost impossible for Poland to recover.

On the whole the English here have behaved very well, though they have always been hampered by the fundamental difficulties arising from our wrong policy from the beginning about reparation. The Americans have been very disappointing; I find it much easier really at bottom to get on with the French than with them. What I miss in your letter is any recognition of the point that if we are to avert a new war in the future, we must really try to build up a new system and realize that, if the new system is to work, it must be of such a kind that ultimately the Germans can co-operate in it. I think also that, like many other people, you very greatly overestimate the weight of the old spirit in Germany. Perhaps, however, this is not correctly expressed. Had we taken the opportunity which was open to us directly after the Armistice, we could have done with Germany what we liked; now we have allowed time for the bad element to come to the top again. The revolution in Germany was, as far as I can make out, as thorough, complete and sincere as any revolution of which there is any record. But we have allowed the effect of it to wear itself out during a period of futile waiting, and we have only ourselves to blame if the effect is beginning to disappear. Of course another great blunder which we made was to hasten on demobilization so rapidly, and the people who clamoured for this were just the people who were clamouring for the most extreme terms against Germany. . . .

Extract from diary   *25 June 1919*

Now that the terms of the Peace with Germany are finally settled, I propose to review those portions of them with which I have been personally concerned, for the purpose of record and criticism. That portion with which I have had to deal has been almost exclusively confined to the territorial settlements on the Continent of Europe.

(1) *Belgium*. I was appointed as second delegate to Sir Eyre Crowe on the Commission on Belgian Affairs. The only point in the terms as ultimately settled which requires notice is the cession of Malmédy and Eupen to Belgium. There was from the beginning general agreement that at least parts of Malmédy should be given to Belgium and in view of the difficulties of determining the area it was agreed that the whole of the *Kreis* of Malmédy should be included. I, however, pressed that this should not be done without the consultation of the inhabitants, and for this purpose put forward the conception of a negative plebiscite, that is one, not in which the inhabitants should be consulted whether or not they wished to be transferred, but one in which there should be given to them an opportunity of protesting against transference.[1] For this idea I am, I believe, solely responsible, and it was adopted. The British and American Delegations were at first unwilling to accept the cession of Eupen also, but having got the principle of the consultation of the population agreed to, we gave way on this point. I am not sure that we were right, and I think had I had more experience, I should have stood out on this.

[1] The minutes of the Commission on Belgian Affairs are found in *Recueil*, IV, C (6).

The matter, however, would have been of less importance had the form in which the population were to be consulted been more satisfactory. The draft of this was open to serious criticism; I hoped that it would be improved by the Drafting Committee, but on the whole they rather weakened than strengthened it, and in the form in which it was inserted in the original provisions of peace, it was open to very serious criticism. It threw upon the Belgian Government the duty of providing for the consultation of the inhabitants and their opinion could only be expressed openly on registers to be kept by the Belgian Government. Obviously this form opens the door both for intimidation and for falsification.

The revision of the terms consequent on the delivery of the German note gave a welcome opportunity for getting this clause revised. The Committee, in consequence, accepted a proposal made by Dr Haskins of the American Delegation which, though rather cumbrous, met the criticism; it threw the responsibility on the League of Nations and provided for secret voting. This was accepted without difficulty and everyone assumed that the necessary changes would be made. At the last moment, however, the Council of Four, for reasons which I have not heard, and as far as I can understand without taking any advice, simply rejected this change, and the clause remains in its original form. The result was most unsatisfactory. Eupen, which is, according to all accounts, almost exclusively German, will be transferred to Belgium, and no real means given to the people of expressing their opinion. Had I known that this would have been the result, I should never have agreed to the cession of Eupen.

(2) *Slesvig*. The Slesvig question was referred to the Belgian Committee. The only matter on which there was any possibility of a difference of opinion was the extent of the territory in which the plebiscite was to take place. The Danes asked for two zones. The French strongly pressed for a third zone, coming down to the Dannewirke. They were undoubtedly influenced by their general desire to separate as many people as possible from Germany and probably also by the wish to make a permanent estrangement between Denmark and Germany. We accepted on the ground that it was desirable to get the whole question settled once and for all, and not to allow any people to say that they had not been consulted. We were also strongly pressed by representatives of mid-Slesvig that there was a strong Danish element there and that they wished to be joined to Denmark. Their leader was Count Holstein, who came to see Carnegie and myself repeatedly, and we also saw a man of the name of Wall, a German peasant from Angelm. The extension of the plebiscite was strongly

opposed by the Danish Government, but as there was every reason to suppose that the plebiscite would be a genuine one, there seemed no reason against extending it. At the last moment we also agreed, at the request of Count Holstein, to include within the plebiscite area the district of Tönning, which is chiefly inhabited by Frisians.

Unfortunately, after this decision had been made, the Danish Government were never informed, and they were very indignant at this action being taken without consultation with them, and contrary to their express wishes. This is a characteristic piece of bad manners on the part of the Allies. A vote of regret was passed unanimously in the Rigsdag. On the revision of the treaty terms, the Committee decided to make no alteration in their recommendations. At the last moment, however, the Council of Four altered the decision and limited the plebiscite to the first two zones. I have no knowledge in this matter either of the particular influences which were brought to bear upon them.

We were also much pressed to make some revision of the financial clause, both by Count Bernstorff, the Danish Minister, and Monsieur Gluckstadt. I drew up a clause which, though it did not meet all their points, would have been an improvement on the existing clause, but it got dropped out, partly owing to delays in our own Financial Department, and partly because, though it was more or less approved at a meeting of the Committee, it never got into our final report. The original clause therefore still stands: it is not well drafted, but it will not do much harm.

(3) *The Saar Valley.* For the general conception of this scheme, I am, I believe, originally responsible. Even when we were in London and were confronted with the French claims of the 1814 frontier, it seemed to me that the best way out of the difficulty was to hand over the mines to France under the title of reparation, making such changes as might be necessary in the Government of the country in order to enable the French to exploit the mines freely. My original idea had been that the country might be definitely taken from Germany and established as a separate state. The suggestion was, I still think, a just one; to transfer the complete ownership of the mines to France would be a means of giving France very valuable property, which would be more than a compensation for the destruction of the coal mines in the north of France, and if it was once done, would create less difficulty than giving her servitudes and options over the other German coalfields. It would be a clear and simple solution, intelligible to everyone, while at the same time it would get rid of the very tiresome French claims to Landau and parts of the Saar. When the

question came up in Paris, I discussed it and put it forward at meetings with the Americans; the results of these meetings were put down formally, but no one took any notice of them. In the earlier discussions we went into some detail as to the extent of the territory which would have to be ceded by Germany, and I always pressed that the frontier should be drawn rather generously, so as to create a district which would be capable of self-government. Eventually I had an opportunity of drawing the Prime Minister's attention, together with that of Mr Balfour, to this solution, and he took it up. The result was the appointment of the Saar Valley Commission on which I was the British representative. In accordance with instructions, we worked first on the basis of giving the ownership of the coal mines to France, but without any change in Government. We worked this out in some detail but came to the conclusion that any such system would be impracticable, and reported accordingly. The Council of Four then of themselves suggested the solution that the district should be put under the direct government of the League of Nations. I had an opportunity of talking over the matter with the President and explained to him how much I disliked the extension of the mandate system to Europe, in which he concurred, but he was bound, as he explained to the Four, by his own utterances, not to require any permanent cession of German territory. The Committee then worked out the scheme as it now stands; it was read through in detail by the Council of Four and approved by them, they making certain alterations in detail. Given the premisses, it is I think about as good as it could be.

The chief block in the original draft was the provision that if Germany did not buy back the coal mines for gold at the end of fifteen years, the whole district should go permanently to France. This was obviously indefensible, but when I protested against it, Tardieu, supported by the American, took the line that it had been specifically approved by the Council of Four and could not be changed. In consequence of the German protest, we had an opportunity to revise this, which we took, and Mr Lloyd George and the President both stated strongly that it was a provision which they could not possibly agree to and that it was quite outside their intention. I ought to have urged the point more strongly at an earlier period. However, the result is satisfactory in that this clause has been changed and one substituted for it which is, I think, quite satisfactory.

Unfortunately, there was no machinery for bringing this scheme to the notice of the Reparation Commission and we had no knowledge of the reparation clauses. The result was that it became apparent that if Germany was deprived of the Saar Basin mines, of the Silesian mines, and if France and other countries also had an option on the produce of the Westphalian fields, payments in coal would be more than Germany could stand. I had hoped that the Saar scheme would bulk much more largely than it has done in the reparation provisions. It was unfortunate that the payment to be made by Germany was undefined, so that she did not really get the advantage which would otherwise have come to her from the value of the Saar mines. I think the scheme would have received more support if it had been put forward much more strongly then was done as one of the most important parts of the French indemnity.

Reviewing the whole matter, I still feel that the suggestion was a sound one, especially as it has now been drafted; the temporary separation of this district from Germany is not a greater price than she should be called upon to pay; the very fact that it is of so exceptional a nature makes it stand out as a landmark which was essentially to be desired, and a clear-cut comprehensible system such as this is in the long run a better method of giving satisfaction to France than the more complicated system adopted by the Reparation Committee. There seems every reason to hope that for the people of the district itself the arrangements, even if they dislike them, will be not disadvantageous. Above all, we have got rid of the French claims to the 1814 frontier; there is no reason why the plebiscite at the end of fifteen years should not be taken as a final and honest settlement, provided of course that the Commission does its work well.

(4) *Alsace-Lorraine.* My appointment on the Alsace-Lorraine Commission was quite unexpected and contrary to my own wishes. I foresaw from the beginning that it would be a most difficult piece of work. The French of course put up claims which seemed to me politically very foolish, and in many details quite unjustifiable. Many of them were matters on which I had no qualification to give an opinion and I was reluctant to be put in a position where I should have to carry on acute controversy with them on questions of which, though each small in itself, were in their bulk important. In particular, I had always strongly taken the view that the French were very ill advised not to have made some opportunity for enabling the people of Alsace-Lorraine to give public expression to their desire to be united to France. For this, however, I could get no support; the view of the Foreign Office has throughout been that this was a point which must be left entirely to the French and, when I asked for instructions, I was told to take a back seat and leave the matter to the Americans.

The French had put forward their proposals at a very late stage and we only had about a week or ten days to deal with them. We were practically compelled to accept their proposals as the draft for consideration, and all that we could do was to eliminate the most offensive elements. This meant a long wrangle over numerous points of detail in which I had to call in the help of Keynes and Falk for financial matters and of the Economic Section for others. We were successful in getting a considerable number of changes; three points, however, had to be reserved for the Council of Four. On one of these the Prime Minister at once gave way; on the other two the French proposals were rejected almost without discussion.

The ultimate result remains profoundly unsatisfactory; we have accepted the French proposals which were complicated and invidious for discriminating between the different classes of the population in Alsace-Lorraine; there is no provision for an amnesty, though I tried to get one inserted, and no protection of any kind for the German-speaking people or the German language. Many of the financial clauses are unfairly stretched against both the German Government and the German population of Alsace-Lorraine, and there are tiresome little provisions which will probably cause difficulty in the future. In particular, the provision that it shall be held that the country was annexed to France as from the date of the Armistice, is, I think, unjustifiable, but no doubt it is a practical necessity for the French. With much difficulty I got in a clause protecting the inhabitants against penal prosecution under French laws which had not been proclaimed. The Kehl clause started in a very offensive form; we had long meetings about it and eventually have so modified it that it might in fact become the basis of an arrangement for the joint working of the ports of Kehl and Strasbourg, which would be really advantageous to both sides.

During the course of the discussion I stated quite frankly to Tardieu that though we did not refuse him our support, I felt bound to say that I much disliked the whole scheme of this chapter and thought that they were very ill advised in their treatment of the matter.

(5) *Danzig.* The one section of the treaty for which I am really responsible, and for which I am prepared to accept responsibility, is that concerning Danzig. From the very beginning of the preparation of the work in London, there had been great discussions about Danzig. While we were at the Foreign Office, the general agreement was that the town should not be given to the Poles but that some arrangement must be made by which the port would be. The discussion of the question in Paris was postponed for a very long time and it was eventually given to the Polish Committee. This apparently was controlled by the French and the American, Lord,

took a strong Polish view. They were supported by Esme Howard, who had changed his opinion after coming to Paris, and Paton, who came out from Oxford and brought very great knowledge and persistence; and Tyrrell, who was our representative on the Polish Commission, seems to have gone over to this view. As he wrote to me from London, he was supported even by Namier. I had really no official standing on the matter for, like all similar questions, it was treated throughout as a Polish and not as a German question. There was no one appointed specially to consider things from the German point of view. Really this should have been Crowe's business but he did not use the opportuinty; I had a sort of roving commission, more from the P.I.D. point of view than any other, to deal with German problems. I used this repeatedly in order to draw attention to the Danzig question and tried to get some decision from our people, but of course this was in vain.

The Polish Commission reported in favour of giving Danzig to Poland. The Prime Minister refused to accept the report of the Commission, although it was unanimous; for this he was bitterly attacked in the press, for unfortunately both the report of the Polish Commission and his speech got out. He was very indignant about this and threatened to go back to England if this sort of thing happened. The whole report of the Polish Commission, practically, together with the map, was published in a French Polish paper. He was obviously in a position of great difficulty in getting any revision of the report of the Committee and, presumably on Philip Kerr's recommendation, asked me to go and see him. In consequence I was, without any formalities or official instructions, told to discuss the matter with Mezes of the American Delegation. We put forward a scheme which I had suggested to him and which, with certain modifications, is identical with that which appears in the treaty. I discussed it with the Prime Minister and also, together with Mezes, with the President. We had great difficulties in determining whether Danzig should be put under Polish sovereignty or only united with Poland as a sovereign state by treaty. My first suggestion was that it should be a sovereign state, and this was in accordance with the Prime Minister's instructions. In deference to the strong pressure brought to bear upon me by Howard, Paton, Kisch and others, I went to the Prime Minister and asked him to allow me to put it under Polish sovereignty with guaranteed autonomy. This he refused – I think rightly. I also discussed the matter with Paderewski, Kerr and I lunching with him alone. He did not like this arrangement and said that it would be political suicide for him to accept it, but I tried to reassure him by strengthening the clauses as to the Polish control of the port and the right of Poles to coast protection. After Mezes and I had agreed on the scheme, which we sent up officially, I lost sight of it for some time. I never found out when it was definitely adopted by the Four.[1] The whole situation was rather difficult, because in fact I arranged the thing with the Americans, and the French were entirely left out.

However, the scheme, practically as we drafted it, was eventually sent down to the Drafting Committee. They made some changes not without importance, in particular setting up Danzig as a free city immediately on the conclusion of peace, while we had arranged that it should not come into its sovereignty until the treaty with Poland had been arranged. To this I attach great importance for, as I pointed out to Monsieur Paderewski, this bound Danzig to accept the conditions which the Allies might determine.

The arrangement for having a High Commissioner at Danzig as the representative of the League of Nations, in order to settle all these questions, I put forward, as I thought that this would be a more satisfactory way of doing things than merely putting in a general clause that the treaty should be arranged by the League of Nations. The idea was that he should be their representative on the spot with practically full powers, though if he could not come to an agreement, there would be of course the final appeal to the League.

The alterations put in by the Drafting Committee caused a good deal of trouble; I had a great difficulty in getting a copy of the treaty after they had passed it and, in consequence, neither Mezes nor I saw the alterations made until it was too late. I had a hard fight to get them to alter the clauses and restore them to their original form, but eventually did so by getting Mezes to send a note to the President; the result of this was a direct order to the Drafting Committee to restore them.

The most vital objection to the whole scheme, which was made by Crowe, was that it was a house of cards which would not stand. My view has always been that this was true supposing we were to revert to a condition in which there was acute national rivalry, supported by large forces. The whole arrangements for Danzig, West Prussia and East Prussia are strategically quite impossible. This I look on not as a disadvantage, but as an advantage. It seems to me the right thing frankly to build up a system which cannot be maintained unless the League of Nations is strong enough to impose peace and disarmament. I tried to get a paragraph into the answer to the German note explaining this, but it was dropped out of the

[1] The Council of Four approved in principle the establishment of Danzig as a free city on 1 April 1919. See Mantoux, I, 110–12.

report of the Committee dealing with the matter because General le Rond objected, and I was not able to get it in later. This is, I think, a very serious omission, for there was a great opportunity of putting forward this conception.

Another weakness is connected with this point. The whole situation on the eastern frontiers of Germany depends on the Allies having sufficient resources to impose it both on the Poles and on the Germans; unfortunately we have apparently no troops for this purpose, and at the time of writing (27 June) I feel the gravest apprehension lest there will be a violent explosion by the Junkers and German Nationalists, which may wreck the whole thing. This is characteristic of the difficulties we have to meet with here. It is no good drawing up terms of peace unless the practical measures which are required as part of the policy adopted are taken. There is a grave lack of co-ordination in this matter, and it is still possible that this may wreck the whole scheme. I have, for instance, had more than once to point out that under the treaty the Poles have no right to send troops into Danzig. The military were obviously inclined to suggest that Polish troops might at once be introduced into the city so as to help the Allied and Associated Powers to take over the control. This would be fatal.

Another point which arose was that of a Polish navy. Some of the Poles want to have some of the German fleet given to them in order to be able to start their own fleet as against the Germans in the Baltic. This I think would be fatal. On the other hand, I agreed with Howard that they ought to have a few gunboats and one or two unarmed cruisers for ceremonial purposes, and the naval authorities have agreed to this.

(6) *East Prussia*. In connection with Danzig the question came up of the transference of the Marienburg district to Poland. The Prime Minister rightly disliked this and decided on a plebiscite in this district, and Mezes and I had also to deal with this. We put in a clause securing to Poland the complete control of the Vistula, but by his instructions, there was added a clause giving the Germans the right of using the Vistula. I tried to get in a clause forbidding the Germans to erect fortifications in the plebiscite area, but this was put forward too late and had to be cut out as it was inconsistent with other clauses of the treaty. I ought to have got it in again on the revision, but forgot to do so. In agreement with Kisch I put forward a strong request that there should not be a plebiscite in this area; as he pointed out, there was no doubt that the result of a plebiscite would be to give the district to Germany, and it seemed much better to do this frankly without a plebiscite if it was determined that it should not go to Poland.

The practically certain assignment of this district to Germany by a plebiscite brought up again the question of the railway. The chief point which had influenced the Polish Committee in giving Marienburg to Poland was the importance of having control for Poland over the Mlawa-Danzig railway. The change had, however, a considerable advantage because this made the Poles dependent upon Germany for railway communication on this line to Danzig in the same way as the Germans were dependent on the Poles for railway communication across West Prussia. Using this I drafted a clause in the treaty, binding the two countries to a reciprocal agreement, each giving the other railway facilities. I had the greatest difficulty in getting this actually into the treaty; it got omitted somehow or other by the Drafting Committee and I had to go down on the last day to the Drafting Committee myself and insist on its insertion. There was a good deal of confusion about the whole matter of railways because the Ports and Waterways Commission had their own clause, to which they were much attached, which, as it seemed to me, was drawn up without sufficient regard to the political situation. The thing ended by their clause and mine both going in. The opportunity given by the revision of the treaty was used to make slight alterations in both so that together they will, I think, do all that is necessary.

The assignment of West Prussia to Poland as determined by the Polish Commission remained unaltered. On the whole it seems to me that this is defensible, and I wrote the defence of it in the answer to the Germans, basing it chiefly on the historical argument that we have to restore Poland in this part as it was before the partition. It is really the most difficult problem of the whole; I think I feel no doubt as to the justice; whether it will be possible to maintain this arrangement is more doubtful. Everything depends on the general political conditions. If I were sure that the disarmament of Germany could be maintained and similar disarmament imposed upon Poland, I should be inclined to be hopeful. I much regret that there are no specific provisions compelling Poland to restrict her armaments. If we get a situation in which Germany is disarmed and Poland used the opportunity to build up a big army, I foresee the greatest dangers and difficulties.

Note of interview   26 June 1919

I received today a deputation consisting of two Polish Jews, who had just returned from Warsaw and were introduced to me by Mr Posner, a Polish Jew residing in Paris, with whom I have slight acquaintance.

They represented that party among the Polish Jews who are strongly opposed to the Jewish National movement and wish for the most complete assimilation between the Jews and the Poles. They represented that the educational clauses in the proposed treaty with Poland might be very disastrous, as they might be used to encourage the use of the Yiddish language, which they always spoke of as a jargon, and thereby intensify the separation between the Jews and the Poles. This would be used on the one side by the Jewish Nationalists and on the other by the anti-Semites, who would use the opportunity to press the point that the Jews were not Poles and, as they said, would try to drive them into the Ghetto. The particular point on which they were most anxious was the use of the Yiddish language. I pointed out to them the modifications which had been made in the last revision of the treaty and suggested that it might easily be that the real effect of the system would be to ensure that all Jews would be taught Polish properly and that if one wanted to discourage the use of a language, it was not always wise to do this by the legal suppression of it. They laid stress on the danger of Yiddish being used as a medium for accustoming the Jews to talk German.

In answer to a question, they confessed that they represented only a minority (it is of course really only a very small minority) of the Polish Jews, and I impressed upon them the danger of a system of universal compulsory education being used by the Poles in a spirit of intolerance.

After a lengthy conversation I said that, speaking personally, my hope had always been that when we communicated the text of the treaty to the Poles, they would help us in regard to the details by discussing matters of this kind with us. This hope had been falsified owing to the unfortunate procedure which the Polish Delegation here had adopted. They let some weeks elapse, before they made any criticisms on the treaty so that when Monsieur Paderewski's letter was received, it was too late to go as thoroughly into these matters as we otherwise might have done. In addition, by protesting formally against the whole principle of the treaty, they had made it much more difficult for us to enter into personal discussion with them. We had, as a matter of fact, modified the treaty in important matters to meet such criticism of detail as they had given us, and if we had not had the friendly discussion which might have led possibly to further modifications, the responsibility rested entirely with them. I said also that I should be glad to receive any precise suggestions for alteration of the text which they liked to send me, though it was now in all probability too late for any further change to be made.

27 June 1919

Note. On 27 June Mr Headlam-Morley presented a memorandum on the draft treaty with Austria and the notes presented by the Delegation of the Austrian Republic, in which he put forward certain proposals for alterations in the treaty. He considered that it was necessary to revise the whole structure of the treaty and made detailed suggestions for this purpose.

Extract from letter to Mr Namier (F.O.)   *30 June 1919*

... I am afraid I do not quite understand even now your view about the Polish treaty. I gather that you are inclined to think that it is unsatisfactory in that it will do enough to annoy the Poles and not do enough to protect the Jews. It is however very difficult to satisfy everyone, and in the end one succeeds only in disappointing everyone. Of course the fundamental difficulty is this, that we refuse throughout to do anything which might in the slightest degree give any countenance to the Jewish National claims. That would, I am sure, have been perfectly impossible and unjustifiable. We have had a lot of trouble about the Jewish educational clauses, and in the end modified them considerably. I had always hoped that after the treaty was communicated to the Poles they would send a detailed criticism which we could consider and discuss with them if possible personally, as it is much better always in cases of this kind to talk over matters freely and openly. This was made impossible because they kept us waiting nearly a month for their answer and when it came it was to a large extent a protest against the whole conception of the treaty. For this Dmowski was of course responsible, and he was I think encouraged by the French Foreign Office. Our difficulty was that we always knew that there were influences there working against the treaty altogether, and one could never be certain until the very last moment that it would get through, as the time was so short and delay would have been so easy. I had an enormous amount of trouble and worry in watching every stage so as to be quite sure that it did not get hung up somewhere; however, I got the Four to send a definite order that it should be prepared in time.

Posner came to see me at the end of last week and brought two Jews who had just returned from Poland, belonging to the Intellectual Assimilants. They were very strongly against doing anything to encourage Yiddish, and Reichmann, whom I also saw, took the same view. I believe you do not agree with this; I am inclined to do so and therefore supported changes which were intended to have this effect. We were very much hampered by the opposition of Hudson, the American, who was extremely obstinate and difficult to deal with. We had to take it back twice to the Four on two successive days, and he refused even to accept their decision but always wanted to go back to his private recollection of something he and President Wilson had said to one another. The truth is that he was very much in the hands of Marshall. I did not like the situation at all, as I got the feeling that what the Americans were thinking of was much more the vote of the New York Jews than the real advantages to be won for the Jews in Poland; I am left with the firm conviction that this political Jewish element may in fact be a very dangerous factor in the League of Nations. The whole thing had ended with a definite difference between Marshall and the American Jews on the one hand, and Lucien Wolf and his Committee on the other. I am afraid that we shall look on this from completely different points of view. I have no opposition to Zionism in the proper sense of the word, viz: the settlement of the Jews in Palestine, if that can be properly carried out, but the other aspect of Zionism by which, while the Jews are to get – if they do – their own state in Palestine, they are also to become an international nationality, influencing every other country, seems to me to be most dangerous.

Whether or not the new system will work will have to be seen; so far as I see it, the really important thing is placing the clauses which give the Jews full protection of the law under the guarantee of the Court of the League of Nations. This throws the whole responsibility on the League of Nations; all depends upon whether it becomes effective. However that may be, the general result has been, I think, still further to discredit Dmowski, and our letter to Paderewski will, I hope, be understood rather in this sense.[1] I am told that Paderewski was very pleased with it.

Now that the treaty with Germany is signed, if at any rate the Germans do not do something foolish in the east, it will I hope be possible to tackle the Polish question more successfully. The difficulty hitherto has always been the apprehension, which is not entirely ill founded, of an outbreak of German militarism on the Polish frontier; I hope that the Germans are sufficiently sensible to see how much harm this would do to them. If they keep the peace and evacuate the territories without trouble, then the chief excuse for Polish militarism will have been removed. I wish they could have put in the treaty some clause definitely referring to Polish disarmament; it is an intolerable situation to the Germans that they should be obliged to disarm and no reciprocal obligation be thrown upon Poland. But I know we differ fundamentally on this aspect of the question. As far

[1] See P.P.C. VI, 629–34.

THE FINAL SCENE · 177

as I can understand your view, you would almost welcome unjust Polish gains as against Germany, provided that there was strict justice on the eastern frontier of Poland; I am afraid that it seems to me that in the long run the Germans are more important than the Little Russians.[1]

It is quite impossible to follow all that goes on in East Galicia, but the last decision, by which it is apparently to be given over to Poland, seems to me to be quite incomprehensible. Here it is above all the Americans who are responsible; as so often is the case, they let us down on the most important points. I can see no sense of intelligence in their policy.[2]

Extract from letter to Mr Koppel (F.O.)   30 June 1919

Now that it is all over, I have no doubt you would like to hear how we have all been getting on. We were kept more or less in suspense up till Friday afternoon as to whether the Peace would really get signed on Saturday; the Germans did just what I expected they would do and I confess what I myself would have done in their place. I think they were quite right in their last offer but one, to agree to sign everything except the surrender of the Emperor, etc., and the acquiescence in taking over the full guilt of the war. These are matters of honour in which they were certainly right to protest right up to the very last moment. I have heard – I am not quite sure whether it is true – that even at the last moment they might have got some concession about the Court before which the Emperor and others would be tried,[3] but they sent in their final note of acceptance an hour sooner than they need have done, because they had

[1] The Ruthenians, i.e. the Ukrainians of East Galicia. The term 'Little Russians' generally denoted Ukrainians under Russian rule.
[2] By the end of May the Poles, in defiance of the Supreme Council's efforts to secure a cease-fire, had defeated the Ukrainians and overrun all of Eastern Galicia. Shortly thereafter, reports began to reach Paris of a Bolshevik drive into Eastern Galicia as part of an attempt to join hands with Bela Kun's forces in Hungary. When in late June the Council of Foreign Ministers took up the question, it had to choose between ordering a Polish withdrawal, thereby opening up Eastern Galicia to the Bolsheviks, or of sanctioning Poland's military occupation. Reluctantly, it chose the latter.
At the same time and at the insistence of Balfour, the Council agreed to resolve the issue by putting Eastern Galicia under a mandate with a plebiscite to be held at some future date to determine the wishes of the inhabitants. However, at the insistence of the American Delegate, Robert Lansing, the Council also agreed to make the Poles the mandatory power. Its decision, which the Supreme Council promptly endorsed, created the 'quite incomprehensible' impression to which Headlam-Morley refers. See P.P.C. IV, 848–55, as well as Headlam-Morley's memorandum on Eastern Galicia (11836).
[3] This rumour, however, was without foundation.

heard that the troops at Cologne were going to begin their march into Germany at 6 instead of 7 o'clock.

We all went out to see the treaty signed on Saturday; we put on our best clothes for the first time since we came here and went out in motors. With that admirable tact which is characteristic of the British Government, all the ladies of the Delegation were also sent out, with tickets for the terrace outside, taken there in three motor lorries, uncleaned, with tarpaulin covers; they had to stand up and were packed like herrings. We drove quite comfortably; there were soldiers along the route and as we neared Versailles considerable, but not very large crowds. I went with Nicolson, and tried to look as if I was quite accustomed to driving under these circumstances with cheering crowds and soldiers saluting. The Square at Versailles, for the first time that I have ever seen it, really looked fine, as it was lined with lancers in their blue uniform and tin hats; one had some sort of conception of how it might have looked in olden days. We got out at the main entrance and went up the grand staircase, which was lined by the Garde Républicaine, and went through all the state rooms to the Salle des Glaces. All these physical surroundings were as magnificent as they could be. On the other hand, I do not think that the ceremony was really well done. The plenipotentiaries were on a very slightly raised dais in the middle of the room, but unless one was quite in the front row it was very difficult to see what went on. They sat round three sides of a square and the treaty was on a small table on the centre of the fourth side. The room of course was crowded. There was very little ceremony or dignity. The plenipotentiaries all walked in casually with the crowd; they ought to have had us all seated first and then have announced them and let them come in with some kind of dignity. When they were all seated, the German Delegates were brought in; they passed close to me; they looked like prisoners being brought in for sentence, but on the whole bore it very well. Müller was a tall, unkempt man, rather like a typical German professor. As you will see from the papers, there were no speeches of any kind except a short opening of the sitting. The Germans signed first and then all the other Delegates. Sitting where I was, the most conspicuous feature was the Private Secretaries, especially Ian Malcolm[1] and Philip Kerr, flitting about. When the signing was finished, the session was closed, and the Germans were escorted out again like prisoners who had received their sentence. Nobody got up or took any notice of them, and there was no suggestion that, the peace having been signed, any change of attitude was to be begun. Looking back, the whole impression seems to me, from a

[1] Ian Malcolm, M.P., Mr Balfour's personal secretary.

political point of view, to be disastrous. The one thing which was forced on one by the whole scene was that it was the revenge of France for 1871. It took place in a building which was really erected on the ruin and humiliation of Germany; it was also the room in which Germany, having won a victory, inflicted a great humiliation upon France; France now once more having got the upper hand was having her revenge for the injury done to her, and in every detail complied with the utmost insult to Germany, and it was merely an episode in the secular rivalry of two nations which has been the curse of Europe. As a matter of fact, what was really being done was not merely to make peace with Germany, but to sign the Covenant of the League of Nations, but of this no one seemed to think. France again was up and Germany was down, but it was a France which is not strong enough to maintain her position by herself, and is entangling the world to make the new system merely a support of France against Germany. Just the necessary note of reconciliation, of hope, of a change of view, was entirely wanting.

After it was over, I went out on to a balcony and the scene from there was extraordinarily beautiful and magnificent, for all the gardens were full of people and soldiers, the fountains were playing, and one was very glad to have been there.

The only people who were absent were the Chinese, who at the last moment refused to sign.[1] I think they were right, but it is a bad augury for the future, for it may imply that China will throw herself with Russia and Germany against the League of Nations, and that would be a serious thing. However, my Polish treaty got signed, and as a matter of fact the guns began to fire just at the moment when Paderewski signed.[2] I hear that he is delighted with our letter to him, which you will no doubt see, and went about, as his way is, shaking hands warmly with both hands and thanking them all for the beautiful letter they had written and the nice things they had said about Poland. So I think this is one good thing done, though I am afraid we shall not really have pleased either the Jews or the Poles. Two days before the treaty was signed, Hurst and Malkin had a great business getting the seals for all the British Delegates to fix to the treaty. I went down to the Quai d'Orsay in the morning to see the treaty itself, but unfortunately there was such a crowd there and such confusion that I was not able to find my way into the right place. Practically none of

[1] Rather than formally endorse the Supreme Council's decision to transfer to Japan the special rights in Shantung formerly held by the Germans, the Chinese Delegation in the end refused to sign the Treaty of Versailles.
[2] Following the formalities in the Hall of Mirrors, the Polish treaty was signed in another wing of Versailles.

our people had any seals of their own and Miss Dougherty had to be sent out going round the shops of Paris to buy seals for the British Delegation.

In the evening the British Government gave us all a special dinner with one extra course, and free champagne; if Carnegie is still there, he will be duly impressed if you tell him that this was served in the dining-room as well as the restaurant. I dined with Temple Franks,[1] Lord Sumner[2] and Lord Cunliffe,[3] who are the two bad men of the Conference; they always go about together and are always summoned when some particularly nefarious act has to be committed. There were two dances in the evening (one for the staff) and a certain amount of mild exhilaration; some of the Delegation went out and as far as I understand indulged in a little mild mafficking, including Webster, Curtis and Simpson. Even Carr took his Miss Dougherty out, and Miss Hughes and I walked soberly down the Champs Elysées, but there was really very little to be seen.

Things will, I think, change here now very much, especially as the Four have ceased to meet. As far as I can make out, I am the only person who regrets it, but as I often got them to do what I wanted, I have a certain feeling of gratitude towards them. No doubt things will become more orderly, but they will be much duller. I do not in the least know how long I shall be here. I have still got some work to do about the treaties with Greece, Romanian, etc., and I do not know whether I shall be wanted for the Austrian treaty or not. I should like to get it completely revised and am making some efforts in this direction, but I do not know if they will have any success. The German treaty was overdone, but much of it was defensible; the whole structure of the Austrian treaty seems to me to be merely ludicrous and stupid.

---

[1] W. Temple Franks, the Board of Trade's Comptroller of Patents, Designs and Trademarks as well as adviser on economic affairs to the British Delegation.

[2] See pp. 187–8.

[3] See p. 210.

APPENDIX

∽∭∾

The biographical notes are arranged alphabetically, under the name or title by which the people were known at the time. Heads of Delegation of major Powers are not included. The titles of books written by the people concerned are given, but only outstanding books or those relevant to the matter in hand are mentioned. No attempt has been made to give a full bibliography. The notes are based on information given by a number of generous contributors. We have aimed at relevance and interest rather than uniformity.

ABRAHAM, EDGAR. An Indian Civil Servant. He was one of the British Secretaries to the Supreme War Council and to the Council of Ten at Paris. He assisted Philip Kerr in the drafting of the pre-Armistice note of 5 November 1918. It was he who suggested the substitution of 'aggression' for 'invasion' in order to secure compensation for the loss of merchant shipping.

BAILEY, JOHN (1864–1931). Educated at Haileybury and New College, Oxford, where he was contemporary with Frederick Kenyon, A. C. Headlam and Walter Morant. Called to the Bar, Inner Temple 1892. A distinguished literary critic and writer of essays and belles-lettres. During the war he served in the Intelligence Department and in the P.I.D. He was responsible for information on France and Italy. He devoted much time and care to the preservation of the countryside and helped to build up the National Trust, of which he became chairman in 1923. Author of *The Claims of French Poetry* (1923), *Dr Johnson and his Circle* (1913), *Milton* (1915), etc.

BAKER, PHILIP. See Noel-Baker.

BERTHELOT, PHILIPPE (1866–1934). Acting Director of Political and Commercial Affairs at the Quai d'Orsay, later Secretary-General until 1932. According to Lloyd George, he was a diplomat of great ability, but as he was closely attached to Briand he was pushed into the background by Clemenceau. French representative on the New States Committee. He afterwards played an important part in the Turkish settlement and in the drafting of the A Mandates.

BEVAN, EDWYN (1870–1943). Educated at Monkton Combe and New College, Oxford. A student of the history of religion and philosophy in the pre-Christian and early post-Christian eras. During the war he worked in the Propaganda Department of the Department of Information and then in the P.I.D. He was responsible for information on internal conditions in Germany. Lecturer in Hellenistic History and Literature at King's College, London, 1922–33. Author of *House of Silencus*, Volume on *Christianity* in the University Library, and *Symbolism*.

BLISS, GENERAL TASKER H. (1853–1930). A plenipotentiary Delegate at the Peace Conference. Representative of the United States on the Supreme War Council. He had supported the setting-up of a unified command. In 1918 he insisted on armistice terms which would make it impossible for Germany to resume war. At subsequent renewals he opposed the imposition of further and more drastic provisions which would weaken the democratic government in Germany. In February 1919 he proposed the immediate enforcement of the final naval and military terms of peace. Demobilization could then take place. Clemenceau turned it down since the Allies would lose the most effective means of imposing the Peace on Germany. Bliss was opposed to the occupation of German territory. Author of 'The Armistice' in the *American Journal of International Law*, Vol. 16.

BOURDILLON, FRANCIS BERNARD (1883–1936). Educated at Charterhouse and Balliol College, Oxford. Lecturer in German, University College, Reading, 1908–14. Modern Language Lecturer at Balliol, 1913–15. Served in Admiralty Intelligence Department 1916–19. At the Peace Conference he was the British representative on the subcommission to study the eastern frontiers of Poland. He was a member of the Upper Silesian Commission 1920–2, and of the Irish Boundary Commission 1924–5. Secretary of the Royal Institute of International Affairs 1926–9.

BOWMAN, ISAIAH (1878–1950). Director of the American Geographical Society. He was one of those instrumental in setting up the Inquiry. A man of integrity and considerable administrative ability, he had frequent differences with Mezes, who had intended to exclude him from the American Delegation. Bowman was responsible for the reorganization and administration of the Inquiry. At Paris he was 'chief of territorial questions'. Himself an expert on the geography of Latin America, he had little previous knowledge of the problems with which he had to deal. See L. E. Gelfand, *The Inquiry*.

BRATIANU, JONEL (1864–1927). He came of purely Romanian stock, an agrarian aristocracy with no cosmopolitan connections. Entered Parliament in 1895. As Prime Minister he showed circumspection during the first years of war and obtained favourable terms when Romania joined the Allies in 1916. The invasion of Transylvania with forces lamentably ill equipped led to disaster. He resigned rather than accept the humiliating terms imposed by the Central Powers in the Treaty of Bucharest. Prime Minister once more in 1918, he worked closely with King Ferdinand. Plenipotentiary Delegate at Paris. Romania obtained great accessions of territory; her population was almost doubled. None the less he protested strongly, especially against the proposals for the protections of minorities. These he held infringed the sovereign rights of Romania which was not a 'new state'. He left the Conference in June. The treaties with Austria and Hungary were signed by other members of the Delegation. The minorities treaty was accepted with some modifications by a Coalition Government in December 1918. Prime Minister in 1922, he exercised near-dictatorial powers. He achieved a measure of reform giving rights of citizenship to stateless Jews. See Temperley, *History of the Peace Conference*, Vols. V and VI; Sherman David Spektor, *Rumania at the Paris Peace Conference* (New York, 1968).

BRIAND, ARISTIDE (1862–1932). Entered the Chamber as a Socialist Deputy in 1902. He was Prime Minister of France for two short periods before the war and again from 1915 to 1917 when he formed a small war Cabinet with Lyauty as Minister of War. He was out of office at the time of the Peace Conference. After the Peace he pursued a conciliatory policy as Prime Minister, 1921 and 1925. As Foreign Minister (1925–32), he worked closely with Stresemann during the Locarno period. He also strengthened the Little Entente and negotiated the Briand–Kellog Pact.

P

BROCKDORFF-RANTZAU, COUNT ULRICH VON (1869–1928). Entered diplomatic service in 1894, served in Budapest and Copenhagen. A diplomat of the old school, he was known to hold liberal views. On the recommendation of Ebert, he was appointed Foreign Minister under the government of the Commissars of the People in December 1918. The appointment was renewed by the first parliamentary republican Government in February 1919. Leader of the German Delegation at Versailles. His speech and attitude on the reception of the treaty (9 May 1919) provoked anger and disapproval among the Allied statesmen. (He was a nervous speaker and his failure to rise was probably due to extreme stress.) He resigned rather than sign the treaty. Appointed first German ambassador to the Soviet Republic in 1922. He favoured German-Russian friendship as the best means of resisting pressure from the West – but not to the point of war. Resigned in 1925 as a result of differences with Herr Stresemann. See Alma Luckau, *The German Delegation at the Paris Peace Conference*; Richard M. Watt, *The Kings Depart*.

BUTLER, HAROLD (1883–1951), K.C.M.G. 1946. Educated at Eton and Balliol College, Oxford, Fellow of All Souls 1905–12. Entered the Civil Service in 1907. He was Assistant Secretary to the Ministry of Labour when it was formed in 1917 under Mr Barnes, the first Minister. At Paris he was a member of the Committee on the International Labour Organization. Together with Mr Phelan he drafted the British proposals which eventually formed the basis of the I.L.O. He was assistant to Mr Barnes at the International Labour Conference at Washington (October 1919) at which forty-eight nations including Germany and Austria were represented. Deputy Director of the I.L.O. under Albert Thomas, whom he succeeded in 1932. After the onset of the industrial depression he went on a mission to the United States which prepared the way for their joining the I.L.O. in 1933. In 1932 and again in 1938 he gave advice on industrial conditions and social reform to the Egyptian Government. Retired 1938. Warden of Nuffield College, Oxford, 1939–43. Author of *Industrial Relations in the United States* (1927), *The Lost Peace* (1941), *Confident Morning* (1950), etc. See also J. T. Shotwell, *The Origins of the International Labour Organization* (New York: Columbia, 1934); Anthony Alcock, *History of the International Labour Organization* (1971).

CAMBON, JULES (1845–1935). Grand Cross of the Legion of Honour. Served in the war of 1870. He had administrative experience in Africa and in France. As Governor-General of Algeria, he sponsored a moderate policy of decentralization (1819–97). Ambassador at Washington. He helped to negotiate peace after the Spanish-American War of 1898. Ambassador in Madrid. *Persona grata* in Spain, he used his influence to mitigate Franco-Spanish rivalry in Africa. Ambassador in Berlin, 1907–14. He exercised a moderating influence by firmness and restraint in the Agadir crisis. He was consistently careful and courteous but came to believe that in the long run war would be inevitable. Secretary-General to the Inter-Allied War Council. He was a plenipotentiary Delegate at the Peace Conference. Chairman of the Commission on Polish Affairs and on Greece and Albania. President of the Conference of Ambassadors until 1922. Elected to the French Academy in 1919.

CARNEGIE, E. FULLERTON-. Member of the P.I.D. Expert on Scandinavian countries. He was present at Paris during the early part of the Conference and advised on the Schleswig-Holstein issue. He returned towards the end to help in the drafting and final preparation of the treaty. His wife was German. Carnegie had a charming personality. He and Headlam-Morley were close friends. They lived near by in Wimbledon and their wives gave each other much-needed moral support. Carnegie afterwards inherited estates in Scotland.

CARR, EDWARD HALLETT. Historian, born 1892. Educated at Merchant Taylors' School, London, and Trinity College, Cambridge. Temporary clerk at the Foreign Office 1916. Attached to British Delegation at the Peace Conference. He was assistant to Headlam-Morley on the New States Committee. Afterwards served in Paris, at the Foreign Office and in Riga. Assistant adviser on League of Nations affairs 1930–3. Wilson Professor of International Politics, University of Wales. Tutor in Politics at Balliol College, Oxford, 1953–5. Fellow of Trinity College, Cambridge. Author of *Michael Bakunin* (1937), *The Twenty Years Crisis 1919–1939*, *History of Soviet Russia* (Vols. I–VII), *German-Soviet Relations between the Two World Wars 1919–1939* (1951), etc.

CARTON DE WIART, BRIGADIER-GENERAL ADRIAN, V.C., C.M.G., D.S.O. (b. 1884). Educated at the Oratory School, Edgbaston, and Balliol College, Oxford. He was born in Brussels. His father was a naturalized British subject who worked as an international lawyer in Cairo. He served with distinction in the Boer War and in the First World War and was wounded eight times, losing a hand and an eye. A member of the British Delegation at Paris. When General Botha retired owing to ill health, he became leader of the Inter-Allied Mission to Poland. After the Peace Conference he was attached to the newly appointed military mission. He lived in Poland off and on till the outbreak of war, on the estate of Prince Charles Ratziwill near the Prypet Marshes. In 1939 he was once more attached as military adviser to the Polish Government. In 1941 he commanded an unsuccessful attack in central Norway. Shot down on a flight to Yugoslavia, he was a prisoner in Italy till 1943, when he was released after being sent on an armistice mission to Portugal. He married the Countess Frederica, daughter of Prince Fugger Babenhausen and Nora Princess Hohenlohe. Author of *Happy Odyssey* (1950).

CECIL, LORD ROBERT (1864–1958). Third son of third Marquess of Salisbury. Created Viscount Cecil of Chelwood in 1923. Educated Eton and University College, Oxford. Parliamentary Under-Secretary of State for Foreign Affairs May 1915–July 1918. Also Minister of Blockade February 1916–July 1918. Assistant Secretary of State for Foreign Affairs July–November 1918 (resigned over Welsh Church disestablishment). Leading Government protagonist of the League of Nations from 1916. British League of Nations Delegate at Paris Peace Conference. Also chief British representative on Supreme Economic Council February–July 1919. He was a consistent advocate of Anglo-American friendship. Lord Privy Seal 1923–4. Chancellor of the Duchy of Lancaster November 1924–August 1929 (resigned over British naval policy). Represented British Governments at Geneva between the wars. Churchman, lawyer, High Tory, with a 'cross bench mind'. His uncompromising dedication to the League earned him international esteem but cost him support in the Conservative party.

CLERK, SIR GEORGE RUSSELL, K.C.M.G., C.B. (1874–1951). Educated at Eton and New College, Oxford. Joined the Foreign Office in 1899. Served in Addis Ababa and Constantinople. Private secretary to Lord Curzon, who in 1919 acted as Foreign Secretary in the absence of Mr Balfour. Owing to the absence also of Hardinge, Crowe and Tyrrell, Clerk was for a time in charge as acting Permanent Under-Secretary. He served as a special Delegate of the Supreme Council on Missions to Bucharest and Budapest. Ambassador in Turkey 1926–33.

CROWE, SIR EYRE, K.C.M.G. (1864–1925). Educated in Germany (Gymnasium in Düsseldorf and Berlin). Private tuition in England and France. His father, Sir Joseph Archer Crowe, was originally a journalist and a connoisseur of Italian and Flemish art. In 1861 he made a special report for Lord John Russell on German opinion in regard to unification. He afterwards served in the Consular and in the Diplomatic Services in Düsseldorf, Leipzig and Berlin. He moved in liberal artistic circles, married Asta von Barby, a lady-in-waiting at the Court of Saxe-Coburg-Gotha, and made friends with the Crown Princess (later the Empress Frederick). Joined the Foreign Office as a resident clerk in 1885, took a leading part in the reforms of 1903–6 and was head of the Western Department. On instructions from Sir Edward Grey, he wrote the famous Memorandum on Relations with France and Germany (1907): in France public opinion might be ill informed and vacillating, politicians mutually disloyal; in Germany a gifted people, eminent in art, philosophy and science, justly proud of an efficient and honest administration, was not unnaturally desirous of expansion overseas. None the less he emphasized the extreme danger of further concession to German demands. It mattered not whether they were the result of an indiscriminate self-assertion or a deliberate bid for domination. Our own security and the peace of Europe depended on maintaining the balance of power. This required consistent loyalty to the Anglo-French Entente. (FO 371/257. Gooch and Temperley, Vol. III, p. 397.) During the war he served in the Contraband Department. He was a member of the Phillimore Committee (1917–18) which considered proposals for a League of Nations. At Paris he was Assistant Under-Secretary of State; British representative on the Greek and Albanian and on the Belgian and Danish Commissions. He favoured a moderate peace and the consistent application of the principle of nationality. From 1920 to 1925 he was Permanent Under-Secretary of State. He was author of the note of 11 August 1923 which condemned the occupation of the Ruhr as a breach of the Treaty of Versailles. He helped to frame the London Agreement of 1924 and took part in preparing the way for the Locarno treaties. He married his cousin, Clema von Bonin.

CUNLIFFE, WALTER (b. 1855). First Baron Cunliffe of Headley, created 1914. P.C. Lord of Appeal in Ordinary. Governor of the Bank of England 1913–17. He established close relations with Lloyd George as Chancellor of the Exchequer. When McKenna was Chancellor, Cunliffe asserted the domination of the Bank of England over the financial policy of the Government. Bonar Law succeeded McKenna in 1916. There followed a time of extreme tension. Contrary to Cunliffe's advice, Bonar Law issued the War Loan of 1917 at a low rate of interest (5 per cent) and proved successful. He resisted Cunliffe's contention that Treasury officials (especially

Sir Robert Chalmers and Mr Keynes) had exceeded their powers by 'meddling' in the affairs of the Exchange Committee (Cunliffe did in fact try to force their dismissal). Finally by countermanding Cunliffe's attempt to control the gold reserves that had been deposited in Canada Bonar Law asserted the principle of Treasury control over financial policy. Cunliffe was a member of the Committee appointed by Lloyd George to report on the sums to be extracted from Germany in December 1918. He was one of Lloyd George's nominees to the Reparations Commission at Paris and was chairman of the Sub-Committee on the Financial Capacity of Enemy States. See Lord Beaverbrook, *Men and Power 1917–18* (1951); Robert Blake, *The Unknown Prime Minister* (1955); H.-M., P.C.M. (Reparations), 11924.

CURTIS, LIONEL (1872–1955). Elected Fellow of All Souls 1921. C.H. 1949. Educated at Haileybury and New College, Oxford. He served in the South African War and was afterwards private secretary to Lord Milner and one of the leading members of the 'Kindergarten'. The meeting in Paris (p. 132) led on to the foundation of the Royal Institute of International Affairs (Chatham House). Himself a man of moderate means, Curtis showed extraordinary energy and resource in extracting large sums of money from wealthy patrons for the endowment of the Institute. He afterwards advised the Government on constitutional reform in India and in Ireland. He was an enthusiastic advocate of federalism for the British Commonwealth which was to lead on to a world state. Author of *The Commonwealth of Nations* (1916), *Dyarcky* (1920), *With Milner in South Africa* (1951). See also Arnold Toynbee, *Acquaintances*.

DAVIS, HENRY WILLIAM CARLESS (1874–1928). Historian. C.B.E. 1918. Educated at Weymouth College and Balliol College, Oxford. Fellow of All Souls. Director of the Dictionary of National Biography 1902. Joined the War Trade Intelligence Department 1915. Member of the War Trade Advisory Committee 1916. Regius Professor of Modern History at Oxford University 1925. Contributed to Temperley's *History of the Peace Conference*. Author of *England under the Normans and Angevins* (1905), new editions of *Stubbs Select Charters* (1913), etc.

DAWSON, WILLIAM HARBUTT (1860–1948). Historian. Hon. D. Phil. Königsberg 1936. Educated at Skipton (Eringsled) School; private; Berlin University. He had been engaged in social and educational work. He was a prolific writer, especially on German history, literature and politics, his purpose being to interpret German life and institutions to English readers. In spite of the war he remained sympathetic to Germany. At this point he was on special assignment with the *Manchester Guardian* to cover the Conference. His reports can be found in the Scott Papers, British Museum Add. 50909. Author of *The Evolution of Modern Germany* (1908), *German Socialism and Ferdinand Lassalle* (1888), *Social Insurance in Germany* (1913), *The German Empire 1867–1914* (1919), *Richard Cobden and Foreign Policy*, *Germany under the Treaty* (1933), etc.

DMOWSKI, ROMAN (1864–1939). Head of the Polish National Committee in Paris and subsequently chief of the Polish Delegation to the Peace Conference. Dmowski was leader of the National Democratic Party, socially conservative, clerical and anti-Semitic. His original objective was the union of all ethnically Polish territories in an autonomous state under the Russian crown, which would, he believed, lead ultimately to independence. His party, therefore, co-operated with the Russian Government until the Revolution, whereupon Dmowski overtly worked for a large and independent Poland which would also include the former Polish eastern territories in which the Poles were a minority. Author of *La Question polonaise* (1909).

DRESEL, ELLIS LORING. He was sent by the American Government on missions of inquiry to Germany at the end of 1918 and again in 1919. He interviewed leading politicians, bankers and economists. At first his reports were on the whole reassuring, but later he warned of the dangers of a drastic treaty and the effects of malnutrition. The substance of his reports reached Lloyd George through Philip Kerr. A number are to be found in the Lothian Papers, GD 40/17/72. See also Arno J. Mayer, *Policy and Diplomacy of Peacemaking*.

DRUMMOND, SIR (JAMES) ERIC (1876–1951), K.C.M.G. 1916, P.C. 1933. Succeeded as sixteenth Earl of Perth 1937. Educated at Eton. Entered Foreign Office 1900. One of the private secretaries to the Prime Minister 1912–15. A member of the British Delegation at Paris, secretary to Mr Balfour. First Secretary-General to the League of Nations 1919–33. British ambassador in Rome 1933–9. It was he who on 28 September 1938 received from Count Ciano the message from Mussolini which reached Mr Chamberlain during the House of Commons debate and led to the summoning of the Munich Conference.

DUTASTA, M. P. French ambassador at Berne. Secretary-General of the Conference. He performed the formal functions but was rather pushed into the background by the activity of Sir Maurice Hankey.

ERZBERGER, MATHIAS (1871–1921). Entered the Reichstag in 1903. One of the more left-wing leaders of the Catholic Centre Party and of the Catholic trade unions. After the outbreak of war in 1914 he urged annexations in the east and west. In July 1917 he promoted the Peace Resolution (no annexations, no indemnities). He was at least in part responsible for the dismissal of Bethman-Hollweg. Leader of the German Commission which signed the Armistice on 11 November 1918. A man of great energy and courage, he was, rightly or wrongly, held to be an opportunist with inordinate ambition. Murdered by a right-wing fanatic in 1921.

FILOPOWICZ, TITUS (b. 1883). Member of Pilsudski's faction of the Polish Socialist Party and his trusted emissary. According to Mr Namier, Filipowicz had in 1905 belonged to the Polish Socialist Party. In 1917 he was imprisoned by the Germans but in 1918 became Polish chargé d'affaires in Vienna under the Regency Council; as a follower of Pilsudski, he supported the project of replacing Russian rule in the territories seized by Catherine the Great by independent or autonomous states of Belorussia and Lithuania federated with Poland. Namier, who saw this plan as 'Polish imperialism', was not flattered by the suggestion that we would welcome Monsieur Filipowicz because the latter had also been a bitter enemy of the National Democratic Party.

FOCH, FERDINAND (1851–1929). Marshal of France 1918. Field-Marshal in the British army 1919. A devout Roman Catholic. Educated at the Polytechnique and École de Guerre, of which he was afterwards Commandant. He was an accomplished strategist and a great leader of men. In April 1918, after the first onslaught of the German offensive, he was appointed Supreme Commander of Allied Troops on the Western Front. In October 1918 he was confident that the next stage of the Allied offensive, an attack between Metz and Strasbourg, would lead to complete defeat of the enemy. None the less he advised the political leaders to conclude an Armistice; since they could secure all that was necessary, not another drop of blood should be shed. He consistently sought to include in the armistice terms political conditions for indemnity and security. Clemenceau at first encouraged him to put forward the most extreme French claims but was afterwards embarrassed by his persistence. At the Peace Conference Foch urged the setting-up of an East European army, which supplied with Allied arms and material could, he held, beat back and defeat the unorganized Bolshevik forces. Author of *Des principes de la guerre* (1903), *De la conduite de la guerre, La Manœuvre pour la bataille* (1904).

FULLERTON-CARNEGIE, E. See Carnegie.

GIELGUD, CAPTAIN LEWIS EVELYN. According to August Zaleski, who represented Poland in talks with Voldemaras on Polish-Lithuanian relations in April 1919, Captain Gielgud, of Lithuanian descent, was appointed as British observer to the talks by Lloyd George. He was withdrawn when the talks reached a stalemate. See M. K. Dziewanowski, *Joseph Pilsudski: A European Federalist*, pp. 119–21.

HANKEY, SIR MAURICE, K.C.B. (1877–1963). Created Baron Hankey of Chart 1939. Educated at Rugby and Royal Naval College, Greenwich. Assistant Naval Secretary and afterwards Secretary to the Committee of Imperial Defence 1908–14. During the war he was Secretary to the War Council, to the War Cabinet and to the Imperial War Cabinet. During the Peace Conference he was Secretary to the British Empire Delegation, British representative on the Secretariat of the Council of Ten and after 19 April 1919 Secretary to the Council of Four. His minutes are reproduced in *Foreign Relations of the United States: Paris Peace Conference 1919*. After 1919 he became Permanent Secretary to the Cabinet and built up the Cabinet Secretariat. He also acted as Secretary to numerous wartime and post-war conferences. Hankey had a prodigious memory and was endlessly hardworking and efficient. He had already during the war begun to give advice and to prepare memoranda. He was chiefly interested in military matters and in the Empire. At Paris he was fully occupied with his secretarial duties, the keeping of minutes, distribution of papers and transmission of instructions. For information Lloyd George relied upon Philip Kerr. Later Hankey did begin increasingly to interfere in matters of policy. After his retirement he joined Chamberlain's War Cabinet in 1939 but left the Government in 1942. (He could not get on with Churchill.) He opposed the policy of unconditional surrender, the indiscriminate bombing of Germany and the trial of war criminals, chiefly on humanitarian grounds. Author of *The Supreme Command 1914–18* (1961), *The Supreme Control at the Peace Conference 1919*. See also Stephen Roskill, *Hankey: Man of Secrets*, Vol. I (1970).

HARDINGE, CHARLES, P.C., K.C.M.G. (1858–1944). Created Viscount Hardinge of Penhurst 1910. Educated at Harrow and Trinity College, Cambridge. Entered Foreign Office in German Department 1880. Served in Constantinople, Berlin, Washington, Sofia, Bucharest and Paris. Assistant Under-Secretary 1906–10. He attended Edward VII on his visits to European capitals. Viceroy of India 1910–16. Once more Permanent Under-Secretary 1916–20. He took part in the Foreign Office reforms in 1906 and 1919. At Paris he was, at Sir Maurice Hankey's suggestion, designated as Organizing Ambassador. He was a firm supporter of the Anglo-French and Anglo-Russian Entente. To keep Russia and Germany apart was, he held, essential for the security of Europe. Author of *Old Diplomacy*. See Zara Steiner, *The Foreign Office and Foreign Policy 1893–1914* (Cambridge, 1970).

HASKINS, CHARLES HOMER (1870–1937). Dean of the Harvard Graduate School. An outstanding medievalist, he specialized in Norman institutions and the transmittal of Greek and Arabic learning to Western Europe. Member of the Inquiry 1917. Member of the American Delegation. He was concerned chiefly with German frontiers in the west. See Haskins and Lord, *Some Problems of the Peace* (1920); *The Inquiry*.

HEADLAM, THE REV. ARTHUR CAYLEY, D.D. He was born at Whorlton Hall on 2 August 1862, and died there on 25 January 1947. He was Headlam-Morley's elder brother. Educated at Winchester and New College, Oxford. Fellow of All Souls College, Oxford. Editor of the *Church Quarterly Review*. Rector of Welwyn. Principal of King's College, London 1903–13. Regius Professor of Divinity at Oxford and Canon of Christ Church 1918. He was consecrated Bishop of Gloucester in 1923. Headlam was an eminent theologian, interested also in archaeology and ancient history. He was one of the leaders of the movement for Christian reunion. He had special knowledge of the Greek Orthodox Churches and was bound to them by many ties of friendship. Tolerant and liberal in his own field of activity, he tended to reaction in politics. At this time he thought the treaty would prove too lenient to Germany. He had great respect for his brother's character, intellect and judgement. Author of *History, Authority and Theology* (1907), *The Doctrine of the Church and Christian Reunion, Bampton Lectures* (1920), *The Life and Teaching of Jesus the Christ*, Vol. I (1923), etc. See also Ronald Jasper, *Arthur Caley Headlam* (1960); A. Headlam-Morley, 'A Biographical Essay', in A. C. Headlam, *The Fourth Gospel as History* (1960).

HERRON, PROFESSOR GEORGE DAVIS. An American clergyman, lecturer and writer who to a certain extent had President Wilson's confidence. He had been nominated as one of the American representatives at the proposed Prinkipo Conference. In January 1919 Wilson used him in an unsuccessful attempt to achieve agreed revision of Italian claims under the Treaty of London.

HEWART, THE RT. HON. SIR GORDON, K.C., M.P. (1870–1943). Attorney-General. A member of the Legal Section of the British Delegation. Vice-President of the Commission on the Responsibility of the Authors of the War and the Enforcement of Penalties.

HOWARD, SIR ESME, K.C.M.G. (1863–1939). Created Baron Howard of Penrith 1930. Educated Harrow and private studies abroad. Joined Catholic Church 1898. Joined Diplomatic Service 1885. Served under Lord Caernarvon in Ireland, Rome and Berlin. Retired 1892. He had great charm, a romantic adventurous spirit and some thought a certain instability of judgement. Fought in the South African War, was captured and escaped. He returned to the Diplomatic Service and as Consul-General in Crete dealt skilfully with the Venizelos revolt. In Stockholm during the war, he was successful in achieving the maximum application of the blockade without alienating the Swedes. A member of the British Delegation at Paris. Adviser on Polish affairs. British representative on the Inter-Allied Mission to Poland. Ambassador in Madrid 1919; Washington (with great success) 1924. Author of *The Theatre of Life* (1935).

HURST, CECIL, G.C.M.G., K.C.B. (1870–1962). Educated Westminster School and Trinity College, Cambridge. Legal adviser to the Foreign Office. He was a member of the Phillimore Committee on the League of Nations (1917–18). Represented the Foreign Office on the Legal Section of the British Delegation. Together with the American David Hunter Miller, he prepared the Hurst-Miller draft for submission to the League Commission. He was chiefly responsible for the legal drafting of the treaties. A judge of the Permanent Court of International Justice 1929–42 (President 1934–6). One of the United Kingdom members of the Permanent Court of Arbitration at The Hague. In 1930 he gave his vote in favour of the legality of the Austro-German Customs Union proposal, which was rejected by the casting vote of the President. He was the principal founder of the *British Year Book of International Law*.

JOHNSON, MAJOR DOUGLAS W. (1878–1944). A geographer on the faculty of Columbia University. As a member of the Inquiry, he came to Europe in spring 1918 to study the relationship between physical geography and military strategy in the drawing of boundaries. He sought to establish liaisons with those in France and England who were preparing plans for the Peace. At the Peace Conference he was an adviser on Italy. He favoured the cession of Fiume to Yugoslavia. See Gelfand, *The Inquiry*.

JONES, CAPTAIN CLEMENT, C.B. Afterwards Sir Clement Jones, K.C.B. Assistant Secretary of the War Cabinet and of the British Empire Delegation he worked closely with Sir Maurice Hankey.

KERNAN, MAJOR-GENERAL F. J. The American member of the Inter-Allied Commission to Poland. Sir Esme Howard said of him that 'he could not understand what it was all about and would have liked to have drawn a cordon round all those warring peoples and let them fight it out in peace'. In March he delivered to the Polish and Ukrainian Commanders the notes by which the Supreme Council hoped, without success, to establish an armistice.

KERR, PHILIP HENRY (1882–1940). Succeeded in 1930 as eleventh Marquess of Lothian. His mother was Lady Anne Fitzalan Howard. Educated at the Oratory School, at Edgbaston and at New College, Oxford. He served under Milner in South Africa – the youngest of the famous 'Kindergarten'. He gained administrative experience and was one of the first to show concern about the relations of Africans and Europeans. Together with Lionel Curtis, he founded the *Round Table* (1910) and was first editor. In 1916 he became private secretary to Lloyd George and served him in this capacity at Paris. A man of great integrity, humility and intelligence, he did what was humanly possible to inform his chief and pass on the expert information he received. He drafted the Allied reply to Brockdorff-Rantzau on German responsibility for the war and was responsible for the preface to the Treaty of Versailles. He ceased working for the Prime Minister in 1922: he was one of the very few who established a lasting relationship of friendship and respect with Lloyd George. Kerr was a member of Ramsay MacDonald's Cabinet in 1931 and Chairman of the Indian Frontier Commission. A believer in Anglo-German friendship, he came to recognize the injustices of the Treaty of Versailles, especially in its economic aspects. He knew little of Germany at first hand and was led for a time into grave misjudgements about Hitler and the Nazis. His gifts proved most fruitful as Secretary of the Rhodes Trust, 1925–39, and as ambassador in Washington from 1939 until his death in 1940. By his frankness, sincerity and understanding, he did more than any one man to break down the barriers of distrust and misunderstanding. See Lionel Curtis (ed.), *American Speeches of Lord Lothian*; J. R. M. Butler, *Lord Lothian*.

KEYNES, JOHN MAYNARD (1883–1955). Economist and philosopher. Educated at Eton and King's College, Cambridge. Created Baron Keynes of Tilton. Fellow of King's College. He joined the Treasury in 1915 and was head of A Division, responsible for external debt. Principal representative of the Treasury on the British Delegation at Paris. He was not a member of the Reparations Commission which ignored and overrode the advice of the Treasury. As a member of the Supreme Economic Council, he prepared a plan for European reconstruction. This was turned down by the Americans. He then retired and returned to King's College. After the Second World War his advice on inter-governmental indebtedness was heeded both in Europe and America. Keynes's economic theories were to a certain extent applied in practice and as a result the Western world escaped the depression and financial crises that followed the First World War. Author of *Economic Consequences of the Peace* (1919), *A Revision of the Treaty* (1922), *A Tract on Monetary Reform* (1923), *The General Theory of Employment, Interest and Money* (1936), 'Dr Melchior' in *Two Memoirs* (1947). See also R. H. Harrod, *Life of John Maynard Keynes*.

KISCH, COLONEL FREDERICK (FRED) M. (1888–1943). Educated at Clifton College, Royal Military Academy, Woolwich, and School of Military Engineering, Chatham. Commissioned Royal Engineers 1907. Brigadier-General 1941. He came of a cultured Jewish family, at one time settled in Prague. His father was an Indian Civil Servant. Fred Kisch served in India and arrived in France with the Indian Corps in September 1914. Wounded at the second battle of Ypres. Transferred to Mesopotamia, where he was seriously wounded 1915. Appointed to General Staff (Directorate of Military Intelligence) at the War Office. Concerned at first with the Middle and Far East; after November 1917 exclusively with Russia. Head of Military Intelligence in Russia. He held that small-scale assistance to anti-Bolshevik forces was ineffective and wasteful. After January 1919 he advised against intervention. A member of the Military Section of the British Delegation at Paris. Assistant to Sir William Tyrrell on the Polish Commission. He was British representative on a Committee set up in Paris in April to recommend armistice terms between the Poles and Ukrainians in East Galicia. On the recommendation of Dr Chaim Weizmann, with whom he formed a lasting friendship, he was chosen head of the Jewish agency in Palestine 1923. He learnt Hebrew and made his lasting home in Palestine in 1923. With firmness and endless patience, he sought to resolve the differences between the various Jewish organiza- tions, to work loyally with the British administration and so far as human- ly possible to mitigate the hostility of the Arabs. He enjoyed the confidence of two outstanding High Commissioners, Lord Samuel and Lord Plumer, and won at least partial acceptance of his contention that increased im- migration would raise productive capacity. Retired in 1931. Together with Hubermann he founded the Palestine Symphony Orchestra. A Palestine citizen, he was still on the reserve of officers. He served continuously in the Western Desert. Chief engineer for the Eighth Army 1941. In com- mand of sappers, he was responsible for water supply, for roads and air strips, for demolition in retreat, for the clearing of 'lanes' through enemy airfields in advance – as at El Alamein – and for the securing of harbours at Tobruk, Benghazi and Tripoli. He was killed by a mine explosion shortly before the capture of Tunis. Author of *Palestine Diary* (1938). See Norman Bentwich and Michael Kisch, *Brigadier Frederick Kisch* (1966).

KOPPEL, PERCY (1876–1932). Educated at Bradfield College and Magda- len College, Oxford. Called to the Bar, Inner Temple 1900. Board of Education 1903–5. During the war he worked at Wellington House, in the News Department of the Department of Information and in the P.I.D. He was responsible for administration, and when Tyrrell and Headlam- Morley were both away at Paris he was in charge of the Department (under the general supervision of Sir John Tilley). First Secretary and Councillor at the Foreign Office 1920.

KRAMARSCH (KRAMÁŘ), DR KARL (KAREL) (1860–1937). Studied at Prague, Strasbourg, Berlin and the École Politique, Paris. Elected deputy in Austrian Parliament 1891. As leader of the Czechs he worked by con- stitutional methods for a federal solution of the Austrian problem. After the outbreak of war he realized this was in vain. He was the founder of the New Slavism based on support of Tsarist Russia. Whilst Masaryk and Benes worked in exile, Kramarsch suffered persecution at home. Forged documents were used to secure a death sentence for high treason in 1915. This was commuted to life imprisonment. Released on accession of the Emperor Charles in the amnesty of 1917. After the October revolution of 1918, elected President of National Council, and then first Prime

Minister of Czechoslovakia. First plenipotentiary Delegate for Czechoslovakia at Paris. A member of the League of Nations Commission. Resigned 1919. A conservative and ultra-nationalist, he led the National Democrats in opposition to Masaryk and Benes. He had hoped for Russian friendship but was never reconciled to the Russia of the Soviets. He showed great generosity to Russian refugees in Czechoslovakia.

LAROCHE, M. A Minister Plenipotentiary in the French Delegation. Chief of the European Section in the Quai d'Orsay. One of the French representatives on the Commission for Belgian and Danish Affairs, and later President of the Commission on the political clauses of the Austrian treaty.

LAWRENCE, LT.-COL. T. E. (Lawrence of Arabia; 1888–1935). Educated Oxford High School and Jesus College, Oxford. Fellow of All Souls College, Oxford, 1919. He first travelled to the Middle East as an archaeologist. During the war he worked in the Arab Bureau under Sir Ronald Storrs, through whom he became closely associated with Abdullah and Feisal, sons of Husain the Grand Sheriff of Mecca. A born leader of men, he joined with them in raising the Arab revolt. Under Allenby's command, Lawrence proved himself a brilliant strategist. He disrupted the Turkish communications and after great hardship and privation led his faithful band to Damascus. He was strongly opposed to the Sykes–Picot agreement. At the Peace Conference he acted as adviser to the Emir Feisal. Afterwards he served for a short period as adviser to the Middle Eastern Department of the Colonial Office. Abdullah was established as ruling prince of Jordan and Feisal as king of Iraq under British mandates. He sponsored the republication of Doughty's *Arabia Deserta* (1921). Author of *The Seven Pillars of Wisdom* (1935). See also David Garnett (ed.), *Letters of T. E. Lawrence* (1938); Arnold Toynbee, *Acquaintances*.

LEEPER, ALEXANDER WIGRAM ALLEN (1887–1935), C.B.E. (1920), C.M.G. (1935). Educated Melbourne Boys' Church of England Grammar School; Trinity College, University of Melbourne; and Balliol College, Oxford. Assistant, Egyptian and Assyrian Department, British Museum, 1912. Member of the Neutral Press Committee, Home Office, 1915–January 1916, then 1916–March 1917 News Department of the Foreign Office. Head of the Balkan Section of the Intelligence Bureau, Department of Information, 1917–March 1918, and in March 1918 made a temporary clerk and member of the P.I.D. Wrote extensively for *The New Europe*, chiefly on Central European affairs. A member of the British

Delegation to the Peace Conference, where his gifts as a linguist proved invaluable. Joined the permanent staff of the Foreign Office in 1920, assistant private secretary to Lord Curzon, 1920–4. Allen Leeper was seconded to the Australian Government in 1924 to advise on the formation of a Department of External Affairs. Served in Vienna 1924–8, and in 1928 returned to London where his chief concern was with the Disarmament Conferences and air disarmament. In 1933 made Head of the League of Nations and Western Department. His scholarly work, *Medieval Austria* (1941), shows the depth and range of his intelligence and integrity.

LEEPER, REGINALD (REX) WILDING ALLEN (1888–1968), C.B.E. (1919), C.M.G. (1936), K.C.M.G. (1945), G.B.E. (1948). Educated Melbourne Boys' Church of England Grammar School; Trinity College, University of Melbourne; and New College, Oxford. Son of Alexander Leeper, noted classicist and first Warden of Trinity College, Melbourne. Rex Leeper joined the Bombay Company, served in Bombay and Madras. Invalided to England in July 1915. January 1916 joined the News Department of the Foreign Office, and in March 1917 in charge of Russian Section of Intelligence Bureau, Department of Information. In March 1918 made a temporary clerk and member of P.I.D. Wrote extensively for *The New Europe*, chiefly on events in Russia. During the Peace Conference he contributed valuable memoranda on Russian affairs. Remained in the Diplomatic Service, serving in Riga, Constantinople and Warsaw. Transferred to the Foreign Office 1929, Head of the News Department 1935, where he was consistently aware of the dangers from Germany. Ambassador to the Greek Government 1943–6, then to the Argentine Republic 1946–8. His incisively analytical mind and brilliance at mastering languages were greatly to be admired. Author of *When Greek Meets Greek* (1950).

LE ROND, GENERAL. Adjutant-General to Marshal Foch. A member of the French Delegation. He played an important part in the territorial settlement, especially in Eastern Europe. French expert on the Polish Commission, member of the commissions on Czechoslovak affairs, Romania and Yugoslavia. With Dr Lord, Col. Kisch and others, he was appointed to negotiate an armistice between Poland and the Ukraine (16 April).

LORD, ROBERT H., PH.D. (Harvard). He had studied in Vienna, Berlin and Moscow. A specialist in Polish history. He joined the Inquiry as one of its youngest members in 1918. He was an ardent admirer of Poland, her people, her language and her literature. As the Polish expert on the

American Delegation, he supported the most extreme demands of the Poles without any consistent regard for national or ethnic factors. He was a member of the Inter-Allied Mission to Poland, January 1919, and of the Polish Commission in Paris. See Haskins and Lord, *Some Problems of the Peace* (1920); Gelfand, *The Inquiry*.

LOUCHEUR, LOUIS (1872–1931). Minister of Industrial Reconstruction. A member of the French Delegation responsible for labour questions. In the controversies over reparations he took a more moderate line than Monsieur Klotz, the Minister of Finance.

MACK, JUDGE JULIAN W. A leader of the old Jewish community in the USA which was established before the great stream of immigration from Russia and Romania. A supporter of Justice Brandeis. Brandeis differed from Dr Weizmann, the great Zionist leader, in holding that the National Home in Palestine should be supported by individual enterprise on an economic, not a political basis. Weizmann sought to organize the Jews in the diaspora to give corporate financial and moral support for the gradual building-up of an independent political society in the historic land of Israel. At Paris the American 'non-Zionists' strove to win for Jewish minorities recognition as autonomous cultural entities. Judge Mack assisted Louis Marshall in drafting proposals to this effect which they pressed upon Col. House and President Wilson. They won a rather confused support from Mr Hunter Miller. See C. A. Macartney, *National States and National Minorities* (1933); Oscar I. Janowsky, *The Jews and Minority Rights 1898–1919* (Columbia University Press, 1933).

MALLET, SIR LOUIS, K.C.M.G., C.B. (1864–1936). Entered Foreign Office 1888. Served in Brazil, Rome and Cairo. Précis writer to Lord Lansdowne. Private secretary to Sir Edward Grey. Assistant Under-Secretary of State 1907–13. Ambassador to Turkey. Zara Steiner describes him as 'the most avid anti-German in the Office'; see *The Foreign Office and Foreign Policy 1892–1914.*

MANCE, BRIGADIER-GENERAL H. O. (Royal Engineers), C.B., C.M.G., D.S.O. A member of the Military Section of the British Delegation. He was British representative on the Commission on International Ports, Waterways and Railways, and on the Sub-Commissions on Freedom of Transit and on the Kiel Canal.

MARSHALL, LOUIS (1856–1929). Lawyer and advocate; a leading member of the American Jewish Congress founded in 1907 to represent American

Q

Jews in national and international affairs. He came of a German Jewish family and belonged to the Reform or Liberal Synagogue. At Paris he worked closely with Judge Mack whom he suceeded as chairman of the Committee of Jewish Delegates. Although a 'non-Zionist', Marshall became deeply interested in the Jewish National Home in Palestine. He admired Judah Magnes, the first Chancellor (later President) of the Hebrew University in Jerusalem. He co-operated with Col. Kisch in winning the support of American Jews for the Jewish Agency in Palestine. He died soon after the first meeting of the enlarged Agency at Zürich in 1929.

MAURICE, MAJOR-GENERAL SIR FREDERICK. He had been Director of Military Operations. He retired in April 1918 and launched a violent attack on Lloyd George, accusing him of using fallacious figures about the strength of the British Army in France. There is an excellent account in A. J. P. Taylor, *English History 1914–1945*. Maurice served during the Peace Conference as military correspondent of the *Daily Chronicle*.

MEZES, SIDNEY EDWARD (1863–1931). Graduated at University of California. Ph.D. (Harvard) 1884. President of the City College of New York. A philosopher and logician. He was brother-in-law of Col. House. At the request of House, and by direction of President Wilson, he brought together the body of experts known as the Inquiry. At Paris they formed a special research section of the American Delegation. See L. E. Gelfand, *The Inquiry;* Charles Seymour (ed.), *The Intimate Papers of Colonel House*.

MILLER, DAVID HUNTER (b. 1875). Lawyer and partner in the New York firm of Miller and Auchinloss. He was an accomplished draughts-man but not originally an expert on international law. He acted, however, as adviser on international law, both to the Inquiry and to the State Department. Head of the Legal Section of the American Delegation. Together with Sir Cecil Hurst, he correlated the proposals of President Wilson and Lord Robert Cecil for the Covenant of the League of Nations. The Hurst–Miller Draft was laid before the League Commission at Paris at its first meeting on 3 February. He was the American representative on the New States Committee. Author of *The Hunter Miller Diary* and *The Drafting of the Covenant*.

MILNER, ALFRED, P.C. (1854–1925). Created first Viscount Milner 1902. Educated Gymnasium at Tübingen; King's College, London; Balliol College, Oxford. He was interested in adult education and was one of the founders of Toynbee Hall. Both in Egypt under Sir Evelyn Baring, and afterwards in South Africa, he proved himself a brilliant administrator, especially in the world of finance. A devoted exponent of an enlightened imperialism, he enacted the policy of reconstruction and reconciliation after the Boer War. He left South Africa in 1905 and joined Lloyd George's War Cabinet in 1916. On a mission to France after the German breakthrough at Amiens, March 1918, he took full responsibility for the unity of command under Foch. Secretary of State for War, April 1918. Secretary of State for the Colonies, December 1918. A Minister Plenipotentiary in the British Delegation at Paris. He advocated a moderate peace of reconciliation. At Paris he was chairman of a committee which prepared the first drafts for A and B Mandates. Author of *England in Egypt* (1892); Cecil Headlam (ed.), *Milner Papers* (1931–3).

NAMIER, LEWIS (born Bernstein; 1888–1960). Educated at Lemberg, at University of Lausanne and at Balliol College, Oxford. Naturalized British subject 1913. Knighted 1952. He was born in East Galicia under the Habsburg Monarchy. Son of a Jewish landowner who had become an assimilated Pole and a Roman Catholic. In early manhood he changed his name to Namier and returned to the Jewish allegiance of his ancestors. He was not a Jew by religion but became an outstanding supporter of Zionism. His historical studies led him to a profound admiration of the British Constitution and the British contribution to world affairs. During the war a member of the Intelligence Bureau and of the P.I.D. A consistent advocate of the principle of nationality, he held that the Habsburg Monarchy should be liquidated in favour of independent national states, and that the German Austrians should, if they wished, be allowed to join with Germany. He opposed what he considered the excessive Polish demands, especially on their eastern frontiers. Lecturer in Modern History, Balliol, 1920–1. Political secretary to the Jewish Agency for Palestine 1920–31. Professor of Modern History, Manchester University, 1931–53. He introduced a new historical method based on the rigorous substitution of accurate detail for generalization. Author of 'The Downfall of the Hapsburg Monarchy' (a brilliant chapter in Temperley's *History of the Peace Conference*, Vol. IV), *The Structure of Politics at the Accession of George III* (1929), *England in the Age of the American Revolution* (1930). *Diplomatic Prelude 1939* (1945), *Europe in Decay* (1949), *In the Nazi Era* (1952), *Vanished Supremacies* (1958), etc. See also Julia Namier, *Lewis Namier* (1971); Arnold Toynbee, *Acquaintances*.

NAUMANN, FRIEDRICH. A Christian Socialist and member of the Reichstag on the left wing of the Catholic Centre Party. In 1915 he published *Mitteleuropa*: Germany, Austria and Hungary should be joined in an organic federal union, based not on nationality, but on a common cultural and historical heritage, which would be used to promote economic and industrial efficiency and prosperity. The book was translated into English and won some approval in liberal circles by the moderation of its language and the repudiation of German 'nationalism'. Headlam, as he then was, rejected it in uncompromising terms (in this he was supported by Arnold Toynbee). He held that in a disguised form it was a plea for German domination – according to Naumann's plan other smaller states would be drawn to the new Central Europe: 'from Constantinople to Antwerp, and from Riga to Trieste there would be one great organization, one army, one financial and commercial system, and this will be German'. See J. W. Headlam, *The Issue* (1917).

NICOLSON, THE HON. HAROLD (1886–1967), K.C.V.O. 1952. Educated at Wellington and Balliol College, Oxford. Joined the Foreign Office in 1909. A member of the British Delegation at the Peace Conference. He was especially concerned with the former Habsburg Dominions and with Greece. Served afterwards in Tehran and Berlin. Resigned from the Diplomatic Service 1927. He was encouraged, one may presume, by his wife Victoria Sackville-West to devote himself to literature. M.P. (National Labour) 1935–45. He was strongly opposed to the Munich Agreement. Author of *Verlaine* (1921), *Tennyson* (1923), *Peacemaking 1919* (1933); biographies of his father *Lord Carnock* (1930), *Curzon The Last Phase* (1933) and *King George VI* (1952); *Diaries*, edited by Nigel Nicolson (1966), etc.

NOEL-BAKER, PHILIP J. (b. 1889), P.C. 1945. Educated at Bootham School, York, and King's College, Cambridge. Commandant of the Friends' Ambulance Unit 1914. Adjutant of the first British Ambulance to Italy (Silver Medal for Valour). Head, under Lord Robert Cecil, of the League of Nations Section of the British Delegation at Paris. Principal assistant to Sir Eric Drummond 1920–2. British Delegate to the Assembly of the League of Nations 1929–31. He worked closely with Lord Robert Cecil in the League of Nations Union and with Arthur Henderson at the Disarmament Conference. A fervent and consistent supporter of the League of Nations, he stressed the importance of the rule of law in international affairs. Vice-Principal of Ruskin College, Oxford, 1918. Sir Ernest Cassell Professor of International Relations, University of London,

1924–9. M.P. for Coventry 1924, for Derby 1936. Minister of State, Foreign Office, 1945. Secretary of State for Commonwealth Relations 1947. British Delegate to the General Assembly of U.N.O. 1946. President of Cambridge University Athletic Club 1910–12. Captain of British Olympic Track Team 1920 and 1924. Commandant of British Olympic Team 1952. One of the founders, with Sir Cecil Hurst, of the *British Year Book of International Law*. Author of *The League of Nations at Work* (1925), *The Geneva Protocol* (1925), *Disarmament* (1926), *The Juridical Status of the British Dominions in International Law* (1927), etc.

PADEREWSKI, IGNACE JAN (1860–1941). The greatest pianist of his time. Entered the Conservatoire in Warsaw at the age of twelve. Afterwards studied with Letschetisky in Vienna. He was a devoted interpreter of Handel, Mendelssohn, Schumann, Debussy, Liszt, and above all Chopin. After the outbreak of war, he organized a Polish Relief Committee in Switzerland and raised funds by lectures and concerts in the USA. When the USA entered the war he acted as Delegate of the National Committee and recruited Polish volunteers for the Foreign Legion, commanded by Gerneral Haller. Paderewski formed an affectionate friendship with Col. House and through him exercised some influence on President Wilson's pronouncements in regard to Poland. In December 1918 he returned to Poland with the British Military Mission. Landing in Danzig, he travelled first to Posen, where his arrival led to a rising against the Germans. He was greeted with popular enthusiasm in Warsaw and Cracow. After lengthy negotiations with Pilsudski, he became Prime Minister and Foreign Minister, with Pilsudski as Head of State. He returned to Paris in March 1919 as plenipotentiary Delegate. He retired from politics as the result of an election defeat in November 1919 and returned to his musical career. He died in New York in 1941, shortly after the celebrations of the Golden Jubilee of his first appearance in the USA.

PAGET, LADY MURIEL (1876–1938), C.B.E. 1938. Daughter of the twelfth Earl of Winchelsea and Nottingham. Married Sir Richard Paget (Bart.). A philanthropist of great courage and indefatigable energy. She established invalid kitchens in London in 1905 and helped with the Belgian Refugee Committee in 1914. She organized and administered an Anglo-Russian Hospital in Petrograd 1915. She was with the Russian army in Romania during the typhus epidemic in 1917. After the Revolution she left Russia under Red Army escort through Siberia to Japan. In 1919 she went to Czechoslovakia at the personal request of President Masaryk to administer hospitals and child welfare work. She returned to Russia in 1924 to organize relief for distressed British subjects abandoned in the Revolution. Expelled in 1938. Neville Chamberlain strongly repudiated a Soviet charge of espionage.

PARKER, ALWYN, C.B., C.M.G. (1877–1951). Educated at Harrow and in Germany. Head of Contraband Department of the Foreign Office 1914–1917. Librarian of the Foreign Office 1918. Private secretary to Lord Hardinge. He was responsible for the organization and accommodation of the Political Section at Paris. A director of Lloyds Bank 1919–47.

PATON, HAMISH JAMES (1887–1967). Philosopher and classical scholar. Educated Glasgow High School and University, and at Balliol College, Oxford. During the war he served in the Intelligence Division of the Admiralty. He gathered a prodigious quantity of Polish statistical data. Paton, instead of Namier, was summoned to Paris in February 1919 to replace Howard as adviser on Polish affairs. He played an important part in drafting the Polish settlement. His work in preparing the so-called Curzon Line has been too little recognized. (See Arnold Toynbee, *Acquaintances*, p. 67.) Professor of Logic and Rhetoric at the University of Glasgow. 1937 Whites Professor of Moral Philosophy at Oxford. He contributed chapters on the Polish settlement in Temperley's *History of the Peace Conference*. Author of *The Good Will* (1927), *Kant's Metaphysic of Experience*.

PENSON, SIR HENRY, K.B.E. (1864–1955). Educated City of London School and Worcester College, Oxford. Chairman of War Trade Intelligence Department 1916. Director of the Intelligence Branch of the British Delegation. He organized the Intelligence Clearing House which was intended to co-ordinate the work of the different sections. Lecturer and Tutor in Modern History and Economics at Pembroke College, Oxford, 1919–22. Author of *Economics of Everyday Life*.

PERCY, LORD EUSTACE (1887–1958). Seventh son of seventh Duke of Northumberland. P.C. 1957. Created Baron Percy of Newcastle 1957. Joined Diplomatic Service 1911. In 1918 he prepared one of the Foreign Office draft proposals on the League of Nations. At the Peace Conference he was Mr Balfour's private secretary. He retired from the Foreign Office to enter Parliament as Conservative Member for Hastings. President of Board of Education 1924. A member of the second National Government 1935, and resigned a year later. His chief interest was in education. The success, indeed the survival, of democracy would depend on sound education, at every level from primary school to technical college. He was Rector of King's College, Newcastle (previously Armstrong College). President of Committee appointed by R. A. Butler to report on proposals for collaboration between universities and technical colleges 1944. Chairman of Burnham Committee 1953–6. Author of *Democracy on Trial* (1931), *John Knox* (1937), etc.

PHILLIPS, J. W. He and Headlam (as he then was) had worked together in the Board of Education under Sir Robert Morant. They were among the first of the Staff Inspectors for Secondary Schools appointed in 1902.

PILSUDSKI, JOSEPH (1867–1935). Born near Vilna, a border country where Poles, Lithuanians and White Russians meet. He was expelled from Kharkov University and spent five years in Siberia. He was the first leader of a 'Socialist' anti-Russian movement – he was never interested in Marxism. Living in Austrian Galicia, where the Poles enjoyed a measure of autonomy, he organized and trained an underground revolutionary force. After 1914 he was encouraged first by the Austrian G.H.Q. and then by the Germans to raise a Polish army in conquered Russian territory. An ardent patriot, Pilsudski intended his legions to win the independence of a united Poland. He refused to serve the interests of the Central Powers, and after the Russian Revolution he was imprisoned at Magdeburg. Released in November 1918, by a German Workers and Soldiers Council, he returned to Warsaw. He took over power from the Council of Regency established under German control, and became Head of State and Commander-in-Chief. In January 1919 a measure of internal unity was achieved by agreement with Paderewski. First Marshal of Poland 1920. He sought to establish a greater Poland in federal union with Lithuania and Ruthenia. He was responsible for the seizure of Vilna and for the invasion of the Ukraine in 1920. He repulsed the subsequent Russian invasion at the gates of Warsaw and obtained a frontier east of the 'Curzon Line' by the Treaty of Riga. Retired in 1923; seized power May 1926. Prime Minister 1926–8. War Minister till 1933. He was closely associated with Col. Beck and favoured the bipartite agreements with Russia and Germany. See M. K. Dziewanowski, *Joseph Pilsudski: A European Federalist*; P. S. Wandycz, *Polish-Soviet Relations, 1917–1921*.

POLLOCK, SIR ERNEST MURRAY, K.B.E. (1861–1931). Created Viscount Hanworth. Educated Charterhouse and Trinity College, Cambridge.

Conservative M.P. for Warwick and Leamington 1910–23. Solicitor-General 1917. Attorney-General 1922. A successful lawyer – a quick though not deep intelligence. At the Peace Conference he was a member of the Legal Section of the British Delegation.

POSNER, STANISLAV (1858–1930). A leading member of the Polish Socialist Party. In 1906 he retired from politics and lived for many years in Paris. A liberal historian, he was a close friend of Lewis Namier, with whom he regularly corresponded. In 1921 he returned to Poland. Member of Parliament 1922–30. He was concerned with adult education and was one of the founders of the Council for Political Freedom.

POWICKE, FREDERICK MAURICE (1879–1963). Knighted 1948. Educated Owens College, Manchester, and Balliol College, Oxford. Fellow of Merton College, Oxford, 1908–15. At Paris he was a member of the Intelligence Clearing House. Professor of Medieval History, Manchester University, 1919–28. Regius Professor of Modern History at Oxford 1928–47. President of the Royal Historical Society 1933–7. Author of *Studies in the History of the Angevin Empire* (1913), *Stephen Langton* (1928), *Medieval England* (1931), etc. He followed to some extent the line taken by C. H. Haskins at Harvard in showing how the history of England can be modified and developed by the study of Norman evidence.

REICHMANN. He was afterwards chairman of the central committee for assimilating German Jews who claimed that they were *deutsche Staatsbürger jüdischen Glaubens*. He was interned in a concentration camp in 1938 but came to England with his wife in 1939 and became a British subject. From 1948 until his death in 1964 he worked as secretary to the Restitution and Compensation Organization under Mr Norman Bentwich, the Chairman.

RENNER, DR KARL (1870–1950). Socialist leader. Elected to the National Assembly of Austria–Hungary in 1908. A sincere Marxist, he was also a believer in nationality and the right of self-determination. After the collapse of the Habsburg Monarchy he became Chancellor, then President of the new republic of Austria. In 1919 he signed the Treaty of Saint-Germain. In the pre-Nazi period he supported the *Anschluss* of Austria with Germany. He was imprisoned for a time by Dollfuss. In 1945 he formed the first Austrian Provisional Government and was afterwards elected President. During the Russian occupation he stood firmly for the independence of Austria and for a democratic as against a one-party system of government. Once more he urged the return of the South Tyrol. He died in office at the age of eighty; his tolerance and steadfastness won for him wide support outside his own party.

SAUNDERS, GEORGE (1859–1922). Journalist. Educated Dundee High School, Glasgow University, Balliol College, Oxford, Bonn University, and Göttingen University. Berlin correspondent for the *Morning Post* 1887, for *The Times* 1897–1908. He was profoundly distrustful of German policy and came to think that conflict would prove inevitable. Saunders condemned as equally insincere the liberals who espoused the cause of the Boers and the Government who, from time to time, expressed a desire for Anglo-German *rapprochement*. He was accused by Bulow, the Chancellor, and Metternich, the ambassador in London, of deliberately poisoning Anglo-German relations by seeking out and publishing anti-British comment in obscure journals run by cranks and reactionaries. There was talk of his explusion but this came to nothing. From 1908 to 1914 he was *Times* correspondent in Paris. A firm upholder of the Entente, he was none the less critical of Poincaré's policy and at one time engaged in acute controversy with Tardieu, editor of *Le Temps*. A member of the Intelligence Bureau and of the P.I.D. His wife, Gertrude Hainaver, was the daughter of a Berlin banker. She had a gentle, patient nature, and put up with it all without resentment or bitterness. Saunders was deeply religious. He was devoted to his native countryside, a lover of music and of poetry.

SAZANOFF, SERGEI DIMITRIECH (1861–1927). He succeeded Iswolski as Foreign Minister of Russia in 1910. He tended to vacillate between a policy of conciliation and the strict maintenance of Russian interests, in the Middle East, in the Straits and in the Balkans. He thought that the best hope of peace was to convert the Triple Entente into a definite alliance. During the crisis following the murder of the Archduke Francis Ferdinand he was cautious but firm in supporting Serbian integrity. It was he who, urged on by the military leaders, persuaded the Tsar to decree general mobilization on 30 July 1914. During the war he favoured an autonomous Poland in free union with Russia. This led to his dismissal in 1916. He was ambassador in London until the Revolution. Afterwards in Paris he was designated Foreign Minister of the counter-revolutionary Government of Admiral A. V. Kolchak, self-styled 'Ruler of All the Russias', i.e. of all pre-war Russian territory with the exception of Russian Poland and Finland. Kolchak was Supreme Commander of the White Russian forces, supported by the French and British Governments. When he was captured and executed by the Bolsheviks in the summer of 1919, he was succeeded by General A. I. Denikin, who in turn gave way to General Wrangel, the last White Russian Commander in the civil war. Author of *Fateful Years* (1928). See also G. P. Gooch, *Before the War, Studies in Diplomacy*, Vol. 2.

SCHIFF, JACOB (1847–1920). An American banker. He encouraged recognition of the Bolsheviks in the hope of securing commercial and economic concessions for Western financiers. He is said to have worked behind the scenes in favour of the Prinkipo proposals and the Bullit mission.

SETON-WATSON, R. W. (1879–1951). Educated at Winchester and New College, Oxford. A scholar and brilliant linguist, he had a unique knowledge of the national problems of the Habsburg Monarchy. Together with Wickham Steed (who was then *Times* correspondent in Vienna), he exposed the legal abuses of the Zagreb and Friedyung Trials. From the outbreak of the war, he consistently opposed a separate peace with Austria–Hungary and asserted the right of its component nationalities to autonomy or independence or unity with their kinsmen in neighbouring states. He was instrumental in bringing Masaryk to England and with him founded the New Europe in 1916. In 1917 he joined the Intelligence Bureau under Count (afterwards Lord Edward) Gleichen, and in 1918 he worked in the Intelligence Department at Crewe House. He and Headlam-Morley were in frequent communication both in London and Paris. This probably explains the lack of correspondence between them. (Seton-Watson came to Paris as an independent observer at his own expense.) He was Masaryk Professor of Central European History at the University of London 1922–1949. He was instrumental in founding the School of Slavonic Studies. Author of *Racial Problems in Hungary* (1908), *The Southern Slav Question* (1911), *Disraeli, Gladstone and the Eastern Question* (1935), *Britain in Europe* (1937), *Britain and the Dictators* (1939), *Masaryk in England* (1943), *A History of the Czechs and Slovaks* (1943), etc.

SEYMOUR, CHARLES, PH.D. (Yale). At this time Assistant Professor of History at Yale. He joined the Inquiry in 1917 as an expert on Austria–Hungary. Served on the American Delegation at Paris. A member of the Commission on Czechoslovak Affairs. He dealt also with Yugoslavia and Romania. Together with other American experts, he strongly urged that Fiume be included in Yugoslavia. He edited *The Intimate Papers of Colonel House* (1928). Author of *American Diplomacy During the World War* (1934), *Geography, Justice and Politics at the Paris Peace Conference* (1951), *Letters from the Peace Conference*.

SHOTWELL, PROFESSOR JAMES T. Columbia University. He lectured on contemporary history. Chairman of the National Board of Historical Services 1917, and one of the original members of the Inquiry. (He took credit for suggesting the name.) He was especially concerned with British Empire affairs. A member of the American Delegation (Historical Questions). Member of the Commission for International Labour Legislation. Author of *At the Paris Peace Conference* (New York, 1937). See also Gelfand, *The Inquiry*.

SMITH, SIR HUBERT LLEWELLYN, K.C.B. (1864–1945). He came of a Quaker family in Bristol. Educated Bristol Grammar School and Corpus Christi College, Oxford (First Class in mathematics). University Extension Lecturer and Secretary of the National Association for the Promotion of Technical and Secondary Education. Served on Royal Commission on Secondary Education 1894–5. 1907 Permanent Secretary at Board of Trade. Under Lloyd George in 1915 he organized the new Ministry of Munitions. He was head of the British Economic Section at the Peace Conference. 1921–7 Chief Economic Adviser to the Government and member of the Economic Committee of the League of Nations. 'A great Civil Servant – one of those who not only administered policy but exercised a powerful influence in its formation' (Sir Arthur Salter).

SMUTS, GENERAL JAN CHRISTIAAN (1870–1950). South African soldier and statesman. Educated in South Africa and at Cambridge. (F. W. Maison regarded him as the best law student he had ever taught.) As a guerrilla leader during the South African War, he showed great fortitude in face of danger and physical privation. Later his political opponents held him to be 'slim'. Took part in negotiations at Vereeniging and Pretoria. In 1917 he joined the Imperial War Cabinet and the British War Cabinet. Resigned 1918. He was commissioned by Lloyd George to prepare the British 'case' for the Peace Conference. South African Delegate to the Conference and British Empire representative on the League of Nations Commission. In opposition to Herzog, he supported South Africa's participation in the Second World War. See W. K. Hancock, *Smuts: The Sanguine Years 1870–1919*.

SOKOLNICKI, MICHAEL (1888–1967). He was sent to Paris by Pilsudski at the end of 1918 to negotiate with the Entente. Pilsudski gave him two sets of instructions. The first outlined a desirable Polish boundary in the east. The second stressed Polish support for an independent Lithuania and

Ukraine. He was secretary to the Polish Delegation at Paris. Later ambassador at Helsinki, Copenhagen and Ankara.

SPICER, GERALD SYDNEY, C.B. (1874–1942). Educated at Eton. Clerk in the Foreign Office 1894. Assistant to Sir Eyre Crowe in Western Department. Head of American Department. Permanent Under-Secretary of State 1903–6. Senior Clerk 1912.

SUMNER, VISCOUNT JOHN ANDREW, OF IBSTONE. Created 1913. Educated Manchester Grammar School and Balliol College, Oxford. Called to the Bar 1883. Judge of the King's Bench Division 1909. Lord of Appeal in Ordinary. During the war he was constantly occupied with appeals from Prize Courts before the judicial Committee of the Privy Council. One of the British Empire representatives on the Reparations Commission at Paris. An eminent judge known for his powers of expression in speech and in writing – lucid, cogent, epigrammatic. In youth he was reputed an aggressive radical, later a diehard Conservative.

TARDIEU, ANDRÉ (1867–1945). (He had been ill since 1939.) Served as attaché in Berlin, in Ministry of Foreign Affairs and as Secretary to Conseil des Ministres 1897–1904. Then went over to journalism and politics. Foreign editor of Le Temps until 1914. French High Commissioner in USA 1917. One of the five French plenary Delegates at the Peace Conference. At Paris and afterwards he consistently maintained the need for concrete security against Germany. He acclaimed the occupation of the Ruhr. Prime Minister for short periods in 1929, 1930 and 1932. As head of the French Delegation to the Disarmament Conference, he proposed an international force – in which Germany would not participate (1934). In urging the need for constitutional reform, the stengthening of the executive and the reawakening of the spirit of France, he foreshadowed and indeed inspired the work of De Gaulle.

TORRETTA, MARQUIS DELLA. A Minister Plenipotentiary in the Italian Delegation. He was the Italian representative on the Polish Commission, on the Committee on the Eastern Frontiers of Germany and on the Commission on Greek Affairs.

TOYNBEE, ARNOLD JOSEPH (b. 1889). Educated Winchester and Balliol College, Oxford. Philosopher and historian. Hon. D.Litt. Oxford, Birmingham and Columbia. Litt.D. Cambridge. D.C.L. Princeton. C.H. 1956. Joined the P.I.D. in 1918. Member of the Middle Eastern Section of the

British Delegation to the Peace Conference. Korean Professor of Byzantine and Modern Greek Language, London University, 1919–24. Director of Studies at the Royal Institute of International Affairs and Research Professor of International History, London University, 1925–55. Author of *The World After the Peace Conference* (1925). With the assistance of Miss Boulter (now Mrs Toynbee), he produced the *Survey of International Affairs* from its inception until his retirement. His personal contributions are important, substantial and sometimes controversial, e.g. *Abyssinia* (1925), *A Study of History*, *Acquaintances* (1967), etc.

TRUMBITCH (TRUMBIČ), ANTE (1863–1938). A leader of the Croat nationalists, he escaped from Austria soon after the declaration of war. Encouraged by Wickham Steed and Seton-Watson, he strove for the national rights of the Croats and Slovenes. As head of the 'Yugoslav Committee', he achieved agreement with Paschich, the Serbian Prime Minister. In the Pact of Corfu (1917) they proclaimed the Union of the Southern Slavs in the Kingdom of the Serbs, Croats and Slovenes. (This was confirmed in the Declaration of Geneva, 11 November 1918.) Advised by his English friends, he sought agreement with Italy in common resistance to Austria–Hungary. It was hoped that the Italians would voluntarily give up part of the Adriatic territory promised in the Treaty of London (1915). At Paris Trumbitch represented as Foreign Minister the newly established kingdom of Yugoslavia. He showed moderation in pressing territorial claims as against Romania and Italy. The seizure of Fiume finally broke the possibility of friendship with Italy. See Wickham Steed, *Through Thirty Years*, Vol. II.

TYRRELL, SIR WILLIAM (1866–1947). Created Baron Tyrrell 1929. Educated in Germany in Roman Catholic institutions and at Balliol College, Oxford (when Jowett was Master). Clerk in the Foreign Office 1889. Private secretary to Sir Edward Grey who relied on his aptitude and skill in winning the confidence of foreign diplomats, journalists and parliamentarians. He was a member of the Phillimore Committee on the League of Nations in 1918 and head of the P.I.D. At Paris he was the British representative on the Polish Commission. Both before and after the war he opposed what he considered to be the dangerous pro-German drift in British policy. He stood firmly by the friendship with France. In 1925 he succeeded Sir Eyre Crowe as Permanent Under-Secretary of State. Ambassador in Paris 1928–34. His younger son was killed in action in 1915, the elder in 1918.

VENIZELOS, ELEFTHERIOS (1864–1936). Born in Crete, he took a leading part in the rising of 1897, which led to the evacuation of the Turks. Called to Athens, he was Prime Minister 1910–15. He was helped by Wickham Steed in the organization of the Balkan League. A leader in reconstruction and reform after the Balkan Wars. He consistently supported the Allied cause (he had offered to declare war on Germany in August 1914). This led to constant friction with King Constantine. With Allied support he set up a separate provisional Government in Salonika in 1916, returned to Athens, declared war and secured the abdication of the King in 1917. President of the Council of Ministers and plenipotentiary Delegate at Paris. He was an active member of the League of Nations Commission. He formed a close friendship with Lloyd George. There was perhaps some affinity of temperament, courage, clarity of aim, a magnetic personality – and the readiness when occasion demanded to pursue methods both devious and adroit. He secured territory from Turkey in the Balkans but failed to obtain Smyrna and eastern Thrace. (The extreme provisions of the Treaty of Sèvres were revised at Lausanne in 1923.) He spent the rest of his career alternately in power and in exile, but achieved reconciliation with Monarchy and with the Turks. See Lloyd George, *The Truth about the Peace Treaties*, Vol. II; Wickham Steed, *Through Thirty Years*, Vol. II.

WADE, LT.-COL. He was military attaché in Copenhagen. At the end of 1918 he, together with General Barthélémy of the French army, accompanied Monsieur Paderewski as liaison officers on his return to Poland. He was in Lemberg in January and had repeated interviews with the Ukrainian leaders. In early February he was in Teschen. He made repeated, though unsuccessful, attempts to end the fighting in Galicia and in Teschen. On 15 February he reported to the Inter-Allied Commission in Warsaw. Wade and Barthélémy returned to Paris and reported to the Polish Commission on 12 and 13 March. Barthélémy, who had originally held that the Ukrainians should not be discouraged in their resistance to the Bolsheviks, now took a strongly pro-Polish line. Wade was more circumspect. See H.-M., P.C.M. Galicia 4819/77/55; Howard, *Theatre of Life*.

WARD, DUDLEY. Treasury officer in charge of statistics and member of the Financial Section of the British Delegation. He had expert knowledge of German finance. He worked closely with Keynes. Author of *England's Financial Supremacy* (1917); translations from *Die Frankfurter Zeitung* in collaboration with Keynes.

WEBSTER, CHARLES K. (1886–1961). Historian. K.C.M.G. 1946. Educated Merchant Taylors' School and King's College, Cambridge. Professor
of Modern History, Liverpool University, 1914. A brilliant lecturer and
teacher. Served in France and then in the War Office. He collaborated in
producing the Foreign Office Handbooks and wrote the *Congress of Vienna*
(*Peace Handbooks*, Vol. XXIV, 1918–19). This was the inception of his
later work on Castlereagh. Secretary to the Military Section of the British
Delegation at Paris. Wilson Professor of International Politics, Aberystwyth, 1922–32. An active founding member of Chatham House. Joined
Foreign Research Service under the Foreign Office 1939. With Mr Glad-
wyn Jebb he was responsible for the British contribution to the drafting
of the U.N.O. Charter. Delegate to the Dumbarton Oaks Conference July
1944. Adviser to the United Kingdom Delegation at San Francisco. President at the British Academy 1950–4. Author of *The Foreign Policy of
Castlereagh* (1931), *The Congress of Vienna* (1937), *Foreign Policy of Palmers-
ton 1836–41* (1951).

WIART, BRIGADIER-GENERAL ADRIAN CARTON DE. See Carton de
Wiart.

WOLF, LUCIEN (1857–1930). Educated at private schools, at the Athénée
Royal in Brussels, and in Paris. He came of a cultivated Jewish family. His
mother was a daughter of Ludwig Redlich, banker of Vienna. A successful
journalist writing often for Jewish papers. In 1917 Secretary of the Joint
Foreign Committee of the Jewish Board of Deputies and the Anglo-
Jewish Association. An an 'assimilationist' he opposed the Balfour Declaration. After the death of Nansen in 1929 he became President of the League
of Nations High Commission for Refugees. He was vigilant in observing
the working of the minorities treaties and the condition of Jews in Eastern
Europe. He was not unsuccessful in his dealings with the Polish and Hungarian Governments. Shortly before his death he wrote a strong letter to
Monsieur Titulesco who was then Romanian Ambassador in London.
'Anti-Semitic action has happened elsewhere but nowhere has it been so
violent, so brutal and so widespread – Government servants were to blame
for tolerating this.' (Pester Lloyd, 25 August 1931.) Author of *History of
the Jews in Elizabethan England* (1929).

WYNDHAM, SIR PERCY (1864–1943), K.C.M.G. 1919. Educated at Eton
and New College, Oxford. Entered the Diplomatic Service 1890. A
diplomat of the old school, he served in Berlin, Tehran, Constantinople,
Madrid, Washington, Caracas, Brussels and Rome. He was Envoy Extra-

ordinary and Minister Plenipotentiary to the Republic of Columbia 1911–1918. Sir Esme Howard wrote that he had suggested Wyndham as British representative to Poland. Sir Percy was dejected at his appointment, complaining that Poland was in a state of chaos and could not offer him the compensations of Venezuela, where he could find orchids and butterflies to console him for the revolutions. See Howard, *Theatre of Life*, II, 369.

ZALESKI, AUGUST (1883–1972). Educated at Warsaw and the London School of Economics. He was in London during the war and made contact with the British Government on behalf of Pilsudski. In June 1915 the Belgian ambassador, Émile Vandervelde, wrote a letter of introduction for Zaleski and Stanislav Patek, another emissary of Pilsudski, to Lloyd George, then Minister of Munitions (Lloyd George Papers, D/19/1/1). At Paris during the Peace Conference he advised Paderewski and helped him to keep in touch with the British Delegation. His views were moderate and he did not share the anti-Semitism of the Dmowski group. He was Minister of Foreign Affairs 1926–32 and again during the war, November 1939–July 1943. He succeeded Wladyslam Raczkiewicz in 1947 as president of the Polish Government in exile (later split into the Zaleski group and the Committee of National Union led by General W. Anders). Author of *Merchants' Confraternity of the Old Town of Warsaw* (1913), *Landmarks in Polish History* (1916), *Parliamentary and other Speeches* (1929).

ZAZONOV, SERGEI DIMITRIECH. See Sazanoff.

ZIMMERN, ALFRED (1879–1957). Knighted in 1936. Educated at Winchester and New College, Oxford. His father came of a German Jewish immigrant family, his mother of Huguenot ancestry. He was originally a classical scholar and from 1905 to 1909 was Fellow and Tutor in Ancient History at New College. He had a liberal international outlook and was interested in adult education. For a time he worked as a staff inspector at the Board of Education. Zimmern joined the P.I.D. in 1918. He worked chiefly on proposals for the League of Nations. He was concerned also with labour relations and with measures to combat Bolshevik propaganda. After the war he was Professor of International Politics at the University College of Wales, and from 1930 to 1940 Montague Burton Professor of International Relations at Oxford. With the enthusiastic assistance of Lady Zimmern he inaugurated and directed the Geneva School of International Studies 1925–39. Author of *The Greek Commonwealth* (1911), *Prospects of Democracy* (1929), *The League of Nations and the Rule of Law* (1936). See also Arnold Toynbee, *Acquaintances*.

INDEX

Abbreviations: Headlam-Morley, H.-M.; Intelligence Clearing House, I.C.H.; League of Nations, L. of N.; Paris Peace Conference, P.P.C.; Political Intelligence Dept., P.I.D. Page numbers printed in bold type indicate the main biographical entry.

Germany—*contd*
co-operation, 98; protests at cession of
Upper Silesia, 103 and n.; inherent
dangers in peace treaty proposals, 119–
120, 162–3; answer to peace terms, 130–1;
rights in Upper Silesia, 144, 151; folly
of ruining their industrial potential, 163;
ultimate co-operation in new system,
163–4; and Saar mines clause, 167;
humiliation at Versailles, 178–9
Gibraltar, *quid pro quo* for Morocco, 16–17,
31
Gielgud, Captain Lewis Evelyn, 79 n. 3, **191**
Glatz, assigned to Czechoslovakia, 105
Gleichen, Count (later Lord Edward), xvi
and n.2
Gluckstadt, Mons., 166
Graudenz, 60
Great Britain: declaration of war, xviii;
acquisitions under Sykes–Picot Agreement, 5 n.; lack of competent diplomats
among plenipotentiaries, 8; U.S. view
of her diplomacy, 39; communication
with Germany through Spain, 43 and
n. 2; and the Rhineland, 45–6; post-
Armistice behaviour, 161–2
Great Powers, and enforcement of min-
ority guarantees, 108, 110, 136
Greece, 93; Jews in Salonika, 110
Grey, Sir Edward, xvi, xvii, xviii

Habsburgs, Namier's views on, xxviii
Haller, General Joseph, xxviii, 13 n. 2
Hankey, Sir Maurice, 44 n. 1, 190, **191**;
criticism of reparations memorandum,
xxxiii and n. 2; representative on
Secretariat, 8; and Danzig clause, 63;
and Saar Valley, 65; letters from H.-M.
on New States, 91–2, 93–6, 141; on
Drafting Committee, 119–20, 123–4; on
treaty with Poland, 145–6; on education
of Jewish children, 157–8
Hardinge, Charles Hardinge, Baron, xli,
39 n. 1, 63 and n. 4, 88 n. 1, 92, **192**; and
Fourteen Points, 6; loses interest in negotiations, 8 and n. 1; and the Saar, 23 n.,
86 n. 3; capacity for overall responsibility, 90; minute from H.M. on
Austrian treaty, 121
Harris, S. R., member of P.I.D., 2 and n.
Hartington, Captain the Marquess of, and
I.C.H., 89 and n.

Haskins, Dr Charles Homer, **192**, 206; and
Commission on Belgian claims, 30, 165;
and Anglo-American interchanges, 33;
and Saar Valley, 59, 67, 71, 73, 86–7, 100,
123; and German frontiers, 63 and n. 1;
and Committee on Alsace-Lorraine, 85
Headlam, Rev. Arthur William (father), x
Headlam, Rev. Canon Arthur Cayley
(brother), x, xxxvii, **192**; letters from
his brother on his work with the Peace
Treaty, 78–9, 103–4, 161–75
Headlam, Maj.-Gen. Sir John, x
Headlam, Walter, xi and n. 2, xiv
Headlam-Morley, Sir James Wycliffe:
parentage and early life, x; education,
x–xi; wins Prince Consort Prize, xiii;
further studies in Berlin, xi, xiii; court-
ship and marriage, xii, xiii; interest in
modern Europe, xiv; and Board of
Education, xiv, xv and n.; at Wimbledon, xv; and World War I, xvi ff.;
belief in justice of Britain's cause, xviii–
xix; objections to an agreed peace, xix–
xx; and a concert of Europe, xx; and
Wilson's peace proposals, xxi; opinion
of U.S. Delegates, xxiv; and annexation
claims, xxv–xxvi; rational political
reactions, xxx; relations with Namier,
xxx; life after leaving Paris, xxx; as
historical adviser to F.O.; xxxi; and Institute of International Affairs, xxxi; and
reparations, xxxii; on need for a European protocol, xxxiv–xxxv; and trial
of war criminals, xxxvi; expedition to
Palestine, xxxvii; work on the history of
the war, xxxviii–xxxix; death, xxxix–xl

on his own position and work, 18, 21, 29,
68, 88–90, 98–9, 149–56; on Namier and
the Poles, 20–1, 24–5; on cultural rights
of minorities, 26–7; on 'small-nation'
mentality, 36, 37; on situation in
Germany, 37–8, 42, 43, 51–2; on con-
cept of city-state for Danzig, 40–1; impatience for peace with Germany, 41–2;
on Tardieu, 74; on need to revise the
Peace Treaty, 76, 116, 147, 149; visits the
Saar Valley, 86–7, 87 n., 91, 96, 100–3,
115, 119; personal view of Poland's
future, 107–8; on role of L. of N., xxiii,
xxvi, 20–1, 113; comments on Peace
Treaty, 118–22; experiences at Versailles,
178–80

}